ST ANTONY'S SERIES

General Editors: Archie Brown (1978–85), Rosemary Thorp (1985–92), and Alex Pravda (1992–), all Fellows of St Antony's College, Oxford

Recent titles include:

Mark D. Alleyne
INTERNATIONAL POWER AND INTERNATIONAL COMMUNICATION

Daniel A. Bell, David Brown, Kanishka Jayasuryia and David Martin Jones
TOWARDS ILLIBERAL DEMOCRACY IN PACIFIC ASIA

Judith M. Brown and Rosemary Foot (*editors*)
MIGRATION: The Asian Experience

Sir Alec Cairncross
MANAGING THE BRITISH ECONOMY IN THE 1960s: A Treasury
Perspective

Alex Danchev and Thomas Halverson (*editors*)
INTERNATIONAL PERSPECTIVES ON THE YUGOSLAV CONFLICT

Anne Deighton (*editor*)
BUILDING POSTWAR EUROPE: National Decision-Makers and European
Institutions, 1948–63

Simon Duke
THE NEW EUROPEAN SECURITY DISORDER

Y Hakan Erdem
SLAVERY IN THE OTTOMAN EMPIRE AND ITS DEMISE, 1800–1909

João Carlos Espada
SOCIAL CITIZENSHIP RIGHTS: A Critique of F. A. Hayek and Raymond Plant

Christoph Gassenschmidt
JEWISH LIBERAL POLITICS IN TSARIST RUSSIA, 1900–14: The
Modernization of Russian Jewry

Amitzur Ilan
THE ORIGIN OF THE ARAB–ISRAELI ARMS RACE: Arms, Embargo,
Military Power and Decision in the 1948 Palestine War

Hiroshi Ishida
SOCIAL MOBILITY IN CONTEMPORARY JAPAN

Austen Ivereigh
CATHOLICISM AND POLITICS IN ARGENTINA, 1910–60

Japan's Foreign Policy in the 1990s

From Economic Superpower to What Power?

Reinhard Drifte
Professor and Chair of Japanese Studies and
Director of the Newcastle East Asia Centre
University of Newcastle

St. Martin's Press
New York

in association with
ST ANTONY'S COLLEGE, OXFORD

St. Martin's Press, Scholarly and Reference Division, 175 Fifth Avenue, New York, N.Y. 10010

First published in the United States of America in 1996

Printed in Great Britain

ISBN 0-312-15977-3

Library of Congress Cataloging-in-Publication Data
Drifte, Reinhard.
Japan's foreign policy in the 1990s : from economic superpower to what power? / Reinhard Drifte.
p.   cm. — (St Antony's Series)
Includes bibliographical references and index.
ISBN 0-312-15977-3
1. Japan—Foreign economic relations.   2. Japan—Foreign relations.   I. Title.   II. Series.
HF1601.D75   1996
337.52—dc20   95-26781
                                                  CIP

To Collette

People in the future will probably speak of Japan as a country that once enjoyed a strange, transient prosperity.

in Kosaka, Masataka, '*Keizai pawa no jidai no genso*' (The principles of the economic power era), *Bungei Shunju* (November 1990) 94–104. Translated in *Japan Echo*, vol. XVIII, no. 1 (1991), p. 13.

The point we need to make to our Japanese friends is that their country is being asked to change and bring under mutual rules only those practices that palpably impinge on others in a globally interdependent age – what John Stuart Mill would have called 'other-regarding' behaviour – not to overturn their entire heritage.

in Hall, Ivan P., 'Samurai legacies, American illusions', in *National Interest* (Summer 1992), p. 16.

If the Japanese cannot begin to see less fuzzily where all this is liable to lead, nobody else seems likely to offer more dependable guidance.

in Sydney Giffard in a critique of 'Visions of Japan' during the Japan Festival in London 1991, *The Pacific Review*, vol. 5, no. 1 (1992), p. 79.

Contents

List of Tables

Preface

This book has been planned since 1987 when the Volkswagen Foundation gave me a Visiting Fellow scholarship at St Antony's College in Oxford. First thanks have therefore to go to the two institutions for their support. Due to private and professional circumstances, the outcome of the fellowship was not the 'big' book I had planned but a smaller volume for the Royal Institute of International Affairs in London. As Professor of Japanese Studies at the University of Newcastle and concurrently Director of the East Asia Centre I found it very difficult to find time for research, but sabbatical leaves in 1992 and in 1995 finally allowed me to finish the project. For the 1992 sabbatical leave, thanks have to go to the Japanese–German Center in Berlin which gave me a three-month scholarship for research in Japan and to my host institution, the Institute of International Relations of Sophia University in Tokyo. I am particularly indebted to Professor Royama Michio, then Director of the Institute, for taking me on as Visiting Fellow and for giving me valuable comments.

The Department of Politics of the University of Newcastle gave me special leave in 1995 to finish the book although university matters kept infringing on my time and concentration while the deadline imposed by the 'Research Assessment Exercise' came closer. I am grateful to Simon Brackenbury, a post-graduate student of the Department, for having helped me with the notes and the bibliography, and to Anita Tibbs, my secretary, for help with photocopying and getting books. Dr James Babb, Lecturer for Japanese Politics in the Department, gave me some valuable advice about the structuring of the book. Thanks has also to go to Professor Tanaka Akihiko of Tokyo University for commenting on an earlier draft. Last but by no means least, thanks to my wife who proofread the final draft and put up with the antics of a writing husband.

REINHARD DRIFTE

List of Abbreviations

ACDA   Arms Control and Disarmament Agency (US)
ADB   Asian Development Bank
APEC   Asia Pacific Economic Cooperation
ARF   ASEAN Regional Forum
ASEAN   Association of South-East Asian Nations
AJDF   ASEAN/Japan Development Fund
ASEAN PMC   ASEAN Post-Ministeral Conference
ASW   Anti-submarine warfare
AWACS   Airborne Warning and Control System
BBC   British Broadcasting Corporation
BIS   Bank of International Settlements
CBM   Confidence Building Measures
CHR   Commission for Human Rights
CNN   Cable Network News
COCOM   Coordinating Committee for Export Control
CSCE   Conference on Security and Cooperation in Europe
DAC   Development Assistance Committee
DOD   Department of Defense (US)
EAEC   East Asian Economic Caucus
EFTA   European Free Trade Area
EPA   Economic Planning Agency
EU   European Union
FAIR   Foundation for Advanced Information and Research
FAO   Food and Agriculture Organization
FASID   Foundation for Advanced Studies on International
           Development
FBR   Fast Breeder Reactors
FDI   Foreign Direct Investment
FY   Financial Year (1 April to 31 March)
GATT   General Agreement on Tariffs and Trade
GDP   Gross Domestic Product
GNP   Gross National Product
GSP   Generalized System of Preferences
HDTV   High Definition TV
IAEA   International Atomic Energy Agency
IMF   International Monetary Fund
IPCL   International Peace Cooperation Law

IWC   International Whaling Commission
JET   Japan Exchange Teachers
JETRO   Japan External Trade Organization
JICA   Japan International Cooperation Agency
KEDO   Korean Peninsula Energy Development Organization
LDP   Liberal Democratic Party
MFA   Ministry of Foreign Affairs
MOX   Mixed fuel rods
MITI   Ministry of International Trade and Industry
MTCR   Missile Technology Control Regime
NATO   North Atlantic Treaty Organization
NGO   Non-Governmental Organization
NHK   Nippon Hoso Kyokai (Japan's National Radio and TV
        Broadcasting company)
NIEs   Newly Industrialized Economies
NIS   New Independent States
NPT   Nuclear Non-Proliferation Treaty
ODA   Official Development Assistance
OECD   Organization for Economic Cooperation and Development
OECF   Overseas Economic Cooperation Fund
PKO   Peace Keeping Operations
PKO   Price keeping operations
PMO   Prime Minister's Office
PNG   Papua New Guinea
POW   Prisoner of War
SDF   Self Defence Forces
SDPJ   Social Democratic Party of Japan
SII   Strategic Impediment Initiative
SIPRI   Stockholm International Peace Research Institute
SLBM   Sea-launched Ballistic Missile
START-2   Strategic Arms Reduction Talks-2
TMD   Theatre Missile Defence
TRDI   Technical Research and Development Institute
UNDP   United Nations Development Programme
UNESCO   United Nations Educational, Scientific and Cultural
        Organization
UNICEF   United Nations International Children's Emergency Fund
UNSC   United Nations Security Council
UNU   United Nations University
WHO   World Health Organization
WTO   World Trade Organization

Introduction

Since 1989 the external and internal environment of Japan has been changing considerably. Although rather belatedly in comparison to the faster and more spectacular events in Europe, the end of the Cold War has now become palpable in East Asia as well. Without the end of the super-power confrontation the outside involvement in the Cambodian war could not have been ended. Russia is at present no longer a major concern for East Asia. On the other hand, the degree of American support and involve-ment in Pacific Asia has also become less credible. Conflicts which had been controlled until recently by the superpowers have now become more open and the emergence of regional hegemons cannot be excluded. Power is daily becoming more diffuse. As a result Japan's shadow looms larger than ever and the country has to find new ways of securing its national interests in an increasingly volatile and complex environment. Japan is increasingly willing to act as a major power as this quote by the former Vice Foreign Minister Kuriyama Takakazu shows:

> For medium and small countries, the international order is basically a given framework; their diplomatic goals should be to best adapt them-selves to the existing order, thereby protecting their security and pre-serving their economic interests. . . . Postwar Japan, using such passive diplomacy and maximally utilising the international order supported by the United States, enjoyed peace and prosperity. . . . But today's Japan [with its economic power] should participate more positively in interna-tional efforts to create a new order, thereby achieving its own secur-ity and prosperity. In this sense, Japan's diplomacy should transform itself from that of medium and small countries into that of a big country [*taikoku*].[1]

At the same time the long rule of one single conservative party, the Liberal Democratic Party (LDP), came to an end in 1993 and the country is almost completely absorbed by the search for a new domestic political con-stellation. In addition Japan is facing a real economic crisis which is much more structural than the previous oil crises in 1973 and 1979. The Great Hanshin earthquake in Kobe on 17 January 1995 has not only emphasized the economic concerns and the country's geological vulnerability, but more importantly may have demonstrated the weakness of Japan's crisis manage-ment. The Gulf War in 1990–91 had laid bare Japan's inability to cope in sufficient time with a major foreign policy crisis.

1

THE URGENCY FOR UNDERSTANDING JAPAN'S FOREIGN POLICY

While a time of dramatic change and apparent weaknesses could be considered the worst moment to write a book on Japan's foreign policy, let alone about Japan's power, one can also argue that it is the most interesting and most important time to do so. The present political and economic turmoil only reinforces the underlying assumption of this book that Japan matters more and more to other countries and that it is increasingly using its economic power to influence the options and power resources of international players. Japan is not the only major power which is affected by recession. The way Japan copes with the economic downturn illustrates Japan's resilience and intrinsic strength. Although a new domestic political constellation has not yet been found, external circumstances and the strife for power within Japan drive Japan towards greater assertiveness and more transformation of economic power into political, military and even cultural power. As we will see, Japan's weight in world politics is now so big that doing nothing, either intentionally or because of an inability to make a decision or because of absorption with other issues, can have a very material effect on other countries. More ominously, inaction can have the effect of narrowing Japan's range of options and predetermine future decisions of Japan which may be then even more forceful or unwelcome for others.

Although the issue of Japan as an economic challenge is still the highest on the Japan agenda of most countries, the end of the Cold War and the accompanying uncertainties of the transition to a new period which has been called 'post international politics' makes a better understanding of Japan's power more urgent.'[2] Economic power seems to have become more important than military power; Samuel Huntington expressed it in the following stark terms: 'It is, indeed, probably the most important source of power and, in a world in which military conflict between major states is unlikely, economic power will be increasingly important in determining the primacy or subordination of states.'[3] Whatever the new world order will look like, Japan with its economic and technological foundation will be an important actor in it and it is therefore crucial to gain a better understanding of the major factors involved in Japan's relationship with the outside world. Due to its positive and negative dynamics, global interdependence has the double effect of defusing and enhancing opportunities for the exercise of Japan's power. The diffusion of power has led to the fact that more complex coalitions of state and non-state actors affect outcomes.[4] The nation-state paradigm is not yet finished and the examination of Japan's economic success shows how important the role of the state has been and still is. Coming to some conclusions about the (albeit narrowing) gap of the scope of the nation-state paradigm between Japan and other major countries may be more important than theorizing about the disappearance of that paradigm!

The investigation of Japan's power and its exercise is also urgent because of the either inarticulate or highly emotionally expressed suspicion abroad as well as in Japan about Japan's power potential, intentions and future path. Insufficient understanding of the political economic system easily leads to conspiracy theories or negative assumptions of Japan's intentions. Is the occurrence of a 'strategic breakout' not unavoidable in view of Japan's past and present power? Or are there blind forces at work? Is Japan a 'Godzilla whose thrashing tail flattens buildings quite unintentionally as it blunders about'?[5] Some worry about the gap between Japan's economic power and the country's ability to handle it:

> No matter how powerful a country is militarily or economically, nor how well-meaning its intention to use that power to bring about regional peace and prosperity, its actions can lead to totally undesired consequences if that country cannot judge how to use its power appropriately. Sound judgment demands, above all, in-depth knowledge of the region concerned and the capacity to analyse situations and plan optimal course of action. The next requisite is the conceptional ability to translate this into national policy. These qualities, even more important than the possession of economic power, are sadly lacking in Japan.[6]

Finally the cacophony of opinions and statements coming out of Japan which range from pacifist to right-wing, bewilders most who still assume at least unconsciously Japan to be a homogeneous country with one voice.

The question of Japanese power has implications for the Japan policies of other countries which for example expect Japan to contribute to the international system in a way commensurate with its economic power. They exert strong influence (commonly referred to in Japan as '*gaiatsu*') on Japan to this effect. As a result it is most opportune to appreciate in a more systematic way what sort of power Japan has, how and if at all this power is exerted, whether the demand for 'commensurate contribution' is compatible with the internal and external conditions Japan is facing, and whether those making these requests are conscious of the implications. It is obvious, but often not fully realized, that such contributions imply the exertion of power, and this has important implications for the world system, including for the relative power of the other countries. There are even Japanese who have to ask themselves whether the outside world really wants to face these consequences.[7]

Looming behind the questions about Japan's future path is often the assumption that big economic power leads sooner or later to political power and eventually to military power. The Realist school in international relations has always insisted that 'countries with great power economics have become great military powers, whether or not reluctantly'.[8]

Andrew Hanami argues that 'by providing a means and pressuring Japan to ratchet up incrementally to a level approaching intermittent parity and interoperability across a range of military capabilities, the Americans have caused Japan to become a key mover in the "balance" of power in Northeast Asia'.[9] So when will Japan's 'strategic breakout' happen?

Concern about the future path of Japanese power is most acute in Asia. Against the background of Japan's past actions in that region, Asians are asking themselves about the possibility of Japan turning its economic power into military power as the following statement by the Southeast Asian scholar Chin Kin Wah illustrates:

> In the Asia–Pacific, Japan is already an economic superpower by any measurement (gross national product, level of technology, foreign trade, international financial power, innovation in research and technology, and quality of human resources and organization). These are also the assets and attributes which can readily be converted to military power. As Lee Kuan Yew put it . . . the possibility of Japan as an independent military power at the turn of the twentieth century is a horrendous one, such a possibility being real given the Japanese propensity to be 'Number One' in whatever they seek to accomplish.[10]

THE PUZZLE OF JAPAN'S POWER

Although there is broad agreement that Japan has power, there are considerable differences about exactly what kind of power and in what areas. Is it an economic superpower but a political and military dwarf? How, if at all, is this power instrumentalized and exerted, and particularly to where is this kind of power leading Japan?

Answers to these question depend very much on the respective observer and whether the intention is to warn of Japan's power, whether Japan is to be invited to 'behave' (for example, burden-sharing) according to its power or whether the intention is rather to cloud the issue of power in order to escape some of the consequences of big-power status.

Many observers are puzzled that despite all the apparent components of power which Japan undisputedly possesses due to its economic success at home and abroad, this power seems not to be instrumentalized to achieve any apparent goal, except perhaps narrow economic goals, or if it is exercised for broader economic or even political goals, it is done so reluctantly or at least differently from the way traditional big powers do it. How to explain this 'paradox of unrealized power'?[11] Moreover, Japan's national interests seemed to be achieved in a very cost-efficient way and Japan has therefore been accused of being a reactive state and of being a free rider.

Inoguchi Takashi writes that Japan has the image of being 'adrift, with an *ad hoc*, opportunistic, and short-term pragmatism', but on the other hand projecting the image of an actor 'determinedly and tenaciously steadfast to its national interests'.[12] Kataoka Tetsuya eloquently encapsulated this frustration of the observer in understanding the co-existence of certain classic power components with what he calls 'idle power' in the following way:

> By general consent there is in Japan a strange combination of strength and weakness, resilience and fragility, expansiveness and subservience, aggressiveness and self-effacement, keen competitiveness and placid stupor, cohesion (or 'consensus') and apparent headlessness, and cynicism and innocence.[13]

Not only does Japan seem not to instrumentalize its power, at least not commensurately with its economic power, but there is also no apparent leadership nor master plan for Japan's foreign and economic policies. Van Wolferen obscures this issue more than he clarifies it by speaking in his book of 'the system'.[14] Instead of saying that the buck does not stop but rather keeps circulating, it may be more appropriate to say that the buck often suddenly disappears and may not necessarily reappear.

FAILURE TO UNDERSTAND JAPAN?

The problem of the alleged puzzle of Japan's power is emphasized by the Revisionist school which asserts that social sciences have failed to explain Japan. Karel van Wolferen states when discussing government and interest groups that 'we are dealing not with lobbies but with a structural phenomenon unaccounted for in the categories of accepted political theory'.[15] Chalmers Johnson wrote in 1989 that 'modern East Asia is a junkyard for Western theories of economic development and political modernization, and it is wise to remind ourselves of the area's profound exceptionalism whenever approaching a theory-intensive subject like democracy'.[16]

This author disagrees with such a perspective of the 'failure' of social sciences in view of the available social science literature on Japan, notably the works written by the revisionists themselves. It is also counterproductive and water on the mills of those Japanese and non-Japanese writers about Japan who insist on Japan's uniqueness, either to argue in favour of a Japanese foreign policy which is solely concerned with direct economic benefits or who support an exclusive and protectionist approach to Japan.

What has failed is not social sciences but rather our application of social science approaches and the damage of focusing too narrowly on one single academic discipline, be it the economic, anthropological or political discipline. The problem has been compounded by the popularity of certain schools within disciplines which gained too much prominence because they are useful for certain political interests, such as the liberal economist school which considers that all problems are taken care of in an equitable manner by free market forces, or the culturalist school in anthropology which considers that culture determines everything and therefore nothing can be done about it.

This unsatisfactory use of social science is particularly criticized by Karel van Wolferen who reviews critically the approach of social sciences to the concept of power. Unfortunately he distorts political science approaches to power by not taking into account the diversity of these approaches, instead asserting that social sciences in the postwar period has either eliminated power from its discourse or at least removed its sharp edges.[17] The author will endeavour in this book to avoid any of the pitfalls of either the culturalist or revisionist explanation model and agree with Eisenstadt that the

> problem is not whether 'culture' or 'social structure' (or history) is the only explanation for specific institutional or behavioural patterns, but rather which are the processes through which cultural and structural dimensions of social action are interwoven in different social and historical settings, and how different modes of interweaving influence the specific patterns investigated.[18]

WHAT IS POWER?

Chalmers Johnson and van Wolferen have, however, put their fingers on a serious failure of social scientists analysing Japan: the existence and role of power. There is first of all the widespread association of the notion of power with military power or force, be it in Japan or outside of it. Force is, however, only one means of power. The problem of seeing Japan's economic power automatically leading to military power is a fallacy of the

Realist school in international relations. David Baldwin therefore made the following comment:

> Phrases describing force as the 'ultimate' form of power imply that all forms of power are arrayed on a single continuum of effectiveness or importance. If power is conceived of as a multidimensional phenomenon, it is harder to think in terms of such a continuum. If one thinks of power as situationally specific rather than generalized, the idea of an 'ultimate' form of power does not make much sense.[19]

The understanding of power is not made easier by the way the term is understood in Japan. The Realist understanding of power is still very prevalent, and even the word 'power' is disliked because of its association with coercion. In the Japanese cultural context this runs against the general preference for the notions of harmony and consensus. Moreover, power relationships are ignored or obfuscated, which is very serious because of the contextual character of power.

This ignorance and obfuscation of power is supported by a Japanese tendency to avoid clearly defined abstract notions, relying instead on the evocation of a certain atmosphere by using such notions, as for example in the case of 'internationalization' (*kokusaika*). This notion can mean many things to many different people, and its instrumentalization ranges from refuting foreign criticism about Japan not opening its market to social engineering in order to make Japan more like other Western industrialized countries. There are also important political and ideological reasons to cloud Japan's 'true' power as well as its instrumentalization, which go beyond cultural and behavioural factors. The recognition of Japan's power is sometimes unwanted because it may be politically inopportune, it may harm relations with other countries or it may provoke demands for more Japanese international burden sharing.

The process of instrumentalization of the concept of power can be illustrated by the use of 'internationalization'. In his Diet speech in January 1986, former Prime Minister Nakasone referred to Japan having to become a '*kokusai kokka*' (international nation) and said that Japan must increase its contribution to and acceptance of the international system as well as increase its responsibility as a major actor in the world.[20] On another occasion Nakasone defined the build-up of defence power as an important duty for Japan as an international country ('*boeiryoku seibi wa kokusai kokka Nihon no juyo na sekimu*').[21]

Particularly relevant to our discussion is the fashionable use of the word '*taikoku*' (big power) in many connotations which obscures and banalizes the notion of power. An anecdotal illustration of this sanitizing attempt of 'power' is the title of one session of a symposium organized by the *Japan Times* in 1987 which was called in English 'Japan as a world power', but in Japanese *'Nihon wa kokusai kokka naru ka?'* (Can Japan become an international nation?).[22] The Komei Party used for example the slogan *'Kogai taikoku kara kogai senshin taikoku'* (From pollution big power to pollution avant garde big power) for its party programme. The government in 1992 spoke of Japan as an *'enjo taikoku'* (development aid big power).[23] In June 1992 the Miyazawa cabinet published a Five-Year Economic Plan (1992–96) 'Sharing a Better Quality of Life Around the Globe' which is called in Japanese *'seikatsu taikoku go-kanen keikaku'* and this would have to be translated as 'Five-Year Plan for a Livelihood Big Power'.[24]

After having thus obscured the concept of power, ritualistic promises by Japanese leaders that Japan will not become a 'big military power' (*gunji taikoku*) or even 'big power' (*taikoku*) lack strength. Moreover, the value of this promise is eroded by the fact that Japan has been constantly expanding and is even now technologically upgrading its military force while other constraints like the one per cent ceiling on defence spending or the use of space for military purposes have been abandoned. In addition, Japan's military force is that of a big military power if seen in its regional context which is a legitimate context for its neighbours (see Chapter 2).

Faced with the above problems in the understanding of Japan's effective pursuit of its national interests in the global arena we have to clarify the notion of power. Power is one of the major topics in political science but there is no agreement on the concept of power. Power is understood here as the ability and will to exert influence over the perceptions, intentions, material circumstances and bargaining power of others. Power is therefore alternatively referred to in this book as 'influence'.

Power has many material and non-material components. We are most familiar with the impact of physical features such as geography, resource endowment and demography. But non-material features such as international experience, institutional status and cultural emanation are increasingly relevant. Joseph Nye has called power based on such non-material and economic features 'soft power' or 'co-optive power' because one country gets other countries to want what it wants in contrast to the hard or command power of ordering others to do what it wants.[25] 'Proof of power lies not in resources but in the ability to change the behavior of states.'[26] In other words, 'power over outcomes' by setting the agenda and structuring the situations in world politics is becoming more important.

The various elements of power can be very ambivalent. They may need additional circumstances or a catalyst before becoming relevant. For example, rich resource endowment can be an important precondition of economic power, but can also be a liability if it means maintaining uneconomic extraction capacities instead of buying raw materials on the open world market at cheaper prices although this involves also questions of economic security. Economic power can lead to cultural power but only if that culture is endowed with certain conditions such as international attractiveness, and vehicles/agents to spread it abroad.[27]

Traditional realism says that the workings of the international system can be explained through the underlying distribution of power. The structural power approach attempts to go deeper and to explain the diffusion of power and the power exerted by the contingent framework. Whereas relational power like agenda setting is an important power in a world with an overflowing agenda, structural power affects the structure through which outcomes are settled. Relational power accrues to Japan by the simple circumstance of being one of the biggest importer of raw materials, energy supplies and foodstuffs, and by the export of a constantly upgraded range of manufactured products in specific and highly important sectors. However, by influencing the rules which govern this exchange Japan will be even more powerful. A third level is the level of influencing ideas, knowledge and truth. The latter is particularly difficult to prove empirically but is obviously very important for our broad definition of power and the creation of consent. Power analysis quickly reveals that not all outcomes are based on intentional power or on actors. A meaningful concept of power has therefore to include the possibility of unintended influence if one conceives power as a way of effecting.[28] If the analysis is solely based on an agent or is actor-based, this cannot be achieved. The complex array of Japan's economic power can have implications and reverberations which were not planned or even foreseen by any actor, but may well be exploited by a concrete actor to further a particular interest.

DEPENDENCE OR INTERDEPENDENCE?

Closely linked to power is the question about dependence vs. independence as a result of power relationships. It is very important to differentiate between these terms because of the confusion in public discourse (unintended or not) about them. Dependence is often equalled with vulnerability, but even interdependence has often a negative or at least ambivalent connotation. Clarity is particularly needed in the case of a country like Japan which is perceived as moving on a continuum which ranges for some from utter dependence on one state, the US, to dominating that same state.

John Kroll suggests that vulnerability measures dependence, but sensitivity measures interdependence. If vulnerability focuses on the costs of breaking relations, sensitivity can be said to focus on the costs of maintaining interdependence.[29] Others explain the ambiguity of interdependence by making a difference between sensitivity interdependence and vulnerability interdependence. Sensitivity refers to changes within a structural framework whereas vulnerability refers to effects of changes of the framework itself.[30] The question then arises whether interdependence can be seen as a form of power relations or as an alternative to power relations. Robert Gilpin argued that interdependence 'establishes hierarchal, dependency, and power relations among groups and national societies' because the relative gains differ.[31] Theorists who perceive interdependence as an issue of vulnerability also see it as a form of power. If one considers interdependence in terms of sensitivity then it can be seen as a new form of relationship beyond power where neither state can act without some form of coordination with the other.

Also relevant here is whether interdependence has increased, particularly after the end of the Cold War. Keohane and Nye propose three characteristics of what they call 'complex interdependence'.[32] First they observe an increase of transgovernmental and transnational channels, thus reducing the coherent and closed nature of the nation-state. Secondly, national interest has become a collection of sub-national interests, and military security no longer dominates the agenda as before. Finally, the significance and effectiveness of military power to solve international conflicts, notably those on economic issues, has become doubtful. We want to argue that all these changes also affect Japan, and that Japan is actually benefiting and thus deriving power particularly from the second and third point more than any other country because of its dependence on the US for its military security. On the other hand, Japan is affected differently by the first point and derives power from it: While the state and the private sector are benefiting from the increase of transgovernmental and transnational channels, the close cooperation between the government and business means that business can operate more effectively across borders and Japan's sovereignty is thus less diminished.

THE HEGEMONIC DISCUSSION

In discussing the external environment of Japan's foreign policy and the issue of power exertion/leadership, the theory of hegemonial stability provides some useful pointers. The external environment in the last 50 years has been shaped by the East–West confrontation and American domination on a global as well as regional level. This situation has led to the theory of hegemonial stability which holds that the maintenance of an open and liberal world economy requires the existence of a hegemonic power.[33] A hegemon uses its influence to create international regimes and this influence is mainly based on economic power. Since the US is seen as the hegemon so far but is now weakening, will Japan take over its role? Robert Gilpin doubts that Japan will replace the US as a global hegemon because of its inward-looking foreign and economic policy and lack of military power.[34]

Looking at Japan's position in the Asian region, Fukai Shigeko doubts the validity of Gilpin's prediction at least for the region because Japan has become more open towards imports from Asia and because the relative weight of military might has declined.[35] But she agrees with Gilpin and others that Japan is not (yet) willing to be a global hegemon because of the lack of a domestic consensus on any value beyond economic growth. She believes, however, that Japan has already become a new regional hegemon as defined by Antonio Gramsci. According to Fukai, 'Gramsci defined hegemony as a relationship, not a domination imposed by force, but of consent generated by political and ideological (or intellectual and moral) leadership'.[36] In order to prove this effort at creating consensus in Asia she measures 'Japan's political and organisational efforts aimed at the formation of an international and a domestic consensus on a regional integration regime' and Japan's manufacturing of 'networks of economic interests through a coordinated use of economic aid, technical cooperation and private sector FDI'.[37] Her conclusions about Japan's hegemony are not final, particularly in view of the question of how Japan will tackle the growing gap of inequality in Asia, but the approach adds to the urgency of understanding better Japan's soft power and not only its hard power.

The first chapter will look at the conditions and circumstances shaping the foundation of Japan's foreign policy and its ability to pursue national interests. The foreign policy of any country is conditioned by the interaction between its domestic political economy and the external environment, moderated by ideology and behavioural patterns.

The concept of political economy has been defined by Yamamura Kozo as 'the political and economic institutions that determine the structure of incentives shaping political and economic interactions'.[38] It is not possible in the framework of this book to give a complete and exhaustive overview of Japan's political economy and we will concentrate in the first chapter on those aspects which are considered different from the political economies of the major industrialized countries and which matter most for Japan's interactions with the outside world.[39] This focus intends to confront the assertions by many of Japan's political and economic partners that its political economic system is different, allegedly providing the country with certain comparative advantages over its main trading partners.

In the second part we will look at how ideology and behavioural patterns moderate the interaction between Japan's domestic political economy and its external environment. This analysis will provide some background for the understanding of the limits of Japan's structural and relational power in the next chapters and the factors which prevent Japan's conversion of power resources. Behavioural patterns, societal values and historical circumstances are in an interactive relationship with political arrangements: Political arrangements exploit them and thus maintain and reinforce them. Japan's history since the Meiji Restoration gives plenty of examples of how flexible and changeable societal values and ideology are. After the opening of Japan in the last century, Japan's leaders learned from the Western powers that imperialism was the way to confront the international environment. This toppled the isolationist and inward-looking policy of the previous 250 years. Industrialization necessitated the 'invention of new traditions' such as lifelong employment. The defeat in 1945 and the American hegemony created and sustained pacifism. It also allowed Japan to concentrate on economic rehabilitation which later turned into a single-minded pursuit of economic goals, thanks to power structures which easily made the transition from wartime economic planning to economic rehabilitation and later economic expansion. These power structures, in the shadow of American domination as well as the success of economic expansion, fostered attitudes which were not conducive to pursuing an independent foreign and security policy.

In the second chapter we look at Japan's hard power and concentrate on the country's security policy and the factors and circumstances which create and sustain it. The chapter will provide an overview of Japan's changed global and regional security environment and how a fragmented public opinion and a political class in disarray are trying to come to terms with it. The latter part of this chapter will evaluate how this hard power is translated into other power, such as Japan's influence on arms control regimes and the regional security dialogue. At the end we will evaluate all the factors and circumstances which weigh on Japan's future security policy and security options to see whether Japan has come any closer to becoming a major military power which may use hard power to achieve national interests. In order to do so one has to get a more realistic view of what Japan's hard power amounts to now, while at the same time appreciate the different perspectives of Japan's neighbours and of Japan's more faraway partners in the Western world.

The third chapter deals with Japan's economic power or soft power and how it translates at a regional and global level into influence over the options and material circumstances of other countries. The shift of importance from military to soft power has been to Japan's advantage as the world's second largest economy. It will show how trade and investment leads Japan now to influence the international economic regimes which regulate these activities. We have chosen the latest GATT round and the establishment of the World Trade Organization (WTO) to illustrate this influence. With its mounting foreign direct investments (FDI) all over the world, Japan is able to exert economic as well as political influence over developed as well as developing countries. The influence over developing countries is enhanced by being the biggest donor of economic development aid which has an impact on the economic development strategies as well as the political options of these countries, notably in Asia. Within the multilateral aid organizations Japan is trying to shift the emphasis away from an absolute free rein of market forces to more state-led development. As the second biggest contributor to international organizations, Japan has become an indispensable member of most of their activities and the country is increasingly using this power for goals which are beyond narrow economic confines. Japan's growing involvement in the UN has finally led to the Japanese military taking part in Peace Keeping Operations (PKO) which constitutes a major watershed in Japan's foreign policy. The ensuing debate in Japan and resulting Japanese demands for a greater say in UN matters, notably its candidacy for a permanent seat on the Security Council as well as representing Asia, conclude the chapter.

While linking Japan's economic power to political and military power may already be for many readers a novelty, it will appear even more unusual to hear about Japan's growing ability to influence ideas, knowledge and truth. But while the big Western powers have become used to their high- and lowbrow culture being disseminated to other countries indirectly through emanation and economic interaction as well as directly through cultural diplomacy, Japan has only now started with its growing economic expansion to become involved in these activities which have a significant impact on the perception of other people of Japan and on the acceptability of Japanese industry abroad. This new development may be surprising for European and American observers of Japan, but is a different matter for Asians who are swamped but also attracted by the Japanese consumer culture in the same way as Europe was attracted by American consumer culture after the Second World War.

In the final chapter we will trace this development and see how Japan's economic power translates into cultural power and make the connection with Japan's influence on work practices which we observed in the previous chapter. While Japan's cultural power in the Western world is focused on highbrow culture (mainly the arts) and information, the sources and scope for cultural power in Asia are much wider, ranging from the consumer culture to Japanese language teaching. While Japan's growing influence on the hearts and minds of other people is increasing, it does not, however, yet amount to ideological, intellectual or moral leadership, but it is an important element in what we will find to be Japan's 'catalytic leadership' or 'leadership by stealth'.

1 The Political and Economic Framework of Japan's Foreign Policy

INTRODUCTION

This chapter is to set the scene for Japan's foreign policy in the 1990s by giving an overview of Japan's power resources and by outlining the scope and *modi operandi* of these resources. We will look at the interaction between Japan's domestic political economy and the external environment, and how this interaction is moderated by ideology and behavioural patterns. After dealing with the actors we will analyse the size of Japan's economy by breaking it down into trade, investment, financial power and high technology. As we will see in the later chapters, the size and scope of the Japanese economy influences the actions which Japan has to undertake in order to maintain and expand its economy. Its economic might determines the structural, relational and ideological power of Japan towards the outside world.

In view of the worldwide recession which is also affecting Japan, reinforced by the banking crisis and the Great Hanshin Earthquake in Kobe in January 1995, it is often argued that the main pillar of Japan's strength, its economic performance, is giving way. We want to argue that, as in any other country, Japan's power resources lie not only in quantitative indicators but also in institutions and the way the Japanese run these institutions. Japan does not have to occupy the first ten places of the ranking list of the world's biggest banks in order to make its economic power felt worldwide. Its strengths reside rather in its flexibility, adaptability or even opportunism to react to internal as well as external shifts and changes. Ideology (as well as its absence) and behavioural patterns deserve therefore equal attention.

Finally we will address the issue of the compatibility of Japan's political economic system with that of its major Western partners which arises inescapably from the above. If the Japanese system is significantly different, as is asserted now by many Japanese and non-Japanese, one of the main tasks of Japan's foreign policy in the 1990s has to be how to deal with the resulting conflicts, in addition to the tasks of how to address the challenges arising from the interaction between a changing international environment and Japan.

THE ACTORS

There is no one theory or model for explaining the role and interactions of the actors in Japan's political economic system. One can identify the three main actors who are involved in most economic and political decision-making, that is politicians, bureaucrats and business. Their weight and importance has shifted over the postwar period, and not necessarily in a linear process. The bureaucracy in all advanced industrialized countries has a built-in strength accruing from its hold on specialized information and from its longer office-holding compared with politicians and often even with business (particularly small and medium-size companies). The bureaucracy in Japan (we refer mainly to the central government bureaucracy) acquired particular strength in the postwar period because of a long tradition of state control and the continuity of personnel between the war-planning era and the immmediate postwar economic catchup era.[1] In the postwar era many links developed between bureaucrats, politicians and business due to the skilful exploitation of social network links (place of birth, schools, university, etc), provision of jobs for bureaucrats after early retirement by private and public companies (*amakudari*), frequent moves between bureaucracy and the political world, and a pervasive attitude of give-and-take which also provided on the negative side an ideal soil for corruption on a wide scale. At the heart of this corruption is the need for business to oil the wheels of the complicated and costly regulatory system and the ability of politicians and bureaucrats to benefit from it either in terms of money and/or influence. These many links between politicians, bureaucrats and business created insiders and outsiders, and it has become very difficult for Japanese as well as foreigners to cross the invisible but tangible border between the two. An important social value which helped these actors to keep their grip on politics and economics and to protect the border between insiders and outsiders is a strong desire for control and predictability, most clearly manifested in the ethos of the bureaucracy. Control and predictability is best preserved with a limited number of insiders. The cooperation between the three main actors has been successful and sustainable by creating big powerful companies and an effective administration despite unimpressive party politics, but also at the same time economic prosperity which brought tangible benefits to a majority of the Japanese. This political and economic system can be criticized on many accounts because it reinforced a big producer-oriented political economic system rather than a consumer-oriented system, has a considerable democratic deficit, creates corruption, and its foundations seem today after the bust of the bubble economy much less stable than before. These features raise important issues about the political economic system of Japan, such as the nature of the interaction between its actors, the system's sustainability, its democratic deficit and its compatibility with the outside world.

A. The Politicians

The role of politicians has traditionally been to keep the hands of the bureaucrats free from political interference in politically non-sensitive areas. Politicians have been too dependent on the bureaucracy and business to be able to dictate their own terms, and have more often than not been amplifiers or instruments of bureaucratic and business interests as partly demonstrated by the unending series of corruption cases since the Lockheed scandal in the 1970s. Politicians have an enormous need for funds to run their electoral campaigns and to keep their constituency satisfied due to the past multi-seat constituency system. These funds can only come from business.[2] It is unclear how the new law on constituencies and electoral funding will affect this relationship with business. Corruption may become worse because the new constituencies demand more votes, which means more money has to be spent which the state funding system may not be able to provide.

Since 1993, arguments can be found which suggest either that the bureaucracy has become stronger or that politicians have become stronger because of the political stalemate. Both interpretations are valid, depending on individual issues and circumstances. But it is also true, as a Japanese diplomat put it, that the bureaucracy feels now more vulnerable than before because they are exposed to more rigorous scrutiny in the absence of political cover which they enjoyed before.[3] Today politicians of changing coalition governments can score points against each other by attacking a ministry, particularly if it is headed by a politician from a rival party. The changes since 1993 have also made politicians sink even deeper into parochialism because they are absorbed in finding a new political constellation.[4]

Due to the culmination of scandals and fear of losing power, two groups from the LDP, numbering over 50 members of parliament, split off from the LDP in June 1993 and supported a no-confidence motion which led to the fall of Prime Minister Miyazawa Kiichi. It was not so much the result of the July 1993 Lower House elections which led to a coalition government between a breakaway LDP faction and the hitherto perennial opposition party, the Social Democratic Party of Japan (SDPJ), but rather the splitting up of the LDP and the willingness of one LDP breakaway faction, the Japan Renewal Party, to form a coalition with an opposition party. In fact it tends to be often overlooked that the July election was a great victory for the conservative forces and the SDPJ lost heavily. This is important to recall in order to judge the possibility of a major foreign policy shift after the politicians again find more time for foreign policy. In the 1990 election the LDP had won 275 seats, but in the 1993 July elections, the LDP received 223, to which have to be added 105 seats from breakaway factions of the LDP.

Nowhere is the limited role of politicians more obvious than in Japan's foreign policy. A major exception has been the politically sensitive area of security policy where Prime Minister Yoshida Shigeru played a high-profile and crucial role when setting up the present US-oriented foreign and security policy of Japan in the late 1940s and early 1950s. A similar case is Prime Minister Kishi Nobusuke's revision of the Japan–US security treaty in 1960. But in an era of high economic growth and a stable US-dominated regional environment it was not very attractive for politicians to become involved in foreign policy, let alone in security policy. In the 1980s, when economic growth rates declined and the budget deficit offered fewer opportunities to satisfy voters, there was a somewhat increased interest of politicians in foreign policy. Foreign demands for a greater opening of the Japanese market and more Japanese burden sharing created a mood encapsulated in the slogan 'internationalization' (*kokusaika*), which was instrumentalized by Prime Minister Nakasone Yasuhiro (1982–87) who domestically benefited considerably from a high-profile foreign policy. Photos in the offices of Japanese politicians showing them with foreign politicians are now obligatory and allow them to bask in the enhanced prestige which Japan enjoys as an economic superpower. With the fall of a unitary LDP government and the search for a new political constellation politicians are generally too preoccupied with party politics and hardly have time for the economy, let alone foreign policy. Nevertheless some politicians like Ozawa Ichiro have made statements about Japan's new post-Cold War foreign policy which aim at giving Japan a more prominent role in international relations.[5] In March 1991 Ozawa, the then Secretary-General of the ruling LDP, side-stepped the Ministry of Foreign Affairs (MFA) to visit Moscow in order to trade the Northern Territories for aid to Russia (see Chapter 3). In Sepember 1990 the LDP elder Kanemaru Shin conducted private negotiations with North Korea and committed Japan, to the great annoyance of the MFA, to pay reparations even for the postwar period because of the absence of diplomatic relations. The new electoral law will most likely not enhance the attraction of foreign policy for politicians because the present political upheaval will take some time to crystallize a new party spectrum and politicians will have to come to terms with the new demands of the single-seat constituency. This may not exclude the possibility that flamboyant and single-minded politicians who seek a higher profile at home may use highly politicized and visible foreign policy issues for their benefit.

The role of politicians in foreign policy is also limited by factors such as language ability or information about other countries. It is well known that Japan lacks adequate foreign language teaching although this is improving. It still has to rely on a very small group of people which van Wolferen derides as the 'buffers'.[6] Even its existing human resources are not adequately or efficiently used.[7]

Japan is a country almost saturated with all kinds of information. The quality of this information is, however, open to question, and the lack of primary information is a case in point. In a 1992 survey of Diet members on their information sources on the United States it was found that 33 per cent of the LDP members of the House of Representatives reported high levels of contact with Americans, but only 11 per cent of LDP Upper House members reached this high level of contact.[8] Numbers for the SDPJ and the Komeito were much lower with only 9 per cent and 13 per cent respectively. Language is another problem: Only 10 per cent of LDP members and 4 per cent of the opposition party members admitted to being able to handle a discussion in English. In terms of information sources about the United States, 36 per cent reported watching CNN (which is available in Japan in Japanese) and 31 per cent reading *Newsweek* (a Japanese-language version is published). Information in English from the United States was read by only 3 per cent. The most important Japanese sources of information on the United States and on Japanese–American relations was for 75 per cent of the LDP Diet members the bureaucracy, followed with 68 per cent by the media, businessmen with 30 per cent and other politicians with 26 per cent. For 79 per cent of the opposition Diet members, the media were the most important source. The bureaucracy itself is heavily influenced by the mass media.[9]

B. The Bureaucracy

It is the interaction between the bureaucracy and business which is the most crucial for the understanding of Japan's political economy.[10] The analysis is made difficult by the fact that those two actors are in fact not two homogeneous actors but contain competing elements within themselves. The bureaucracy can be split not only by inter-ministerial and inter-agency turf battles, but sometimes also by intra-ministerial competition. For example, in the Ministry of Finance the Tax Bureau (*Shuzei kyoku*) rivals with the Budget Bureau (*Shukei kyoku*). In addition there is intra-agency competition, as for example between the various ministries and agencies involved in Japan's Official Development Assistance (ODA). Business, not even big business, is as unified or homogeneous as institutions like the big employers' federations such as the Keidanren or the Nikkeiren make it appear. While outside observers envy or bedevil Japanese business for the support it gets from the bureaucracy, there is also strong criticism of the bureaucracy for its weakness and unresponsiveness in many cases affecting foreign interest such as the opening of the Japanese market. Kent Calder explained Japan's intermittent responsiveness by describing Japan as a political system which is 'in the throes of perpetual domestic conflict, driven by political cycles, interest-group pressures, and bureaucratic machinations in complex inter-relationships with one another'.[11]

The strength and power of the government and the bureaucracy over the economy is not so much based on the size of the national budget or the number of public servants (which are both rather small in comparison with other Western developed countries) or statutory powers, but on its link-ages to enterprises, the working of the polity and the cultural context. The relationship between the bureaucracy and business has been summarized succinctly in the following way:

> Japan's state is neither dominant nor subservient to private business; it is instead tied into 'relational' networks enmeshing politics in multiple formal and informal linkages across the business–government frontier. Political coordination is based more on organizational intelligence and strategic financial incentives than on coercion and tends to blur the line between the private and the public realm. In a similar vein, relations among private businesses involve 'controlled competition' – a combina-tion of fierce market competition for customers on the one hand and cooperative relations among networks of banks, manufacturers, and their suppliers on the other.[12]

The privileged funding situation of Japanese companies may serve as an illustration because it has received particular attention, going beyond the circumstances of the easy access to funding during the real estate-based credit bonanza of the bubble economy era. The central bureaucracy had a major role in allowing this easy access, and according to a recent research project it is involved in three distinct ways:

> First, government has a direct role as a participant in financial markets. Several government-owned financial intermediaries are involved in lend-ing funds collected by the Postal Savings system to industrial borrowers. In this role, they are directly competitive with private financial institutions. Secondly, government ministries enter as the regulators and controllers,

but also protectors of, private financial institutions. Finally, government sets the legislative environment in which private relationships and property rights are determined. . . . Borrowers from government financial institutions have found it easier to borrow from private institutions than firms with no government loans.[13]

C. The Ministry of Foreign Affairs

The part of the central bureaucracy most involved in foreign policy is obviously the Ministry of Foreign Affairs (MFA). Despite being the window of Japan to the outside world it receives less attention than MITI (Ministry of International Trade and Industry) or more recently the Ministry of Finance. The reason for this neglect has to do with the increasingly multifaceted tasks of the MFA in contrast to more delineated tasks and objectives of other functional ministries and agencies. Moreover, with the growing internationalization of traditionally domestic policies the MFA is only one among many other players and it has become more of a go-between and mediator who tries to remind other players of the implications of a given issue for Japan's overall diplomacy or for a given bilateral relationship. This role also brings with it turf battles with other ministries and agencies where the importance of a given issue disappears behind the question who has won how much.[14] Even local administrations are now involved in international relations and are conducting their own diplomacy. The MFA is structurally in a weak position because it has no clear domestic constitutency or parliamentary interest group (*zoku*) like other ministries and agencies. It has, however, some influence with industry thanks to the fact that 76.4 per cent of its budget is ODA-related (out of a total budget of ¥55.3 billion as of FY 1995–96). Out of this ODA amount, 12.3 per cent is for contributions to international aid organizations.[15] Based on 1987 data, the budget of the MFA ranked fourth with US$2.97 billion, behind the US ($8.28 billion), Germany ($5.35 billion) and Britain ($3.36 billion).[16]

A substitute for this structural weakness is, as in any other country, the strong backing from an authoritative government as was the case to some extent during the premiership of Prime Minister Nakasone. However, even he relied to a certain extent on private emissaries or private 'advisory committees' which tend to sideline the MFA. Usually, however, the Prime Minister is not a strong figure because he is the outcome of factional politics (lowest common denominator) and has to rely on an office which is weakened by small size and a rapid turnover of staff. Prime Minister Nakasone tried to strengthen the prime minister's coordination and control function of the bureaucracy by reorganizing the Prime Minister's Office (PMO).[17] Several new coordinating offices were created: the Councillor's Office on Internal Affairs, the Councillor's Office on External Affairs, the Security Affairs Office, and the Research and Intelligence Office. For various reasons this reorganization has not improved the decision-making.[18] One issue is the understaffing of the Prime Minister's Secretariat which has altogether 176 staff (Office of External Affairs 19, Security Affairs Office 24, Research and Analysis Office 24). Moreover, most of the staff of the PMO is on loan from other ministries, or at least the heads of sections are on loan. The MFA is in this way well represented on the staff of the PMO, but not at a level that the Prime Minister could exert strong control over the MFA.

The MFA's task and position is also more difficult in relation to other advanced industrialized countries because of staffing and funding restrictions. The staffing level reached as of March 1995 a total of 4889 (compared with 4416 in 1991), of which 1911 were in the Ministry itself and 2978 were abroad.[19] This can be compared with the figures for other countries (see Table 1.1).

A considerable part of the staff is on loan (*shukko*), be it in Tokyo or in overseas missions. As of March 1995 out of the 2978 staff abroad, 481 were on secondment from other ministries.[20] In 1987 there were 53 officials from the MFA to other governmental offices, and 712 officials came from other governmental offices on loan to the MFA, half of them at missions abroad, as well as 40 from the Defence Agency.[21] As of March 1995 the MFA had 181 embassies, 69 consulates-general, two consulates and six permanent missions or delegations.

The MFA was heavily criticized after the Gulf War in 1991 because of its alleged inability to predict the event and the way the International Peace Cooperation Law (IPCL) was handled (see Chapter 3). In a report of the Provisional Council for Promoting Administrative Reform, headed by Inamori Kazuo (president of Kyocera Corp.) deep cuts in the Ministry's personnel number, abolishment of its examination system and appointment of more ambassadors with private-sector background were demanded. In the end, however, the final report did not go as far as this and personnel numbers continued to increase. The examination system, which is different from that of all other ministries and agencies, was kept. In order to adapt the MFA to the changes in international affairs (for example new areas like high technology, foreign workers, drug issues) and to the growing visibility of Japan abroad (for example, number of Japanese tourists and residents abroad) the Ministry has recently undergone structural changes. But budgetary constraints oppose significant increase of personnel and these

Table 1.1 International comparison of staff in
ministries of foreign affairs (1990)

US	15 900
UK	8 204
France	6 632
Germany	6 546
Italy	4 855
Canada	4 606

Source: *Far Eastern Economic Review* (18 July 1991).

changes have to be done within the administrative guideline of 'scrap and build' which allows hardly any personnel increase but relies mainly on reorganization.

Whereas the administration and disbursement of ODA constitutes the MFA's financially most important activity, it is also in charge of Japan's security policy despite some competition from the Defence Agency and sometimes even MITI. The role of the MFA in security policy goes back to the occupation period and the negotiation of the Japan–US San Francisco Security Treaty of 1951. It stayed in charge of security policy as a function of the overall relationship with the US. The MFA thus became the guardian of the relationship with the US and all issues were subordinated to the maintenance of it. In the meantime the importance of the Defence Agency and the Self Defence Forces (SDF) in security policy has increased because of direct contacts with their counterparts in the US. When defence technology became an issue, first as a matter of the Coordinating Committee for Export Control (COCOM) and then as a new dimension of Japanese–American security cooperation, MITI created a Security Export Control Division in its International Trade Administration Bureau. At the beginning and during the Toshiba incident (1987) the MFA did not recognize MITI's role in this matter as it pertained to security policy.

D. Business

A crucial point for the understanding of the bureaucracy–business relationship is the size of the business entities which most enjoy the support of the bureaucracy. In order to wield more influence the bureaucracy has to concentrate on the big companies although because of their growing size they are also less amenable to bureaucratic control. At the same time the global market place is favouring big global companies and this fact promotes concentration of corporate players. The present recession is hastening this process of concentration by squeezing out smaller players who cannot cope with the rapid rise of the yen and the need to restructure. The foundation for this corporate power is the increase of overseas investment which has increased at a higher rate than world production or world trade. This applies notably to the Japanese multinational companies which are mostly synonymous with *'keiretsu'*.[22] The trend towards bigger corporate players seems to be unstoppable within Japan's economic system and stronger anti-monopoly laws will not have much impact on the size of these corporate players:

> Only by rigorous state intervention could further concentration be checked. But there is absolutely no chance of it. The history of the Japanese Antimonopoly Law is a history of emasculation. . . . The conclusion to be drawn from the prevailing conditions is that the concentration of economic power in Japan will continue. The world has to come to terms with the fact that the conglomerates will get even bigger and wield more clout than ever. Their irresistible attraction will lead to other independent companies seeking to join the industrial groupings. Belonging to a kigyo keiretsu may be a matter of survival.[23]

The tendency of the bureaucracy to favour 'controlled competition' and to prevent 'excessive competition' (*kato kyoso*) to the benefit of big companies is now very well documented. One case of how the bureaucracy colluded with the established big companies to prevent a new Japanese company (not a foreign company!) from entering the league of big players and which came out into the public relatively early was provided by a Japanese entrepreneur who wanted to use a loophole in the regulations in order to import oil and thus undercut the established companies.[24] The tolerance of cartels for various purposes (export cartels; recession cartels; rationalization cartels) strengthens the hands of big companies and is an illustration of its close links with central bureaucracy. Another example is 'bid rigging' (*dango*) by construction companies which is illegal and could not have continued for such a long time without the collusion of the bureaucracy which – apart from direct personal gains accruing to certain bureaucrats – saw it as a way of maintaining a controlled, predictable and orderly market.[25] A recent example of helping big companies through (legal) cartel building for the sake of economic (or rather financial) stability is the way the government intervened in 1992 and helped the banks to cope with their losses in real estate and their bad loans by establishing a joint 'bad loan' company.[26] Another example is the measures used by the government to support stock exchange prices which were ironically called PKO (price keeping operations).[27] The Bank of Japan used more than $35 billion between January 1993 and May 1994 to keep the yen's rise towards the dollar under control in 'one of the most sustained and costly campaigns to control currency values ever attempted'.[28] In the end the Japanese endeavour failed and the yen continued to rise below the threshold of ¥100 to the dollar. While the intervention by the Ministry of Finance-controlled Bank of Japan may have been aimed at providing a breathing space for the government to reduce Japan's rising trade surplus through credible measures to enhance imports, letting market forces provide stimuli would have been much more efficient in providing the political energy to do so.

The close cooperation between the bureaucracy and big companies has now come under more scrutiny in the context of the need to restructure the economy in order to get out of the recession, to respond to foreign demands for a greater opening, to bail out (or not) big companies fatally hurt by the end of the bubble economy and as a result of the changing domestic political alliances. The bureaucracy's ability to continue as before has become more limited due to growing popular opposition to such a cosy 'cohabitation', but by now the majority of the big companies have a strong position, increasingly relying less on the domestic market thanks to growing foreign investment and reliance on other markets. The financial markets in Japan have been opened considerably to the outside in the last ten years, but the tendency is not linear and the current volatility of the international currency markets and the risks involved in introducing advanced financial instruments as Barings' downfall has demonstrated (involving notably Japanese banks) will prevent Japan from opening very fast.

IDEOLOGICAL AND BEHAVIOURAL FACTORS

The above overview has touched upon several historical, ideological and cultural factors which influence the actors and have an important bearing on 'the paradox of unrealized power'. The following section will expand on two features related to these factors: pacifism and leadership. They have a strong impact on the actors, including public opinion, and affect the mobilization of Japan's power resources for its foreign policy.

There is first of all Japan's pacifism which influences not only Japan's security policy but its whole attitude towards involvement in international relations. The long experience of seclusion and peace during the Tokugawa period (1600–1867), the trauma of the failure of imitating imperialism, and the ensuing relatively benign international environment after 1945 have led to and sustained pacifism in Japan. This pacifism has nurtured a widespread apolitical attitude among most Japanese who were able to pursue economic rehabilitation and then expansion and consumerism without having to worry about military security.

Several factors strengthen pacifism in Japan. The defeat in 1945 gave rise to great scepticism about the usefulness of military power. The American war in Vietnam reinforced this attitude. Military power is still more associated with direct use and the invasion of other countries, whereas in other Western countries military power is more perceived as a deterrence, and as an additional and legitimate means to influence other countries (for example by showing the flag).

At the same time this pacifism could only survive because of the existence of the comprehensive Japanese–American security alliance which has since 1952 to a large extent taken care of one fundamental national interest of Japan, that is its external and physical security, as well as other interests (for example, an open international trading regime). While Japan has therefore renounced military power commensurate with its economic power, it has effectively used the power of another country which it could do because of the geostrategic interests of the US and the willingness to subordinate to and/or coordinate its foreign policy with that of the US. In other words, the fact that Japan did not own and exert certain power resources does not mean that such power resources were not actually available for use or needed. This policy is usually referred to as the 'Yoshida line' because it was set up by Prime Minister Yoshida Shigeru, the main architect of Japan's immediate postwar foreign and security policy.

Another factor is Japan's growing self-confidence derived from its economic achievements. There is the feeling that money can buy everything. During the Iraqi invasion of Kuwait many Japanese ignored the implications of Iraqi regional hegemony and felt that whoever would be ruling over Kuwait would have to sell oil, and Japan would have the money to buy it.[29] This attitude was viable because the US led an allied effort to militarily subdue Iraq, which was later financially supported by Japan.

Related to the above point is the general understanding that what Japan did to other Asian countries until 1945 was wrong (either morally and/or tactically) and that it should never be repeated. This recognition of historical debt, as insufficient as this recognition may appear to be to many neighbours of Japan (see Chapter 4), restrains Japan in exerting power.

Pacifism is also supported by a widespread feeling among the Japanese that their country has become such a valuable international asset and that other countries are so dependent on Japan's economic success in terms of access to capital, products and investment, that this situation would deter a security threat.

The clash which resulted from the demands of the Cold War and this pacifism gave rise to two conflicting political streams, which epitomize the dichotomy of Japanese politics until today.[30] On the one hand, there is what can be called the 'System of the Peace Constitution', because it was the 1947 Constitution which became the rallying point of all those who wanted a Japan without military forces and involvement in the struggles of the outside world. In Article 9 of the Constitution, Japan renounced forever the right to wage war and to maintain any sort of military force, and instead put its trust into the 'peace-loving peoples of the world'.[31] On the other hand, however, there is the comprehensive Japanese–US alliance system embracing political, military, economic and cultural areas. The alliance with the US provided Japan with a cost-efficient defence, allowed the readmittance to the Western world, but necessitated the rearmament of Japan and the unequivocal siding with the US during the Cold War period. Each system seems to exclude the other, but in effect the former would not have existed without the comfort of knowing that the US would always be the ultimate protector of Japan's security. In order to make the coexistence of the two streams more palatable to a majority of the Japanese, the conservative leadership focused successfully on economic rehabilitation and, later, economic expansion.

There is a widespread feeling that by being peaceful, notably adhering to the Peace Constitution (*Heiwa Kempo*), Japan will never be threatened. Opinion polls prove this when they reveal that the Peace Constitution in itself is seen by a considerable part of the population as a shield. On the other hand, Japan has been part of the Cold War confrontation and participated in it by strengthening its Self Defence Forces and integrating them into the global American security policy as well as by giving diplomatic support to this policy. Royama Michio therefore questions the foundation of Japan's postwar pacifism, calling it an 'unsophisticated pacifism' (*soboku na heiwa shugi*) with a very truncated understanding of war and peace.[32]

This 'unsophisticated pacifism' and concentration on economic goals has not allowed the development of principles. Some Japanese politicians have stressed that Japan's foreign policy has no principle, calling the country a trading or merchant nation which has to forgo all value judgements in order to survive. Miyazawa Kiichi, a former Foreign Minister and Prime Minister, is supposed to have said that Japanese diplomacy must preclude all value judgements.[33] The negative historical experience of militarism and ideological mobilization of the Japanese people for the Emperor institution and expansionist foreign policy goals has enhanced an inclination which avoids the development of a strong philosophy. As Nakane Chie once put it:

The Japanese way of thinking depends on the situation rather than principle – while with the Chinese it is the other way round. . . . We Japanese have no principles. Some people think we hide our intentions, but
we have no intentions to hide. Except for a few leftists or rightists, we
have no dogma and don't ourselves know where we are going.[34]

This statement may, however, go too far because there is a strong nationalist element in Japan which is instrumentalized by political and economic
forces. Japan's pacifism has led to a strong anti-American inclination with
leftist political forces because the US is seen as a factor which opposes
Japan's pacifism through the Japanese–American security treaty. Rightist
forces nurture nationalism by opposing American pressure on Japan to open
its market, change economic policies towards greater compatibility with
other Western countries and integrate Japan's defence into American security policy. The end of the Cold War and the doubts about America's continued commitment and ability to care for Asian security have strengthened
these two sources of nationalism.

Leadership without Leaders?

The issue of actors and institutions ultimately leads to the question whether
there is a leadership which can mobilize Japan's power resources to promote
the country's national interests abroad. Looking for one leader, however, is
rather misleading in Japan, where power is extremely diffused and where
there are many power-holders. In addition, behavioural patterns do not promote individual leadership.

Japan has had leaders, but even prewar politics did not produce any
outstanding leader like Churchill or a dictator like Hitler. The long rule of
conservatives in the postwar period relied on relatively weak leaders who
managed for longer or shorter periods to keep a coalition of factions in the
LDP together. They were hampered by institutional arrangements like the
weak Prime Minister's Office, the strong bureaucracy and competing power
interests in their own party. The system of changing ministers twice per
year in order to keep the factional balance and the factions' support did
not allow the nurturing of leadership. An exception was to some extent
Prime Minister Tanaka Kakuei (1972–74) who managed to build up a very
strong power position, lasting on well beyond his term as prime minister,
thanks to the pervasive use of funds to corrupt Diet members and leaders
of the bureaucracy on a scale unknown until then. After his fall from
power he showed also that leadership can be best exerted from behind by
using money to shape political forces and establish a factional balance in

favour of his own power. Kanemaru Shin, a senior figure in the LDP and one of the inheritors of Tanaka's political power base, never made it to prime ministership but, thanks to funding the political life of his allies, he became very influential in Japanese politics. His financial power derived from 'smoothing' the relationship between the construction and transport industries and the relevant ministries. By doing it too deftly even for Japanese taste and involving gangsters, he contributed to his downfall.

There are several cultural factors which have supported the political arrangements inhibiting political leadership. The values of harmony, conformity, groupism and conflict avoidance do not encourage leadership. Leadership in the Western sense of 'sticking one's head out' goes against a culture which advocates 'hammer down the nail which sticks out'. The need for consensus, conflict avoidance, and conformity does not allow for the development of concepts and leadership. On the other hand, Tanaka Kakuei enjoyed considerable popularity with the Japanese at large (that is, not just with his constituency for which he secured huge infrastructure projects) because he was unorthodox, forceful and not a former bureaucrat like his predecessors. Prime Minister Nakasone had a rather weak power base in the LDP but he skilfully used the media to address the people directly. By establishing a good relationship with President Reagan he enhanced his stature and prestige with the Japanese.

Nishihara Masashi once wrote in the context of Japan's defence policy but which can be applied to foreign policy in general, '. . . Japanese leaders tend to follow public opinion rather than lead it. They are responsive to public opinion rather than being responsible for it.'[35] Culturally there is a preference for stressing the importance of role model over leadership. Many Japanese consider that leadership through role model is provided by their country's extraordinary economic success, a feeling which is enhanced by the pride in this achievement. This explanation is also in Haga Yasushi's differentiation in the political arena between 'explicit leadership' which is for example strongly proposed by political leader Ozawa Ichiro, against 'implicit leadership' as for example exerted by the late Prime Minister Ohira Masayoshi.[36] Being rich and relying on economic power provides, however, many opportunities to continue to indulge in pacifism and in 'implicit leadership'.

THE IMPORTANCE OF BEING RICH

The foundation of Japan's international status and power is based on its economic achievement. Japan's GDP amounted in 1993 to $4190 billion which is the world's second after the US with $6377 billion and followed by Germany with $1879 billion. The UK's GDP is again only half of Germany's GDP. The nominal growth rate based on yen value has declined from 4.3 per cent in 1991 to −0.2 per cent in 1993 although based on dollar value the growth rate would be higher because of the yen's steep appreciation.

A. Financial Power

The result of Japan's industrial and trade performance has provided Japan with considerable financial might. The appreciation of the yen in 1985 as a result of the Plaza Agreement and the rise in land prices contributed to a tremendous boost to Japan's financial might. From 1972 to 1987 the value of the yen went up by a factor of around 2.6, from ¥360 per dollar to ¥140–150. Within 16 months alone the value of the yen rose by 70 per cent. Land increased in value by ¥200 trillion in 1986 alone. In 1987 Japan became the world's richest country, surpassing the United States in national assets with land, factories and other holdings valued at $43.7 trillion from $28.3 trillion in 1986 and $19.6 trillion in 1985.[37] Although much of the land and share values have taken a deep fall since 1990, it allowed Japan to win considerable advantages and to consolidate its economic power by building up its manufacturing capacity, by winning overseas markets, by enhancing its technological level through increased R&D expenditures whereas others had to cut it, and by investing abroad in financial markets and manufacturing capacities. In real terms, Japan invested in 1990 25.4 per cent of its GNP in plant and new capital equipment, for a total of $660 billion, compared with the US investing $510 billion, or approximately 9.3 per cent of GNP, while Germany invested about $240 billion, or about 15 per cent of its GNP.[38] The yen has continued to rise and is at present around ¥80 to the dollar (May 1995). Japan is still the world's largest net creditor. Its net external assets had increased by 34.1 per cent from 1991 to $513.62 billion in 1992, an increase for 11 consecutive years while overseas liabilities recorded their first decline in 15 years.[39]

B. Technological Power

A decisive indicator of Japan's international competitivity is its technological performance and therefore deserves special mentioning. The better the performance of the financial and manufacturing sectors, the more funds can be put into R&D (if this need is recognized!) and in turn further strengthen the technological base in order to stay ahead or even overtake competitors. The Japanese R&D expenditures increased from only $8.8 billion in 1975 to $100.9 billion in 1992, compared with $62.6 billion and $157.4 billion for the US in the same time period. The figure for the UK in 1991 was $21 billion compared with Germany's $45 billion. Japanese firms spend more on R&D as a percentage of GNP than do their European or American counterparts. The percentage of research spending in GNP for 1992 was 2.96 per cent for Japan, followed by Germany with 2.57 per cent, the US with 2.52 per cent, France with 2.44 per cent and the UK with 2.12 per cent.[40] Between 1981 and 1993 private sector-financed R&D expenditures grew at an average rate of 8 per cent, compared with a rate of 3.9 per cent, 1.6 per cent, 3.9 per cent and 4.6 per cent for the US, the UK, Germany and France, respectively.[41] Another useful indicator for Japan's technological strength is the fact that the technological balance of payments in 1992 became positive, which means that Japan is now reaping benefits from technology licensed to developing countries and thus balancing payments to advanced industrialized countries.

Japan is today undisputedly a major technological power, as is proved by a great variety of aggregate indicators. Although it is second after the US in R&D expenditures and as a percentage of GNP, it is probably first if American R&D expenditures for military purposes are taken out. Japan takes top position in other indicators of input such as R&D expenditures per capita, R&D personnel as a percentage of the labour force, and industrial R&D expenditures as a percentage of the domestic industrial product. The input is reflected in the output such as the share of total world exports in high technology sectors and the share of patent applications. Efficiency of the R&D in terms of high technology products is enhanced by the fact that over 70 per cent of the R&D expenditures are undertaken by civilian companies in comparison to other major industrialized countries where the government accounts for a large share. Japan's technological ability is significantly enhanced by various governmental promotion efforts of high technology, ranging from subsidies and low-cost loans to tax exemption.[42] The importance given to technology is also demonstrated by the fact that in 1993 80 per cent of Japan's intelligence work was in this field, mostly directed against American companies.[43]

As a result Japan has advanced to top positions in critical areas of high technology:

– Japan's semiconductor industry has absolute control in a certain number of key device, equipment and materials technologies.[44] The world market is therefore, for example, vulnerable to the impact of the yen's appreciation.[45] However, the US is still leader in higher value segments of

the market (for example, microprocessors) and Korean companies are making inroads into the mass production segments (DRAM).
– Of the top ten semiconductor equipment suppliers in 1980, all but the tenth were American, in 1990 five of them, including number one and two, were Japanese.[46]
– Japan has become an important partner for the growing number of transnational corporate alliances for technology development. In the period 1980–84 there were 345 between the US and Europe, 274 between US and Japan and 101 between Europe and Japan. These numbers increased to 593, 309 and 150 respectively for the period 1985–89.[47]
– The position of Japan's electronics companies is crucial in determining international standards. One recent example is the new standard of video disks with sound and picture. As in the previous case of the video tape standard, the option is not between a Japanese and a non-Japanese company, but between alliances built by two different Japanese companies.

C. Integration into the World Economy

Particularly relevant for our purpose is the integration of Japan into the world economy.[48] Here very often hasty conclusions are drawn from the size of Japan's economy as well as the visibility of its consumer goods abroad. In fact, however, Japan's position as a world trading power becomes more relative in the light of some trade indicators which are also important in evaluating the perceived importance of the outside world. The value of foreign trade per capita is for exports and imports together $4856 compared with $10 327 for the UK or $8552 for Germany.[49] A similar picture results from a comparison of the rate of dependency on foreign trade which is also related to the size of population. Due to a big domestic market (123 million inhabitants) these figures are low and similar to the US, but they do not diminish the overall importance of foreign trade for the prosperity of Japan. However, in absolute monetary values, the total value of Japan's exports in 1994 was $397 billion, compared with $513 billion for the US and $422 billion for Germany according to the World Trade Organization. Britain came fifth with $205 billion after France. Japan's share in world trade is also relatively low and for exports amounted to 9 per cent in 1992 (compared with the US with 11.9 per cent, Germany 11.2 per cent and the UK 5 per cent) and for imports to 6.2 per cent (compared with the US with 14.7 per cent, Germany 10.7 per cent and the UK 5.9 per cent). Japan has had since 1991 an annual trade surplus of around $100 billion with the rest of the world (1993: $106 billion), over half of it with the US. This compares with a trade surplus for Germany in 1993 of $43 billion and a deficit for the UK of $20 billion. The figure for Japan is particularly high because of the yen's appreciation but reflects also a tendency to focus imports more on raw materials and energy requirements rather than on manufactured goods compared with other Western industrialized countries. Although the share of manufactured goods in Japan's total imports has dramatically increased from 22.8 per cent in 1980 to 55.2 per cent in 1994, notably thanks to the country's growing imports from Japanese-owned production facilities abroad, the figure is much higher for other industrialized countries (1993: US: 80 per cent; Germany: 78 per cent; UK: 79 per cent).

The rising yen, circumvention of protectionism in Japan's major markets and growing globalization of Japanese production have led to an increase in the relocation of production facilities abroad. In 1981 Japan became the world's largest capital exporter. In 1993 the cumulative amount of Japan's direct foreign investment (of which investment in the manufacturing sector is only a small part!) had risen to $422 billion, of which $185 billion went to North America, $84 billion to Europe and only $6.6 billion to Asia. At the end of 1993 Japanese net external assets stood at $611 billion, with $2181 billion assets and $1570 billion liabilities.[50] In 1992 Japan overtook the UK as the world's second largest source of foreign investment, only preceded by the US. At the end of 1992 American outward investment amounted to $489 billion, Japan's to $248 billion and that of the UK to $243 billion.[51] However, because the manufacturing sector has a relatively small share in Japan's total direct foreign investment, the percentage of production abroad was rather low with 16.1 per cent as of 1993. The US has 27 per cent of its production overseas.[52] The high amount of Japanese direct investment abroad compares also with a paltry cumulative foreign investment in Japan of only $30 billion. Finally, intra-firm trade accounts for a high percentage of Japan's trade. Over the past decade, intra-firm trade accounted for 71 per cent of merchandise trade with the US, of which 92 per cent was conducted by Japanese multinationals and only 8 per cent by US-based multinationals.[53] It is also very relevant for the Japanese trade surplus with Europe and the US that in 1992, Japanese affiliates in the US imported $62.2 billion from their parent firms, while US multinationals exported only $6.8 billion to their affiliates in Japan. By comparison, European affiliates in the US imported $41.9 billion from their parent firms, while US multinationals exported $32.2 billion to their affiliates in Europe.[54]

D. Is Japan's Economic Power Declining?

In the last few years books have appeared in Japan as well as outside of Japan which do not just relativize Japan's economic strength but cast doubt on the economy's sound foundation.[55] The main triggers for these books and articles have been the impact of the worldwide recession, the severe banking crisis and recession in Japan, but also a certain lack of perspective of the Japanese. The recession has hit Japan, but although GNP growth has declined, unemployment and bankruptcy figures have increased, the banking system suffers from a severe loan crisis and manufacturing capacity is leaving the country with increasing speed, the overall stability and prosperity of Japan is not threatened. Most alarmist figures are still very moderate in comparison with Japan's major competitors and the fast changes in Japan prove the intrinsic strength and adaptability of the economy. What country could have survived so well such a steep appreciation of its currency as Japan has since the Plaza Agreement in 1985?

A more temperamental reason for this outburst of pessimism in Japan is a general tendency for pessimism which is exploited by the great number of publications chasing readers. The older generation, remembering the difficult times of rebuilding the economy after the war, has always felt that the rapid growth of the economy cannot be sustained and that everything may crumble as fast as it has been built. Moreover business seems not to be too averse to continue to tolerate if not foster a cult of vulnerability ('we have no raw materials and only our brains to rely on for our economic prosperity') which keeps up the morale of a producer-oriented society and may be useful in moderating foreign demands for greater openness of the Japanese market and in keeping down domestic demands for more deregulation and consumer orientation.

This pessimism is also fed by the theory that Japan with growing economic and social maturity will succumb to the same social 'evils' such as welfare and consumption as its competitors in America and in Europe are supposed to have done. The support of this theory is, of course, useful for business and government which wants to keep social expenditures down. It is true that Japan's working hours have become shorter and leisure and consumption attract now much more attention than ever before, while the four little dragons in Asia (South Korea, Hong Kong, Singapore, Taiwan) increasingly encroach on some sectors where Japan excels. Yet Japan is not standing still but surprises the world with its adaptability. Even if the gap between Japan and (for example) Europe should narrow – which seems to assume that the Europeans stand still or do not decline further while only Japan declines – the comparative advantages which Japan enjoys will make a crucial difference.

Other concerns about the Japanese economy are more well founded. One is the rapid restructuring of the Japanese economy which includes the threat over long-established traditions like 'life-long' employment, automatic promotion following the principle of seniority, and a general loss of stability compared to the past. Another more long-term but well-documented and discussed problem is the economic impact of an ageing population which is still low but rapidly rising. But while more workers have to shoulder more retired people, there are still considerable pockets of non- or under-utilized labour, like female workers, who are discriminated against. The Great Hanshin Earthquake of 17 January 1995 has also reminded the Japanese of their vulnerability to natural calamities which can have disastrous effects on growth and prosperity.

E. The Banking Crisis

The banking crisis is particularly symptomatic of what has gone wrong with Japan's economy and is the most dramatic failure of any economic sector apart from the real estate sector to which it is, of course, intimately linked. The crisis reminded people of the futility of money speculation (*zaiteku*) and relying on ever-increasing real estate prices. Japanese banks count a portion of their unrealized stock gains as capital, which makes them very vulnerable in case of a stock market crash or devaluation of land holdings. This is exactly what happened when the stockmarket went down to a record low in 1992. Debts of companies which went bankrupt in 1991 totalled a record ¥8149 billion (£35.6 billion), four times more than 1990. Property and stock market investors accounted for most of the largest failures.[56] The non-performing loans of the banking system due to the fall in the property market were officially estimated to be around ¥40 000 billion (£296 billion) or around 10 per cent of Japan GDP in June 1995 but estimates are constantly revised upwards.[57] The continued weakness of the Japanese economy has in addition led to a fall in total loans advanced.[58] The attraction of Japan as an international financial market has also decreased because of costs and the strict regulatory framework. The number of foreign stocks listed on the Tokyo Stock Exchange went down from 127 at the end of 1991 to 93 at the end of 1994.[59] One can not only talk about the hollowing out (*kudoka*) of manufacturing industry, but even more so of the financial industry. The stockmarkets of Hong Kong and Singapore have expanded at the expense of those in Japan. Futures and bonds are increasingly traded in less regulated Asian places like Hong Kong and Singapore.

In 1994 none of Japan's 20 commercial banks retained the previous triple-A status. Leading Japanese banks reportedly have an average capital adequacy ratio, the main measure of their power to lend, which stands at 9.75 per cent of risks-weighted assets, which is above the 8 per cent minimum set by the Bank of International Settlements (BIS) in Basle. But this

BIS ratio is widely assumed to be artificially high because the Ministry of Finance is allowing banks to overstate their capital.[60] When the BIS ratio was determined in 1988, the Japanese banks were structurally so different in terms of liquidity that a different way of calculation of the BIS ratio for the Japanese banking system was accepted in order to allow Japan to reach the ratio in as reasonable a length of time as the other industrialized countries.

Still, in 1995 11 banks of the world's top 20 banks (by assets) were Japanese, and Japanese banks occupied the top eight places. The fact that their net operating profits are by international standards very low may be a disadvantage in non-Japanese eyes, but profits have never been the main consideration of Japanese companies marching towards the top. In 1993 Japan had the world's second largest government bond market and the second biggest stock market capitalization, while being the world's largest capital importer and the biggest net capital exporter.[61]

F. Weaker but Still Less Weak than Others

Rising investment and the transfer of technology abroad is said to have led to higher unemployment (around 3 per cent) and a hollowing out of the country's manufacturng base, bringing with it a loss of capabilities, increased dependence on external factors and less Japanese control. Japan now imports more colour television sets than it exports and has been overtaken by China as the world's largest producer of colour TVs. Imported cars (often from Japanese subsidiaries abroad like the 'Primera' of Nissan in Washington (Northeast of England)) are taking a growing share of Japan's car market. Japan was overtaken in 1994 by the US as the world's largest producer of cars for the first time since 1980. Domestic production in 1993 was about the same level as in 1983 at just over 11 million units.[62] On the other hand, Japan manages to keep R&D activities and the production of high-value-added products at home, such as liquid crystal display and wide-screen TVs. Japan's manufacturing sector share in GDP has remained steady at an unusually high 31 per cent (similar to Germany's 34 per cent, but higher than the American share of 21 per cent or Britain's at 23 per cent) and is only now decreasing to 27.9 per cent in 1992. It is as yet unclear whether this is more a cyclical or a structural change. The manufacturing sector has also reduced employment at a much slower pace than the drop in manufacturing output might indicate.

Japan's technological base has structural weaknesses such as a lack of fundamental research, lack of a venture capital infrastructure and lack of medium-sized companies in the high technology sectors which would be more responsive to newly emerging technology and to new technology applications. Japan is also weak in system integration (for example, aerospace), software and nuclear technology. The ten-year 'Fifth Generation' computer project had to be ended in 1992 after having created some interesting hardware, but no promising software.[63] Japan's strength is more in products which can be enhanced through incremental improvements rather than technological breakthroughs. It excels in products which can be standardized and thus benefit from mass production technologies (for example, memory chips rather than microprocessors). This has made Japan vulnerable to competition in certain sectors like mass produced memory chips, where Samsung of Korea has now achieved larger scales of production than Japan. Samsung is now the world's seventh largest chip company. Japan's share of worldwide sales of semiconductors has decreased from over 50 per cent in 1988 to 40 per cent in 1994, whereas that of the US moved from a trough of 37 per cent in 1988 to 43 per cent in 1994.[64]

Other problems limiting Japan in using its advantages in technology and domestic market lie in the producer-motivated rather than consumer-motivated approach, bureaucratic rivalries and the general top-down approach in certain areas of high technology.[65] The strength of Japan's corporations and their support from government can also be counterproductive when energy is channelled in the wrong direction as was the case with the standard for High Definition TV (HDTV). Although the Japanese, thanks to their exclusionist market power, were the first to start an analogue HDTV, it turned out that the digital technology of the US is more powerful and the Japanese will probably have to be content again with being the market leader for the hardware, but not for the original technology. A similar top-down approach with the same danger of getting it wrong on a massive scale is also recognizable in the way Japan approaches the Information Superhighway. Thanks to its huge domestic market, high technology, a very sophisticated hardware market and bureaucratic support, there are great opportunities for worldwide dominance as well as great dangers of failing by putting all its eggs into one basket, for example building a massive fibre-optic network which misses the market demand.

The political and economic changes within the last few years have proved that the Japanese political and economic system is still powerful but less successful in dealing with change. The Great Hanshin Earthquake in 1995 demonstrated the weak crisis management of the bureaucracy and the central government because a natural event such as this is against the traditional strength of the Japanese political system, that is, control and predictability. The political turmoil has on the one hand strengthened the hand of bureaucrats, but on the other hand further exposed their fundamental weakness. Bureaucrats are good at the micro level but as the international monetary crisis 1969–71, the 1987 Toshiba scandal and the 1990–91 Gulf War have shown they cannot act independently and with vision. Very often these agencies cannot resolve their inter-agency conflicts without outside intervention and overall guidance by politicians. If politicians are too weak and absorbed with power struggles, decisions are difficult to make. The bureaucracy cannot therefore always benefit from the power vacuum created by the absence of politicians since the political changes in 1993.

Can we therefore conclude that the foundation for Japan's power, its economic strength, is dwindling, making any consideration of the development of this power into other power areas a moot issue? This would certainly be a mistake and miss the intrinsic strength of Japan's political economic system.

Due to the end of the bubble economy and the downturn during the period 1990–93, Japan's foreign investments have very much slowed down. Until 1990, the capital outflow was roughly equivalent to the current account surplus. In 1991 there was a long-term capital inflow of $35 billion, and thereafter the net outflow of long-term capital was far smaller than the current account surplus.[66] The two major motivations for investment will, however, stay and pick up again when the recession eases: the need to find profitable placement for capital and the internationalization of Japan's economy. Increasing production costs at home and access to markets will continue to motivate Japanese companies to invest in manufacturing abroad. More investments abroad will mean more Japanese control of segments of foreign national economies, but at the same time also a growing dependency on other countries and the international economic system for the health and prosperity of Japan's economy.

Japan's liquidity holdings are still very high and will remain so. The international financial market has come to rely on Japanese capital. The extreme size of Japan's financial holdings also has an impact on exchange rates. Japanese financial institutions are still willing to live on smaller margins than other institutions and they continue therefore to be a formidable competition in the international financial market. The sheer size of Japan's financial institutions (banks, insurance companies, the postal savings system) offsets the lower efficiency and profitability of these institutions. The competition is more strongly felt in the banking sector (that is, loan giving), which is as sophisticated as that in other countries, than in the insurance market. Japanese insurance companies are relatively unsophisticated and are restrained by domestic regulations in adopting new financial tools such as derivatives. Japan's insurance companies have reacted to the yen's rise in recent years by staying at home, thus further contributing to Japan's huge current account surplus.

Japan's industrial strength lies in the high average level of technology in its products and processes. There is the relatively high availability of funds which allows investment in new developments and R&D, buying of foreign technology and/or expertise, further automation, foreign direct investment and greater risk safety. There is the industrial structure which allows greater diversification, greater risk taking and better economies of scale. There is a less controversial employer–employee relationship than in most other countries. There is the proven cooperation between government and industry which often is not so much agreement on a specific course, but agreement on a general course or on a general value (that is, protection of Japan's economic interests). Japan is closely linked to the most dynamic economic region of the world. Japan's economy has also still considerable reserves for growth if it really overcomes domestic opposition to deregulate its domestic market to allow new players and thus reduce its high domestic price level.

In many ways Japan is constantly trying to change and to adapt in order to keep ahead. While fundamental change and adaptation is slow and this slowness hurts not only Japan's economic and foreign relations with other countries but also its own long-term economic interests, these delays are also often keeping structural advantages which are considered as unfair and against a 'level playing field' by its foreign partners. Japan is becoming a more 'normal' country, but 'normal' countries are also changing so that in effect the gap may be eroding, but there is still a gap which can be interpreted as a comparative advantage.

IS THE JAPANESE 'SYSTEM' COMPATIBLE WITH OTHER COUNTRIES?

It emerges clearly from the above that the Japanese political economy is different from that of most of Japan's trading partners and that Japan derives considerable benefit from these differences. Japan's economic partners fault these differences for serious trade and investment imbalances with Japan. Is Japan's political economic system therefore incompatible with the most important global players or is there even a 'Japanese conspiracy'? The question would not matter if Japan was generally considered not to be very important or if Japan's takeover of crucial sectors of global politics and economics was perceived as imminent and unstoppable. But the truth of the matter is that Japan is very dependent on the outside world for the perpetuation of its prosperity and welfare. Moreover, due to its global reach Japan is daily becoming more interdependent. The question raised about Japan's incompatibility is therefore as much related to Japan getting an unfair advantage over its competitors as to the accusation that Japan is a free rider of the global system who is doing nothing or not enough to maintain a favourable global environment.

Closely related to the issue of compatibility is the issue of convergence and Japan's political economy moving closer to that of its major industrialized trading partners. From the outside it often appears that despite the constant changes in Japan's political economy, the country is hardly moving, whereas from the inside the changes are dramatic. It depends whether one looks at Japan with the impatience of a businessman or the results-oriented Japan policy of a foreign government aiming at entering the Japanese market, or whether one is confronted with these changes as a resident, consumer or long-time observer.

A. Is Japan's System Conspiratorial?

It is natural that Japan's political economic system is open to conspiratorial suspicions because the hierarchical structure of Japan's political economic system with a decreasing number of actors the closer one approaches the top makes agreeing on fundamental interests easier than in a system with more effective and rigid checks and balances. Transparency of procedures and processes is often lacking due to structures and leadership issues. The barrier which the Japanese language erects between Japanese and foreigners is also not helpful.

However, a conspiracy theory is refuted by most serious authors and scholars, including the Revisionist school, which has unfortunately encouraged some people to see a conspiracy. There is no centrally planned conspiracy. Bill Emmott even argues that there is no national economic strategy and that the definition of any common goal or strategy would merely result in a most general and banal statement because there are too many groups and interests.[67]

The central question is whether Japan's big business federations or individual companies who influence foreign actors are acting as Japanese enterprise with Japan-centred strategies or whether they are acting as global enterprises which have no special allegiance to Japan or any other countries. If the latter is the case then their function for using Japan's economic power for other than Japan-centred economic goals is limited. This question is particularly important in view of the fact that the role of oligopolistic firms abroad has considerably increased with more such companies setting up manufacturing investments in the Western industrialized countries, accompanied by Japanese banks.[68] Related to the interaction between the bureaucracy and business is also the question to what degree private companies have taken over from the government many functions normally the prerogatives of the state.[69] Thanks to what Matsumoto Koji calls 'kigyoism' big companies are states in themselves, providing services normally provided by a state, and receiving loyalties normally reserved for the state. This, in conjunction with the close cooperation between the government and (big) business, may enhance the perception of foreign competitors that they are not dealing with private companies but rather with 'government' which is less acceptable because it further reduces the 'level playing field' and impacts on the very sensitive issue of national sovereignty of other countries.

The first element of the answer is that there are no 'stateless' enterprises with their activities spread in balanced fashion across a 'borderless world'.[70] So-called 'multinational', 'global' or 'transnational' enterprises are only national entities with foreign operations. Although some companies like Nestlé or IBM are more transnational than most others normally mentioned in this category, Japanese companies are even less transnational. A recent US government report came to the conclusion that 'most multinational companies remain firmly rooted in the national technical, financial, and corporate cultures of their home countries', and that it would be unlikely 'that differences in national patterns of technology development, direct investment, long-term finance, and corporate governance will converge'.[71]

The second part of the answer is that Japanese companies act on their own, but depending on their size and structure (involvement in a *'keiretsu'*) they can draw more on the help of their national government than comparable 'multinational' companies can. Their ability to draw on these resources is, however, limited by conflicting other interests and the relative paralysis in the whole political decision-making process.

The multitude of actors and the limits of the collaboration between the bureaucracy and business makes a general conspiracy or even a national economic strategy unlikely. One of the very fundamental strengths of the Japanese system, that is, its unprincipled flexibility or opportunism, also militates against such conspiratorial ambitions. The Japanese polity does not often get bogged down in the devotion to any fundamental principle, be it spreading democracy or 'wasting national energy' in coming to terms with the legacy of its past.

B.   But it is Different...

If Japan's political economic system is not conspiratorial it is certainly different and there are now plenty of statements originating from Japanese as well as non-Japanese to this effect. Very often these statements do not mention that around Japan there is a growing number of countries now reaching increasingly (at least in the economic arena) global importance such as the NIEs which share many features of Japan's political economic system. The issue of 'systemic differences' with the other Western industrialized countries is therefore important beyond Japan. It has to be recognized, however, that the differences between the political economic systems in Japan and the US may be larger than between that of Japan and other Western countries, notably European countries.[72]

International competitiveness has been defined as 'the degree to which a nation can, under free and fair market conditions, produce goods and services that meet the test of international markets while simultaneously maintaining or expanding the real income of its citizens'.[73] It is the part on 'free and fair market conditions' which is very much in doubt, although no country can claim complete adherence to free market conditions. The main arguments brought forward to justify Japan being called 'different' are the following:

1.   The domination of Japan's economic activities by big conglomerates and the tolerance of cartels which indicates a fundamental difference to the liberal economic idea where structural adjustments are carried out by free market forces, for example by more imports.[74] Over 70 per cent of the shares of large companies are tied up in cross shareholdings (*mochiai*) with banks or related corporations.[75] Individuals hold just 20 per cent of the value of all shares, compared with more than 70 per cent in the late 1940s and early 1950s. As a study commissioned by the Ministry of Finance itself found out, the stock market of Tokyo is not really a market.[76] This situation allows cheaper funding and long-term planning.

2.   The subcontracting system allows big companies to use subcontractors as recession cushions and constitutes a considerable barrier to newcomers (foreign and domestic). The subcontracting system has over time ossified and adapted many non-economic features (social features; relocation ground for unwanted staff in big companies, etc).[77]

3.   The close relationship between the bureaucracy and the big economic players; the role of the bureaucracy (MITI, Science & Technology Agency, etc) in fostering applied and now also fundamental research.[78]

4. The ethos of the bureaucracy (as part of a general societal ethos) which values predictability and wants to avoid 'excessive competition'.
5. The relational character of Japanese society which favours cooperation and conformism but can also constitute the breeding ground for political and economic corruption.[79]
6. The existence of many non-tariff barriers (such as regulations, *keiretsu* trading, etc) is enhanced by a nationalistic atmosphere which tends to exclude foreigners and foreign products in favour of domestic products.[80] It has been calculated that these trade barriers inflicted a cost on the Japanese consumer of ¥10–15 trillion in 1989, or $75–100 billion. Due to the appreciation of the yen the cost of protectionism is rising.[81]
7. The existence of institutions and mechanisms which are only on the face of it similar to ours but are run very differently, or do not exist at all in other countries.
8. Market share is the absolute goal of Japanese enterprises, and the political economic structure helps them to achieve this goal without having to pay the full costs which would accrue to a company in a more liberal capitalist system. This has been referred to as the pursuit of adversial trade.[82]
9. A producer-oriented rather than a consumer-oriented system.

Whereas these differences in institutions and political–economic philosophy have been most eloquently documented by the Revisionist school, notably Chalmers Johnson, there are now also increasing numbers of Japanese voices which confirm these findings, either by taking pride in them to protect them or in order to make the Japanese political economic system more compatible with that of the country's major partners and to open new business opportunities to lead Japan out of recession. Japanese writers have referred to Japan's economic system as 'noncapitalist market economy' (*Sakakibara Eisuke*), 'network capitalism' in contrast to America's 'market capitalism' (*Nakatani Iwao*) and 'catch-up capitalism' or 'the capitalism of the latecomer' (*Okita Saburo*).[83] Chalmers Johnson has coined the phrase 'capitalist developmental state' to describe Japan's political economic system whereas others describe it as neo-mercantilist state.[84] In a recent article Johnson has presented various statements and writing by Japanese economists and government officials who admit to the difference of Japan's capitalism.[85]

There is now in Japan a much greater assertiveness about these differences, and some are even recommending Japan's system as a model for other countries. In a report commissioned by the Ministry of Foreign Affairs and written by business leaders, the US is reminded in the context of the much criticized *keiretsu* system that it had failed to learn key lessons about the merits of doing business the Japanese way.[86]

Other Japanese are critical and talk about Japan's 'war-footing' economic system.[87] In its 1995 White Paper the Ministry of International Trade and Industry recommended that Japan's economic system must be adjusted to incorporate market mechanisms more fully if it is to successfully compete with other countries. Government regulations and special business practices are blamed for Japan's high cost structure which also prevents the population from benefiting from the high rise of the yen.[88]

C. From Difference to Incompatibility?

Refuting a conspiracy and finding a growing consensus among Japanese and non-Japanese alike about fundamental differences between Japan's political economic system and that of most of its partners is easier than to come to a conclusion on the question of what this means for Japan's compatibility with the most important players in the world. The underlying problem is to define where difference in degree turns into incompatibility. The question is whether the political economic system is just different as is that of many other major countries (for example, the German system from the American system) or is the difference going beyond a threshold which is arguably intolerable? And what conclusions would have to be drawn by Japan's partners if Japan's systemic differences are intolerable? Or is Japan's political economy bound to become convergent with the majority of other political economic systems and will the problem therefore sooner or later disappear? The matter is made more complex by the fact that many features of Japan's economic system have become more convergent with that of other countries, as for example the ratio of manufactured imports or the number and size of tariffs imposed on foreign goods. On the other hand, many features of its system are not covered by international regimes like that of GATT, such as the *keiretsu* system or the complex distribution system. These issues have to be addressed at least to some extent before we come to the discussion of Japan's hard and soft power.

Some people argue that Japan is indeed a threat to the rest of the world, and after the demise of the Soviet Union, many in the US were willing to consider Japan as the new threat replacing that of the Soviet Union. This threat perception was nurtured by Japan's inroad into what many Americans, in particular defence technology leaders, considered as very strategic

American assets. One CIA-funded study therefore came to the following conclusions:

> Economic domination could precede the imposition of substituted value systems. This is particularly troubling because of the absence of any absolutes or moral imperatives in the Japanese paradigm, unlike [in] the Western paradigm, anchored on the Judeo-Christian ethic. . . . Individual freedoms . . . have created an atmosphere of openness and sharing that has enabled our economic competitors to acquire our most important technology – and they are using it to defeat us, to lower our standard of living, and to threaten our national security.[89]

Chalmers Johnson makes an interesting comparison between Germany and Japan which both diverge from Anglo-American orthodoxy but Germany's difference is, according to him, less disruptive of the global capitalist system because

> German patterns of intraindustry trade are on a par with other industrialized countries; foreign investors own some 17 per cent of German assets compared with one per cent of Japan's; Germany has real political parties and a highly transparent political process; Germany has come to grips with the nations it once victimized and today is deeply embedded in a multinational environment; Germany absorbs refugees; and Germany is actively engaged in foreign aid to the former command economies of Eastern Europe.[90]

He argues that '. . . the study of comparative capitalism indicates that several capitalist countries want to produce more not in order to consume more but to obtain leverage over other countries and to bolster their own national security and autonomy'.[91]

The conclusion drawn by authors like Chalmers Johnson or James Fallow, another 'Revisionist', is that we have to recognize that Japan is indeed different and therefore have to abandon the illusion of Japan just being a different capitalist system and ultimately becoming like the US.[92] Furthermore, they suggest that the US should pursue a more results-oriented managed trade policy towards Japan, adapt some Japanese institutions and procedures to become more competitive and reduce security commitments to East Asia. Others have gone much further and even suggest the likelihood of a Japan–US war.[93] Similar European voices are much fewer, which reflects the lower importance of Japan for the EU. Roy Denman, a former EU official, suggested raising tariffs against Japan, on the basis that Japan 'does not fit into the rules of the modern trading world. . . . Japan is not a democracy; it is an association for the advancement of the interests of

Japan'.[94] Recognizing that the way the Japanese economy is organized and supported, it is unbeatable as a system, Fodella suggests that we have either

> to create a barrier to control that system in order not to be dominated by it, or accept the rule of 'survival of the fittest' even when the fittest is not in the West, a Darwinistic approach [which] is out of date since we created the welfare state and a social market economy rather than 'pure' capitalism as the rule in Europe.[95]

By the former system he understands a differentiated protectionism where the weak are protected and the strong kept under control.

The Japan Federation of Economic Organizations (*Keidanren*) has also recognized officially that Japan's political economic system is somehow different, describing Japan as 'a society in which the company plays an excessively dominant role, the efficiency-first principle, long working hours, poor social infrastructure related to the nation's life, scorn for family life, the burial of individuality, a lack of human comfort'.[96] Faced with domestic as well as foreign criticism of this system, the *Keidanren* proposes '*kyosei*' (economic symbiosis) as a new mode of competition. The idea seems to be that by addressing the above deficiencies the Japanese economy will become more similar to that of its major competitors and thus make it easier for these to compete and coexist with Japan. But in the first instance, it seems to be directed at smaller domestic competitors and only at a later stage to be extended to foreign competitors. The hope is, of course, that addressing these deficiencies, that is exploiting Japan's huge domestic market, will generate sufficient opportunities for business to offset any losses incurred by '*kyosei*' towards foreign competition. The idea ties in with *Keidanren*'s pressure for deregulation and opening of the Japanese economy to address the structural weaknesses as shown by the present economic recession. The concept of '*kyosei*' is still very ambiguous and there has been suspicion that it will result in cosy cartels to overcome the recession. It has also been called a way of sugarcoating the westernization of Japan which was brought along by industrialization.[97] Only the future will tell whether it applies to Western competitors as well, and how the contradiction between competition and harmonious relations can be resolved.

The most famous individual critique of Japan's economic system (not political system) and its compatibility with that of the major Western countries is probably that by Morita Akio.[98] He wrote:

> We are approaching a point where continued competition by Japanese companies operating under a management philosophy alien to that of Europeans and Americans can no longer be tolerated. . . . These differences

of management philosophy are responsible for . . . creating a pricing structure that is impossible for Western companies to beat.[99]

And on another occasion he said:

Western business management typically sell their products at a price that will enable them to pay adequate dividends to their stockholders and good wages and holidays to their employees, and still retain a reasonable level of corporate earnings. With these generous policies, European and American companies, then, cannot compete with the low profit, mass sales approach of Japanese companies. They claim it is unfair for Japanese companies to enter their business domain with prices that are determined according to the market principles of Japan.[100]

To resolve the problems created by the different kinds of capitalisms, Morita suggested more vacations, higher dividend payments, contributions to the community and more environmental protection. By focusing merely on the economic system, he obviously cannot explain the structural reasons and incentives for Japan being as he describes it, and therefore he can only offer an appeal to change it.

Other evaluations of Japan's differences basically agree that we can accept the costs of these differences. A representative of this opinion is Joseph Nye, who plays down the differences by pointing out the end of the bubble economy and changing currents like demography. Although he agrees that the differences will not go away quickly, the recent developments are to alleviate the tension arising from the differences. He argues that the differences have brought the Americans good quality consumer goods and that without Japan there would still be problems like America's low savings rate, its budget deficit and its low productivity growth in services etc.[101]

Some economists even point out that some of the differences are necessary for the stability of the international economic system, such as Japan's trade surplus. In 1990 a report of a Ministry of Finance advisory panel concluded that Japan's surplus is not disruptive to the world economy because it helps to finance the US budget deficit and development aid.[102] While this view may be put down as self-serving propaganda, it was reinforced by the IMF and other economists who stressed the importance of Japan's high savings for the world economy.[103] This is, of course, a rather narrow economist view which does not take into account wider economic, let alone political, aspects of chronic Japanese trade surpluses, but it points out that the looming shortage of capital from the industrial world could trigger a rivalry for scarce funds among Eastern Europe, Middle East, Asia and less developed countries. The only region likely to be a net supplier of funds to global finance markets will be Asia.

Finally some foreign companies have actually become part of the beneficiaries of the Japanese political economic system and are therefore not inclined to oppose it. Faced with foreign pressure to open the market, some foreign companies have been co-opted into domestic oligopolies and benefit as insiders from the protection against outside competition.[104] This has led to the situation that foreign governments, which had been pressing their Japanese counterpart on the opening of certain sectors, either do not get any support (that is, relevant information) from their national companies (or only anonymously, which reduces the effect) or the support suddenly stops.

CONCLUSIONS

Several major points emerge from the discussion in this chapter. Japan has considerable structural and relational power sources. The recent recession and the serious loan crisis in Japan has dented these power resources but not dramatically and the damage has to be considered in relation to the effect of the recession in other countries. Japan derives great strength from the way its political economy is structured and moderated by ideological and behavioural patterns. These features have absorbed to a large extent costs such as unemployment or a collapse of the banking system which would have been more likely in a less regulated and less 'relational' system. On the other hand, these same features manifest themselves on occasion as restraints to exerting political influence commensurate with Japan's economic power and constitute for Japan's foreign policy a major challenge as to how to reconcile fundamental differences between its own system and that of its major partners. Historical, ideological and cultural factors reinforce these constraints as could be illustrated with Japan's pacifism and notion of leadership. While Japan's political economic system is changing and becoming more convergent with that of the major industrialized countries, these changes are often unacceptably slow for Japan's partners and lead to continuous trade conflicts. Proposals for how to deal with these differences range from fundamental criticism to acceptance.

2 The International Environment and Japan's Hard Power

INTRODUCTION

When power is considered, the most readily made association is military power, or hard power. The reason for this is firstly the influence of the Realist school which has still a strong grip on the understanding of international relations. Secondly, Japan's militarist past casts a shadow on the evaluation of Japan's present military capabilities and future intentions, thus reinforcing the tendency to assume that economic power sooner or later leads to military power. Thirdly, arguments based on geopolitical systems theory see Japan's defence policy determined not by politicians and opinion leaders but by systemic factors like geography.[1] Finally, there are plenty of factors which allow for a negative as well as a positive reading of Japan's military potential and intentions. The numerical indicators of Japan's military can for example either be interpreted as Japan being a formidable military power, particularly when seen in the regional context, or a weak military power, particularly when considered against the background of its economic and technological strength, potential threats and the military power of the US. In fact, Japan relies on a mix of hard power (its own and that of the US), and economic power to protect its national security.

CHANGES IN THE STRATEGIC ENVIRONMENT

Whereas the global security environment has been predominantly bipolar until 1989, the regional environment in East Asia has always been more complex since the split between Moscow and Beijing in the 1960s. Nevertheless Japan was firmly allied to the US and followed its lead globally. The oil crisis in 1973, the American withdrawal from Vietnam in 1975, and finally the planned (but later cancelled) withdrawal of US ground troops from South Korea in 1977 shook the Japanese confidence in the American security umbrella, and rising trade frictions with its most important ally added to the concern about the reliability of the American security protection. In addition to these concerns, the US pressured the Japanese government in the 1980s to do more for national as well as regional defence. As a result Japan's defence expenditures saw a marked increase, but at the same time Japan's Self Defence Forces (SDF) were increasingly and much more effectively than ever before integrated into the US East Asian strategy.

Since 1989 Japan has been faced with a new security environment which is presently in a fluid state and is characterized by two conflicting tendencies: considerable risks for the future on the one hand, and peace and cooperative approaches to regional security on the other hand. The Soviet threat, the main rationale for Japan's military build-up and military alliance with the United States, has given way to a Russian Pacific Fleet which is crippled by economic decline, ethnic frictions, and public pressure to reduce its influence on the life of Russia's Far East. The danger from Russia lies now more in the unpredictability of the consequences of political and economic collapse which could lead to the hijacking of the Pacific Fleet and other military units in the Maritime Province by political or military elements which have gone out of central control, and ultimately result in a military dictatorship. More imminent security threats are the confrontation on the Korean peninsula and the growing assertiveness of China with as yet unknown repercussions on the rest of Asia. Yet there is no multilateral or regional security system in the Asia Pacific region and a security dialogue has only recently started. The Realist school of international relations sees danger in any shift of power relations, particularly when one power is singularly weakened like that of the former Soviet Union, creating a power vacuum which other countries may want to fill. The Liberalist school tends to emphasize the cooperative aspects of international relations and therefore highlights the new opportunities for cooperative security in Asia. In real politics, the boundary between the two schools is not as clear cut, and we will see later how Japan's postwar policy is a model of the coexistence of both approaches to international relations. We will see in the following that the adherents of the Realist school in Japan feel now freer than ever before to discuss publicly the dangers inherent in the new security environment of Asia, though this does not necessarily lead to a more assertive security policy, but rather musters the continued support for the reliance on a close Japanese–American security relationship which is now with a more benign looking environment also more difficult to maintain. At the same time the Japanese government has become an active participant in the nascent regional security dialogue and its defence expenditures have dropped.

A. The End of the Cold War in Asia

It was Europe which saw after 1989 the most spectacular changes in its security environment, whereas in Asia not much seemed to have happened. Whereas in Europe people were celebrating the lifting of the Iron Curtain, best symbolized by Germany's reunification, nothing on a comparable scale seemed to have happened in Asia. Although there were positive changes in Asia like the end of foreign intervention in Cambodia or the recognition of South Korea by China and Russia, these changes meant little to Japan immediately after 1989, and it could not claim to have had any influence on these shifts.

The strategic environment in East Asia has always been much more complex and therefore a single event like the end of the Cold War could not have the same dramatic impact on Asia as it had on Europe. The relationship between the US and the Soviet Union and their policies towards the region have always been the most important factor in the East Asian strategic environment but they have had a less significant impact on Asia than on Europe. Although the two wars through which the superpowers came closest to facing each other directly were fought in Asia (Korean War and Vietnam War), the sheer geographic size and cultural/political diversity of Asia has prevented the superpowers from ever achieving the same kind of hold on Asia as a whole or even on one of its subregions.

There was never a Soviet security glacis in Asia as there was in Eastern Europe. Asia's communist countries have enjoyed a greater independence *vis à vis* the Soviet Union and, with the exception of Mongolia, did not have to agree to the stationing of Soviet troops. They are different from each other and were never integrated into a military pact like the Warsaw Pact, but only linked to the Soviet Union through bilateral security agreements. Finally, in contrast to Eastern Europe, communism in East Asia has been developed along more indigenous lines (like Juche or Mao-Ze-Dong-thought) and has been underpinned by some degree of nationalism. This was lacking in Eastern Europe and explains the quick demise of the communist regimes of former Eastern Europe.

Another factor affecting the impact of the Soviet Union/Russia on East Asia has been its orientation towards its European part where most of its élite is from and most of its industry is located. Russia is facing Asia with its economically and demographically least developed region. It is for this economic weakness and geographic remoteness – as well as America's security protection – that the Japanese never took the Soviet threat as seriously as the Europeans. For Japanese observers the Soviet Union was a military giant on clay feet. Culturally there are hardly any links between Soviet

East Asia and the rest of Asia, particularly if compared with the cultural affinity between, for example, Romania and France or Japan and China.

Instead the Soviet Union had been solely relying on military power and considered its relationship with Asia in terms of superpower rivalry. Japan, as the most developed country in Asia, was defined in terms of its alliance with the US and not on its own merits as an economic and technological power or in terms of what a closer relationship with Japan could yield in political and economic advantages.[2]

Basically a reduction of superpower tensions globally or even regionally still leaves regionally generated conflicts untouched or even worse, depending on the nature of the conflict, the diminished influence and presence of the superpowers may reduce an important element of moderation which previously kept hostilities from breaking out.

Here is a short list of all the inherent and latent security challenges to East Asia:

- First of all, many countries in the region are inherently unstable and we have to part with the preconception that growing wealth will somehow inescapably lead to stability. The rapid modernization and industrialization of most Asian countries has created many political and social tensions. The gap between poor and rich is increasing in several countries, notably China. Environmental degradation can easily add a decisive element to a potentially explosive situation. The racial equilibrium in some countries is very delicate. Most countries have no institutionalized procedure of leadership succession.
- Secondly, in the face of the diminishing influence of the superpowers there is a growing concern about the rise of regional hegemons, as happened with Iraq or Iran in the Middle East. In Asia it is India, China, Indonesia and for some even Japan that are seen as potential regional hegemons.
- Thirdly, China has become politically very assertive and is building up its military force. It takes a very ambiguous attitude towards how the territorial conflict in the South China Sea can be solved peacefully.
- Fourthly, the North Korean attitude towards its obligations under the Nuclear Non-Proliferation Treaty (NPT), which it signed in 1985, is very worrying and far from clear. This adds another worrying dimension to the unsettled issue of Korean reunification, which will be unsettling even under the best of circumstances.
- Fifthly, there is the arms race in East Asia which is closely linked to the reaction of the Asian countries to the above four points, as well as their reaction to the concern that an American military withdrawal from

the region would expose the countries of the region to these tensions and confrontations. Anticipating such challenges, most countries in the East Asian region have embarked on an arms race which is often veiled under the explanation of 'catching up' or 'ongoing modernization' of their military forces. But there are also other factors driving the arms race, such as the need to police the Extra-Territorial Economic Zones and sea lanes of communications as well as to defend territorial claims. In some cases an additional factor is prestige conferred by the possession of certain advanced weapon systems. Weapon purchases have also become an important source of high technology because of the increasingly competitive sales environment which forces weapon producers to license more technology and to allow offset arrangements. But in all cases the arms race is fanned by the growing wealth of most Asian countries and the ability to afford expensive weapons. The latter point is enhanced by the dumping of advanced weaponry by Russia (for example, the unprecedented sale of aircraft to Malaysia) and the ensuing competition of European and American arms producers which are facing reduced domestic markets as well as Russia's bargain prices.

B. How to Address the New Regional Security Environment?

The changes in the post Cold War era have led to a greater awareness of the regional strategic environment in the Asia Pacific. Some have even gone as far as arguing that 'the change from worldwide bipolarity to unipolarity makes the global dimension of strategic competition irrelevant at the regional strategic level'.[3] We would not go as far as that, but with Russia's present situation we agree with Akaha Tsuneo that the strategic environment of the Asia Pacific is more immediately relevant to Japan than global security developments.[4] The recent focus on Asia and the calls by many commentators for Japan to look to Asia or to 're-Asianize itself' have also contributed to the greater attention devoted to Asian security (see Chapter 4).[5]

The review of Japan's security policy in the wake of the end of the Cold War has not yet been finished by the Japanese government and defence specialists.[6] Its start was retarded by the reduced impact of 1989 on the Asia Pacific as well as by the domestic political stalemate since 1993. At one time in 1990 five LDP committees were reported to be studying the military alliance with the US and implications of a change, but not much has come out because of other pressing domestic issues and because leaving the arrangements as they are is at present easier than changing them.[7] The government has still not abandoned the National Defence Programme

Outline (*Taiko*) adopted under the Cold War situation in 1976. In January 1992 Prime Minister Miyazawa instructed the bureaucracy to review the Mid-Term Defence Buildup Plan (*Chukibo*) which had been running since December 1990 to achieve the hardware targets of the *Taiko*. In December 1992 the *Chukibo* was revised downward, but until today the *Taiko* has not yet been revised by the National Security Council, the highest defence policy body.

The novelty of the security debate at present is that on the one hand there is now a greater readiness and freedom than ever before to discuss the security situation confronting Japan. This is due to the disappearance of the Soviet Union as a threat, the doubts about America's commitment to stay in Asia, and the resulting need to have a better understanding of many potential threats in the regional environment. The allied war against Iraq and the demands for a Japanese contribution to this effort which benefited Japan's economic interests in the Middle East have only enhanced this debate which has come to centre on Japan's attitude toward Peace Keeping Operations (PKO). On the other hand, those who have always critically viewed Japan's SDF and military alliance with the US, including the Social Democratic Party, now feel even more encouraged to press their demands. The coming to power of the SDPJ, a prime minister from that party and the reduction in Japan's defence expenditure seem to indicate the ascent of those in favour of a 'peace dividend'. As far as the printed media is concerned the split in the debate is, for example, reflected in the proposals by the biggest Japanese daily, the *Yomiuri Shimbun*, to change the Constitution and to give the SDF a clear mandate for national defence as well as participation in PKO, while the *Asahi Shimbun*, a more left-leaning daily, proposed to keep Article 9, scale down the SDF into a force exclusively for Japan's defence, and separate the SDF from PKO.[8]

The conservative forces, however, emphasize the need for a deepening of the military alliance with the US as well as some changes in the allocation of defence expenditures to take into account the growing range of direct and indirect security threats. In August 1994 the Advisory Group on Defence, which had been set up by the previous Prime Minister Hosokawa Morihiro, published its report (Higuchi Report) which took the new security environment and the weakening of the US strength into account.[9] It recommended the following three basic policies:

1.   to promote multilateral security cooperation on a global and regional scale
2.   to enhance the functions of the Japanese–American security treaty
3.   to build up a highly reliable and efficient defence capability based on

strengthened information capability and prompt crisis management capability.

The SDF should concentrate on the following challenges:

1. safety of maritime traffic
2. territorial and air space
3. limited missile attack
4. illegal occupation of a part of the country
5. terrorist acts
6. influx of armed refugees.

The study can be considered to reflect aptly the Japanese mainstream perception and is a good illustration of the perceived importance of the regional environment. The underlying perception of the regional environment has thus not diminished the importance of the alliance with the US, but rather demands the enhancement of its functions.

In the following we will analyse Japan's main regional security challenges before finding out what kind of hard power is at the country's disposal to confront these challenges.

C.   The Rising Challenge from China

The future of China is probably the most difficult challenge for Japan's foreign and security policy, as it is for the whole of Asia and those outside powers involved in Asia's security. China is a rapidly developing country, a nuclear weapon state and a leading regional military power, as well as a global power thanks to its permanent seat on the UN Security Council. All countries, but particularly its Asian neighbours, have a vital stake in China being a stable and peaceful country.

China's official defence budget has doubled in the past five years, with real growth, adjusted for inflation, estimated at about 40 per cent.[10] Independent estimates of China's annual military expenditures vary between $10 billion (SIPRI) and $50 billion (ACDA).[11] In addition, it is safe to assume that many other budget items are hidden in other budget categories. China is constantly upgrading its military potential by buying new fighter aircraft (including Russian SU-27s), Russian missiles and Russian submarines in addition to the products from its own big armament production facilities. Increasingly China is acquiring a blue-water naval capability.

This armament programme raises concern because of China's unresolved leadership succession, unresolved territorial disputes, the unresolved reunification issue, the zero-sum-game approach of China's leaders to foreign and security policy, the Chinese perception of having to regain their country's dignity and place in the world and the region, the huge perception gap between the Chinese élite's self-perception of a peaceful China and that of its Asian neighbours, and China's past record of using military power to attain political objectives.[12] China's economic development is, on the one hand, giving rise to the hope that this will lead to a moderate foreign policy which takes account of China's growing international interdependence. On the other hand, there is equally no historical determinism guaranteeing the benevolent outcome of economic development. Greater wealth can also sustain a more forceful foreign and security policy, particularly in view of China's historical baggage consisting of past experience with imperialism and its past record of using force.

China is a huge country and huge countries are inclined to draw their 'line of interest' further than smaller countries. Very soon China will be a considerable international economic force as a result of the sheer size of its population. Although its per capita income will still be very small, its population size will several times multiply its power as an exporting and importing nation and its GNP will soon have overtaken that of most industrialized countries. This may encourage China to disregard the legitimate interests of other countries. Other countries may, however, be willing to accept China's behaviour because of its huge domestic market which whets the appetite of all major industrialized countries. Moreover, with so many raw materials of its own, China is much less dependent on the rest of the world than most other countries.

Japan is gradually waking up to the security challenge of China and while the Korean nuclear problem has been dominating the agenda of the last few years, there is growing concern about the long-term impact of China. There is, first of all, the prospect for direct competition between China and Japan for Asian resources and markets as well as the environmental threat from China's breakneck speed of economic development to which Japan is nevertheless contributing through its investment and aid. However, the importance of China as a source of energy has diminished considerably because of Japanese diversification of energy sources and China's own rising needs for them.[13] Secondly, Japan is concerned about China's relations with the US. American insistence on human rights, a more balanced trade relationship, intellectual copyright issues and the Taiwan issue makes the relationship vacillate between hot and cold.[14] China views the post-Cold War situation with the US being the only real superpower as worrying, particularly in view of the Second Gulf War and American attempts to create a global as well as regional anti-ballistic missile which would nullify China's nuclear deterrent. On the other hand, Japan is concerned about American military contacts leading to arms sales to China which would further enhance China's military capability.[15] It is interesting to remember that Japan's government did not show too much enthusiasm for COCOM until the Toshiba incident in 1987, but it had always assumed a much more alert attitude towards American arms sales to China when they started in 1981.[16] Finally there is concern that the US and other Western countries, frustrated with Japan's economic advance and growing assertiveness, may play China against Japan.[17]

The post-Cold War era provides a different environment for Japan where the need of a strong China to counterbalance the Soviet Union has rapidly declined. The hope of getting strong Chinese support to keep North Korea on a more rational path has also evaporated. China proved either not to have much influence in Pyongyang or it was not willing to use the remainder of this influence in order not to risk its national security interests, which are not entirely congruent with Japan when it comes to nuclear non-proliferation.

The heart of the problem for Japan is to decide whether it is better to appease China or to stand up in order to protect its own national interests. Japan's natural inclination so far has been appeasement because of a cultural tendency to avoid direct confrontation, because of its negative past legacy notably in China and a resulting guilt complex, because a stronger stance would open many cans of worms in domestic and international politics, and finally because of its growing confidence in its huge economic power as a replacement of military power. During the postwar period Japan was always concerned about China taking up Japan's rearmament and using it as a stick to put pressure on the country, and Japan was wary of offering China any opportunity to take up the issue.

Japan's official attitude now is balancing between engagement of China through trade and political/military contacts on the one hand and demanding transparency and restraint in the military area on the other. The former is, for example, illustrated by Japan's lack of enthusiasm in joining general sanctions against China because of the brutal repression of student demonstrations in 1989 (Tiananmen massacre). Japan broke with its Group of Seven (G-7) partners and resumed official loans to China in 1990 after the G-7 had announced sanctions against Beijing at the Paris summit in July 1989. In August 1991 the then Prime Minister Kaifu Toshiki was the first leader among the major developed countries to visit China.[18] Another example was Japan's appeasement over the fact that in 1992–93 on average once a month Chinese navy ships fired on Japanese trawlers in the East China Sea close to disputed islands in the middle of Japan's sea lanes of communication to Southeast Asia with its many economic links to Japan and to the Middle East. No protest was issued and the Japanese media did not even directly identify the Chinese ships.[19] There have also been reports that for diplomatic reasons the Defence Agency has been understating the number of aircraft violating Japanese airspace.[20]

Faced with China's growing military potential and assertiveness, the Japanese have finally started to discuss security more openly at home as well as with the Chinese.[21] As one of the main providers of investment, trade opportunities and technology, Japan is in a strong position. The Japanese concerns about China are clearly spelled out by people close to the government as this comment by Professor Nishihara Masashi of the Defence Academy indicates:

> Where is China heading? Will it become a hegemonic power, establishing a new regional order under its control by taking advantage of the upper hand it has over its neighbours in size and power? . . . Despite the fact that China and Japan have close ties in virtually all fields, their relationship remains essentially fragile.[22]

And in another interview he said: 'The way they [the Chinese] have behaved in South China Sea may one day be applied to the Senkaku islands. It's a creeping expansionism.'[23]

In 1992 Vice Foreign Minister Kakizawa Koji warned China about buying a Ukrainian-built aircraft carrier.[24] In May 1993 Japan proposed to Foreign Minister Qian Qichen to resume bilateral security negotiations, frozen after Tiananmen, and tried to draw China into regional security discussions. Japanese officials complained to Qian about repeated attacks on Japanese fishing boats in the East China Sea and Foreign Minister Muto raised the issue of China's nuclear testing.[25] In 1993 a leading member of the then ruling LDP, Mitsuzaka Hiroshi, expressed concern about the modernization of China's military and the defence spending increase, signalling a change in the LDP's willingness to vent this concern openly. When Foreign Minister Hata of the Hosokawa cabinet visited China in January 1994 he asked China about the intentions behind the 15 per cent increase in the Chinese defence budget and urged China to abide by the guidelines of the Missile Technology Control Regime (MTCR).[26]

A major concern is China's claim to wide areas of the South China Sea and the Senkaku/Jiaoyutai islands off Okinawa. In February 1992, China passed a Law which proclaims sovereignty over all islands in the South China Sea as well as over the Senkaku islands. In April 1992, a Chinese navy deputy commander was quoted in the Chinese press as saying that it was high time for China to readjust its maritime strategy and to make more efforts to recover the oil and gas resources in the South China Sea.[27]

Seventy-five per cent of Japan's oil imports pass through the South China Sea, as does much of its intra-Asian trade. Japan's assertiveness is shown by the fact that it not only now discusses the issue with China but Japanese companies disregard Chinese warnings about not getting involved in oil prospecting in areas disputed by Vietnam and China. Japanese companies have major stakes in three oil concessions off Vietnam.[28] Japan also has a vital interest in the freedom of the sea lanes and communicated to China its concern when it came to a confrontation in spring 1995 between China and the Philippines over a reef in the Spratly islands.

In order to exert pressure on China, the possibility of reducing aid to China is openly discussed in Japan. In March 1991, the Chief Cabinet Secretary Sakamoto Misoji declared that Japan was yet undecided on whether to curb economic aid to China following Beijing's announcement about a sharp increase in defence expenditures.[29] When Japan negotiated a new multi-year loan package in 1994, Japan pressed China on human rights, defence spending, nuclear testing and pollution.[30] In March 1994, Foreign Minister Hata Tsutomo told visiting Chinese Vice-Premier Zhu Rongji that the size and terms of Japan's next package of official yen loan would be conditional on Beijing's efforts to produce environmental projects and clearer information on military spending. In the end Japan gave a new loan package without insisting on any Chinese compromise in the security area. The Japanese government was very offended when China resumed nuclear testing in May 1995 just after the successful conclusion of the NPT Review Conference and Prime Minister Murayama's China visit. It sent a formal protest to the Chinese government and declared that grant aid would be cut. Although this is hardly inflicting economic damage on China, it is a clear departure from the past.[31]

Another approach is to engage China in bilateral talks as well as multilateral dialogue to increase the level of military transparency and reduce the military build-up. In May 1993, both sides agreed to resume the bilateral security dialogue which had been suspended following the Tiananmen massacre in June 1989. They agreed to hold talks between defence and diplomatic officials, but at the APEC meeting in Seattle in November 1993 China's Foreign Minister Qian asked that only foreign ministry officials be involved.[32] In December 1993 the first Japan–China conference on security finally took place. In February 1995 Admiral Nishi became the first uniformed senior SDF official to visit the PRC. It was reported that he would ask for transparency in China's defence budget and armament programme.[33]

Until recently the geopolitical and strategic interests led the government to treat China as too important to isolate, whereas the Japanese private sector has been led by considerations of risk and profit as the ups and downs of Japanese investment in China prove.[34] While the China policies of these two different actors did therefore not always converge in the past and the Japanese government tended to be more lenient towards Beijing in order to protect these strategic interests, the government has become now more assertive and is applying some pressure on China to moderate its military posture. The major instruments for this pressure are putting China's defence policies on the bilateral agenda, engaging in an open debate about China as a security issue and using Japan's considerable aid power (see Chapter 3 on aid).

D. The Decline of the Soviet Threat

The relationship with the former Soviet Union was always subordinated to the comprehensive relationship with the US. Japan's economic interests in the Soviet Union were very limited after an initial flurry of interest in Siberian raw materials in the 1970s ended in frustration. The US, and at times also China during its anti-hegemony campaign in the 1970s, successfully reinforced the effect of the commercial disappointment by putting pressure on Japan. Within this context the territorial conflict over the ownership of the so-called Northern Territories was allowed to take on an importance out of proportion with the size of the islands. It is characteristic that one of the weakest postwar Japanese prime ministers, Suzuki Sunao, established in 1982 the so-called Northern Territories Day to be commemorated on 7 February, the date of the first Japanese–Russian Agreement in 1855. Today the Northern Territories issue has become the overriding issue in the absence of any other major strategic, political or economic interest of Japan in Russia (see Chapter 3).

Japan's security perception of Russia is concerned with the following four issues: (1) the reliability of command and control over the arsenals of the former Soviet Union; (2) the problem of arms proliferation; (3) the Northern Territories issue; and (4) the overall Asian strategy pursued by Yeltsin.[35] Russia had, according to the Defence Agency's White Paper 1993, 290 000 personnel in the Asia Pacific in 1993, down from 390 000 five years earlier. The border situation between Russia and China has significantly improved since the signing of a border treaty, the agreement in 1992 on border Confidence Building Measures (CBMs), the opening of borders for trade, and the general improvement of Russian–Chinese relations. The Pacific Fleet is gradually being reduced, shipyard facilities eliminated in the Far East and there is discussion about abandoning a Pacific SLBM capacity in the Pacific as a result of START-2 although a military expansion in the Asia Pacific cannot be totally excluded.[36] In 1994 the Russian Pacific fleet decommissioned the only two aircraft carriers it had, the *Minsk* and the *Novorossiysk*, and sold them as scrap to South Korea.[37] As mentioned before, Russia is a major arms exporter, particularly in Asia, and the strengthening of China's military potential through cheap Russian arms exports is worrying to the Japanese. The Russian Far Eastern situation is politically and economically rather unstable.

A particular Japanese concern is the orderly dismantling of the nuclear arsenal of the successor states to the Soviet Union and the continuous Russian dumping of nuclear waste into the Japan Sea. Japan has pledged $100 million to Russia to dispose of its nuclear arsenal, and has concluded similar agreements with Belarus, Kazakhstan and Ukraine.[38]

Under the present situation of a weak central government in Russia faced with vigorous regional tendencies, notably in the Russian Far East, a compromise on the Northern Territories seems to be impossible given Japan's strong stance.[39] On the Russian side, nationalist tendencies have become much stronger, to the extent that a 1991 Russo-Chinese border treaty is openly challenged by the governor of the Maritime Province, Yevgeny Nazdratenko. The Russian military is also not unified on giving up the Northern Territories.[40] On the other hand, Russian military concerns about Japan and the US using military means in case of a political collapse of the situation in the Maritime Province seem even less probable.[41] Japanese intransigence is supported by American backing for Japan's territorial claims. When President Bush visited the Soviet Union in July 1991, he referred to the need to solve the territorial dispute between Japan and the Soviet Union by clearly warning the Soviet leaders about the economic consequences of not showing a more concessionary attitude: 'This dispute could hamper your integration into the world economy.'[42] It is interesting to note that Satoh Yukio, a high official in the MFA, mentions the territorial issue as one of the functions of the military alliance with the US:

> US–Japan security arrangements serve as an important prerequisite for Japan's dialogue with the Soviet Union. Western solidarity has been an indispensable prerequisite for a constructive dialogue with the Soviets in East–West relations. In the same vein, unswerving alliance relations between Tokyo and Washington are essential to the success of Japanese efforts to conclude a peace treaty with the Soviet Union through solving the question of the Northern Territories.[43]

The tough Japanese attitude towards the Soviet Union and the Russian successor state has to be seen against considerable resentment about alleged

Soviet disregard and disrespect for Japan and the resulting hurt national pride in the postwar period. In addition relations with its closest neighbour have traditionally been bad and the late Soviet entry into the Pacific War and the treatment of the Japanese POWs by the Soviet Union only strengthened dislike of the Soviet Union. Japanese bureaucrats, notably in the Foreign Ministry where Japan's policy towards the Soviet Union/ Russia is still concentrated, have for many years strongly resented what they perceive as wilful disregard of their country despite its growing economic importance. Until the beginning of the 1980s the Soviet Union did not pay much attention to Japan because they considered Japan to be a mere appendix of the United States without any policy of its own.[44] Japanese observers got the feeling that the Soviet Union would only take seriously a country with considerable military power. This Soviet attitude changed only when Japan's economic might became all too visible and growing frictions between Japan and the United States indicated even to the most ideological Soviet observer that Japan had also its own agenda of national interests. Japan's military build-up also certainly played a role in this Soviet reconsideration. After the Soviet attitude started to change, Japanese decision-makers who had no great economic interest in the Soviet Union (but realized great Soviet interest in economic interaction with Japan after Gorbachov's Vladivostok speech in July 1986) and were contemptuous of its economic and political weakness, dug their heels in and made it clear that the Soviet Union would have to 'pay' a price for its past disregard, that is, the Northern Territories. In addition the territorial issue is also part of what former Prime Minister Nakasone Yasuhiro called the 'settlement of the postwar era'. With the increasing Russian economic and political difficulties there is no easier target for 'redressing' the record and soothing Japan's hurt national pride. The territorial demand is pursued with such a tenacity that wider global or regional policy considerations such as the possible repercussions on world politics by a further disintegration of Russia suffer. Moreover, the Japanese government is showing little concern about its isolation within the Western group of nations, which tries to take a more constructive attitude towards Russia although Tokyo attempts on the other hand to get their support for its territorial demands. The growing Russian political and economic difficulties support, however, the majority in Japan which never believed that Western economic aid could help much, and since the start of the Russian war in Chechniya, Western enthusiasm to help Russia and attempt to get Japan to participate has markedly diminished. Finally the Northern Territories issue provides Japan with an opportunity to 'rectify' Western perceptions about Japan as is stated by Japan's best known Russia specialist, Kimura Hiroshi:

Japan's persistent demands for the reversion of the islands has also contributed to the correction of the impression prevailing in the world that the Japanese are ' "economic animals" solely intent on pursuing and realizing their material interests'. . . . the return of territory concerns the most important task for any state, as its sovereignty and national prestige.[45]

The security dialogue and the agreement on any confidence-building measures with Russia has also been hostage to the territorial issue and continues to be so. Russia's reduced threat ability has probably contributed to the feeling of reduced urgency in this matter. In 1988 the MFA discussed for the first time a Japanese–Soviet version of the Prevention of Incidents at Sea agreements concluded between the Soviet Union and various other countries (US, UK, France, Italy, Germany and Canada) in the past.[46] Despite the unsettled political relationship, the Japanese government has finally agreed to engage in some sort of confidence-building measures. In June 1992 both sides conducted a policy planning meeting at the Russian Foreign Ministry in which for the first time uniformed military officers took part.[47] In February 1993 senior Russian officers were for the first time invited to a seminar at the Japanese National Institute for Defence Studies.[48] In October 1993 both governments signed an agreement concerning the prevention of incidents at sea between the armed forces of both sides beyond the territorial waters and the air space above them, and a memorandum on cooperation in the field of search and rescue at sea. The latter in particular is very much in the Japanese interest because Japanese fishermen are operating in the fishing waters near the disputed islands and are regularly apprehended and fined.

E. Unresolved Issues on the Korean Peninsula

The situation on the Korean peninsula is Asia's most risk-prone one in the short run as well as in the medium term. Japan's means to influence the situation are limited to a delicate diplomacy of balance between South Korean sensitivities, North Korean political and diplomatic brinkmanship and American concern with nuclear proliferation. In addition, Japan may be able to use massive financial incentives for North Korea to behave peacefully in order to ease the shock of eventual reunification of two extremely different Korean states.

Until 1990 Japan's role in the security of the Korean peninsula was very limited. The security alliance with the US, the economic and political support of South Korea and the legacy of the past did not afford Japan much room for manoeuvre towards North Korea. Instead consecutive Japanese governments pursued a strategy of 'peaceful coexistence' between North and South Korea by supporting South Korea and allowing some limited trade with North Korea. The latter afforded Japan some leeway against South Korea and left a window open for broader relations with the North should the situation improve. Trade was mostly done through those Korean residents in Japan who lean towards North Korea. Economic links were supported by all-party parliamentary delegations to North Korea which provided also the only channel of political communication.

The end of the Cold War and South Korea's *rapprochement* towards the Soviet Union and other East European countries led in September 1990 to a visit by an elder of the LDP, Kanemaru Shin, to North Korea. The outcome was a joint declaration which opened the way for the start of official negotiations to normalize diplomatic relations. Kanemaru, later implicated in a corruption scandal which forced him to resign, is an example of how individual leaders under the long rule of the LDP could provide fresh impulses to Japan's foreign policy. He accepted, to the consternation of some of his fellow politicians and of the MFA, Pyongyang's demand for compensation not only for the colonial period, but also for the 45 years of losses incurred by North Korea in the postwar period because – according to North Korea's perception – the LDP prevented normal diplomatic and economic relations with Pyongyang. The latter was not accepted by the Japanese government. But the ensuing negotiations broke down in November 1992 after eight rounds because of Japan's strong insistence on North Korea's adherence to its international obligations under the NPT and insistence on clarification of the fate of an abducted Japanese woman who was used by North Korea to teach Japanese to a North Korean terrorist. As a result of the October 1994 Framework Agreement between North Korea and the US on the nuclear issue, Japan and North Korea resumed the dialogue. North Korea is vitally interested in Japanese reparations and the full resumption of trade for the survival of its regime. Although the Japanese side would like to further *détente* on the Korean peninsula through normalization of diplomatic relations, and Socialist Prime Minister Murayama particularly pursues this goal, there are many bilateral issues which will make the road very bumpy. In addition, Tokyo has to consider its relationship with South Korea, which watches developments between Tokyo and Pyongyang with great suspicion. While Japan may disagree with some American policies on nuclear proliferation on the peninsula, as occurred in summer 1994 when sanctions against Pyongyang were proposed by the US, Japan has a vital interest in a nuclear-free Korea.[49] In addition, Japan is concerned about North Korea's development of missiles which can reach Japan. Moreover, North Korea is also suspected of having chemical and biological stockpiles which may be used instead of or in addition to nuclear warheads.

The October 1994 Framework Agreement between the US and North Korea provides hope for at least temporizing the nuclear issue until the North Korean regime disappears, if it does not lead to a solution of the issue. Japan is willing to contribute to the financing of the two nuclear light-water reactors which North Korea is promised to receive under the Agreement. The nuclear arming of North Korea, or the continuation of North Korea's nuclear weapon programme by an assertive reunified Korea could have a very negative effect on Japan's nuclear policy, particularly if it goes with a loss of the credibility of America's nuclear umbrella. Another Japanese concern are the likely events which will accompany the reunification of the Korean peninsula. Reunification, even under the best circumstances, that is without armed conflict, will economically and politically destabilize South Korea and lead to many refugees going to Japan. The North Korean economic and social situation would be much more difficult to remedy than that of former East Germany. With its economic power and the carrot of reparations and economic aid, Japan can significantly supplement its hard power towards North Korea.

In the meantime, the end of the Cold War, American encouragement and a lessening of the antipathy which South Korea and Japan have felt for each other have led to more contact in the security field and a greater balance in the otherwise trade and investment dominated relationship. From 1969 until 1994 both countries held 156 meetings for exchanges of military information, and military leaders at the chief of staff level or above have visited each other on 48 occasions since 1965.[50] In April 1994 both sides signed an agreement on the prevention of accidental aerial collision of aircraft from the air forces of both sides. In May 1994 the two navies held their first exercises together as part of the US-led biannual Rimpac manoeuvre.[51] In November 1994 a working-level meeting between ranking South Korean and Japanese military officials took place in Seoul.[52] In December 1994 three Korean warships made for the first time a port call in Japan. The nuclear issue has also led to a high level of meetings between Japan and South Korea because of Japan's direct interest as well as its role in the Korean Energy Development Organization (KEDO).

On the other hand, growing self-confidence in its economic and military strength has led some commentators and military in South Korea to consider Japan if not as an immediate potential adversary then at least as a potential one in future. Talk of Korea's '360 degree defence' has Japan very much in its mind and no longer just North Korea.[53] Perceiving themselves to be a 'shrimp among giants' some Koreans are looking beyond reunification and view with concern Japan's (as well as China's) military potential and the more open debate about defence in Japan.[54] In 1993 a Japanese newspaper reported that from 1996 Japan will shift the focus of army exercises away from Northern Japan to Honshu and Kyushu because of the declining threat from Russia and the volatile situation on the Korean peninsula.[55] Although this move would not be directed against South Korea, it could be used by South Korean military to encourage their '360 degree defence'. The security relationship between both countries will therefore continue to be bedevilled by events in North Korea as well as by negative images, while on a practical level the bilateral security dialogue is becoming stronger.

F. The Japan–US Military Alliance

The main hard power means for Japan to confront its external security are the security alliance with the US and its own military forces. The functions of the Japanese–American security alliance may be summarized in four points.[56]

First, the security treaty provides Japan with nuclear deterrence. Although the end of the East–West confrontation has reduced the likelihood of a superpower nuclear exchange, the American deterrent is still considered necessary against the remaining nuclear (as well as conventional!) threats, be they from Russia, China or North Korea. At the very least the American nuclear umbrella obviates the necessity to acquire a Japanese nuclear deterrence which would set off a nuclear arms race in Asia and deprive Japan of many of its low-cost gains in foreign and security policy.

Secondly, the American naval presence in the Pacific and Indian Oceans is considered as vital for the protection of Japan's sea lanes to Asia and the Middle East with which it has strong trade links.

Thirdly, the security alliance adds credibility to Japan's claims, particularly in the eyes of its Asian neighbours, that it will not use its considerable military power for political purposes and will not expand its military power beyond a certain (although rather ill-defined) threshold.

Fourthly, the alliance still moderates the disputes in other areas of Japanese–American relations although this function of the alliance has considerably declined in the 1980s and particularly after 1989.

1. Burden Sharing
A central issue of the military alliance has been and continues to be the search for a balance between the burden borne by each side. The American

burden has been greater because the US has been militarily the much bigger partner with global interests, and Asian security was only one of several other concerns. Japan, on the other hand, had not only a much more regionally determined view, but was even within the regional framework very restrained by political and economic factors. With the Asia Pacific security environment becoming now much more demanding and America's role in the region more dependent on support from allies like Japan, the search for a more appropriate and politically defensible (not necessarily 'equal') burden sharing has reached a new stage.

The 1980s were marked by American demands for more Japanese military efforts, echoing the frustration over Japan's trade surplus with the US which was attributed to Tokyo having a free ride on the American security umbrella. There was, however, ambivalence in the administration about these demands. In February 1988 Assistant Secretary of Defense Richard L. Armitage responded to Senate and House demands urging Japan to spend more on defence: 'What would the additional funds be used for? A nuclear capability? Offensive projection forces? Professor Kennedy speaks of Japanese carrier task forces and long-range missiles – is that what Congress wants? Will that enhance stability in East Asia?' Deputy Assistant Secretary of Defense for East Asia, Karl Jackson, was quoted as saying that the extent of Japan's military muscle was already 'the best-kept secret in Washington'.[57]

The US is fundamentally interested in staying a Pacific power for security and economic reasons despite its weakened economic power base. It is therefore essential that it can rely on allies like Japan which is, together with Korea, after the forced withdrawal from the Philippines, the only allied territory where it can station troops.[58] The US intends to maintain approximately 100 000 troops in the Asia Pacific, around 40 000 in Japan and 37 000 in Korea, the rest on vessels mostly belonging to the Seventh Fleet. Japan's importance increased after the withdrawal from the Philippines. An American military presence is considered by the Clinton Administration, as by previous administrations, vital as a guarantee for the security of sea lanes, as a deterrent to armed regional conflict and as support for regional cooperation. Japan and most Asian countries agree that a US military presence is important for the power balance in Asia in view of the many potential instabilities in the region and the presence of potential hegemons, which include China, but for many other countries also Japan. As long as the Japanese–American security treaty and American troops in Japan exist, the potential of Japan seems to be contained. This perception is also held by some Americans as illustrated by Major-General Henry Stockpole, the then commander of the Marine Corps in Japan, who said in an interview in March 1990: 'No one wants a rearmed, resurgent Japan. So we are a cap in the bottle, if you will.'[59] The 'cap in the bottle' theme continues to contribute to America's motivation in maintaining the security treaty and a military presence in Asia. It appeared again in an early draft of the Pentagon's 'Defense Planning Guidance' for fiscal years 1994 to 1999 which said that the principal goal of US national security policy should be to thwart the emergence of a new rival to American military supremacy, including a discussion of Japan, Germany and India as potential 'regional hegemons'.[60]

While some of the American demands for burden sharing have stayed the same, others have experienced slight changes. One demand is the support given to the stationing of American troops in Japan, which has increasingly become crucial for the US because of its dwindling resources while the yen has been appreciating. Japan supplies today the most generous host-nation support of any American ally. Under an agreement concluded in January 1991 and other arrangements, Japan has assumed an increasing share annually. In 1994 the Host Nation Programme covered more than 70 per cent of the annual salary costs of the Japanese workers on US military bases in Japan. Together with rents, foregone income and other costs this is estimated by the US to be more than $4 billion per year. An additional amount of approximately $1 billion per year is spent on facilities construction and improvement.[61]

In the 1980s Japan and the US agreed on a division of roles and missions which means that Japan concentrates on the defence of the home islands and sea lane defence up to 1000 nautical miles while the US has responsibility for power projection and nuclear deterrence. The two sea lanes stretch north of the Philippines and west of Guam. According to the Defence Agency, however, the defence of sea lanes is not necessarily restricted to the two sea lanes but 'rather covers a wider surface of waters within the 1000 miles'.[62] Whereas before 1989 anti-submarine warfare (ASW) was emphasized by the US in order to check Soviet submarines in the Northeast Pacific and as a result a joint ASW Centre was established in Yokosuka, this aspect of joint defence is no longer even mentioned in the March 1995 DOD Report. What is now emphasized by the US and where it asks Japan to spend more money on is airborne early warning and ship-borne anti-air capability, and land-based and ship-borne anti-missile capability. In response Japan is buying early warning aircraft (AWACS) and building Aegis-class ships for its fleet.

Finally the US wants to develop together with Japan and then deploy together Theatre Missile Defence (TMD). The Japanese side is very interested in TMD because of the North Korean deployment of intermediate missiles which can reach Japan. North Korea tested in July 1993 a missile (Nodong-1) with a range of 620 miles and there are reports on the development of a two-stage ballistic missile referred to as Nodong-2 with a range of over 2000 miles.[63] Whereas the US aims ultimately to have a global missile defence system to be built from regional sub-systems, the Japanese government has to consider the regional implications on North Korea and particularly on China. It has to ask itself whether such a move would be conducive to making these countries renounce missile development (and missile exports!) or whether it will only fan the missile race because it would nullify their deterrence.

2.   Weapon Technology Cooperation

Japan's military and economic powers also complement each other in the country's arms production capability. The joint development of weapon systems is particularly central to US concerns because it seems to be the answer to American demands for more Japanese military efforts as well as demands for a more balanced defence and economic relationship. The technology issue links burden sharing on the military side with what is either referred to as a more level playing field in the economic field, or as the re-establishment of American technological 'primacy' through the transfer of Japanese technology to the US. Japan is already one of the major US weapon customers, buying in 1994 US arms valued at $729 million, compared with South Korean purchases amounting to $433 million and Singapore with $456 million.[64] The US has been urging Japan since the 1980s to reverse what it calls the one-sided flow of defence technology, hoping that it will reduce funding for new weapon developments and provide access to the rich dual-use technology potential of Japan, ultimately helping US industry to regain its technological strength (which means for others 'primacy') in military and civilian applications.[65] These demands for Japanese technology are based on the fear that the US is losing out in the technological race against Japan, and those who want to make this point like to conjure the concern of national security by linking performance in civilian technology to achievements in military technology. In 1988 the US Defense Science Board identified 22 areas of critical technologies and judged Japan to be 'scientifically ahead in some niches of technology', mentioning six areas specifically.[66] A 1990 Department of Commerce study argued that Japan had an advantage over the US in five of 12 emerging technologies and was ascending in five others.[67] Recently, however, these concerns have abated. A recent White House review of 27 critical technologies showed a US lead in 21 while Japan led in none.[68]

At the end of the 1980s, particularly after the end of the Cold War, Japan became for many Americans the new threat to American national security.[69] Growing American dependence on Japan was perceived as a dangerous vulnerability. The purchase of sensitive American technology and production facilities, notably in electronics, generated concern whether the US government would be able to assure 'production security', which is defined as the existence of assured capabilities to generate surge production rates or mobilization in time of crisis. A report by the DOD Defence Science Board in February 1987 urged less dependence on Japan in electronics by arguing that 'while Japan is a strong and essential ally, its economic interests occasionally differ from those of the US'.[70] Even without any national crisis the question was asked whether Japanese competitors would give their best to a foreigner or hold it back to preserve a competitive advantage. The Japanese diplomat Ogura Kazuo expressed the Japanese frustration with American ambivalence on interdependence in the following way:

> Far from becoming accustomed to dependence on other countries, many Americans want nothing to do with it, particularly if Japan is involved. . . . Nobody objects to Dutch or British investments in the US, but Japanese investments are perceived to be a threat. The reason is quite simply that the American people are not yet psychologically prepared to accept dependence on Japan. And yet we have entered an age when Washington must look to Tokyo for money to fund a war and when the US defense industry would face a crisis without Japanese technology and parts.[71]

American efforts to achieve a more balanced flow of dual-purpose technology have shown rather mixed results for a variety of reasons. Most Japanese defence technology as well as dual-use technology is in the hands of private companies, and the government can therefore not order them to share it with American official or private counterparts. As in the case with 'voluntary export restraints' the American government is pursuing goals which have contradictory side effects: On the one hand, it wants to loosen the close links between the Japanese government and private companies in order to create a 'level playing field' for the economic relationship; on the other hand, it wants to use the strong influence of the government on private business to achieve a reduction of Japanese exports in certain sectors (for example, cars) or access to technology. Another obstacle is legal issues which are surrounded by political complications. Japan has a cabinet policy which does not allow the export of defence technology. In 1983 the Exchange of Technology Agreement made an exception for the US and in December 1985 the modalities of the Agreement were spelled out in the Detailed Arrangements for the Transfer of Military Technologies.[72] Care has been taken by the Japanese side that any such technology can only be used for DOD purposes and not benefit an American company for civilian purposes. Another legal issue is the protection of secrecy. The Japanese private sector is concerned that any transferred technology may become a military secret and could then no longer be exploited for civilian purposes.

The joint development of Japan's next support fighter (code-named FSX) brought all the contradictions and opposing interests of Japan and the US to the fore. After an initial agreement during the Reagan administration, President Bush was forced by domestic pressure groups to reopen negotiations to get a more favourable division of labour. After the troubled FSX joint development, cooperation on TMD is the next big item on the agenda. The US wants it a 'technology-for-technology arrangement' in which military technology will flow from the US to Japan and in return Japanese private companies working on the joint project would pass along dual-use technology to American companies.[73]

In conclusion, one can state that Japan has achieved a much higher bargaining position towards the US in its bilateral defence relationship due to the end of the Cold War, its high technology and its financial power. The latter two are important for the US to maintain its security posture, not only in Asia but worldwide. The security alliance provides Japan with a cost-efficient military capability and thus with hard power without having to incur the political costs which would go with acquiring a corresponding capability. On the other hand, Japan's bargaining position is weakened by the bilateral trade imbalance and the perceived need by Japan's mainstream politicians to keep the US involved in Asia. The US has therefore still considerable leverage over Japan, not only because Japan relies ultimately on the US for its security, but also because the weakening of this security guarantee could lead Japan to having to alienate its East Asian neighbours by embarking on an autonomous defence posture which would create a very negative political, military and economic backlash.

But how sustainable is the future of the Japanese–American military alliance? The basic assumption of successive American administrations has been that they can contain Japan by having a very close political and military alliance and by integrating Japan's military potential as much as necessary into the American East Asia strategy. Taking the American complement away, the Japanese military would not be worth much. However, how sustainable is a relationship where Japan is economically and technologically growing very strong and self-assertive? How long will Japan be content to pay for the 'cap in the bottle' although even the SDPJ now accepts the SDF and the Security Treaty? In a speech at the commencement ceremony at the National Defence Academy, Professor Eto Jun of Keio University recalled what Yamagata Aritomo, one of the Meiji leaders, had called in 1890 the need for defence of Japan's line of sovereignty and Japan's line of interests. He mentioned as one of the challenges for Japan and the US in the post-Cold War era how to compromise on differences concerning the issue of 'line of interest'.[74] It is rather worrying that a defence specialist should use Yamagata's expression, which paved to some extent the way to Japan's expansion in the region. In contrast to Germany, Japan is only linked and constrained by a bilateral relationship with a faraway partner. What happens if the US security guarantee, starting with the nuclear umbrella against China and Korea, begins to unravel or is perceived as unreliable? While the US would have had to react to a Soviet military provocation, such an American reaction is less certain in the case of North Korea acquiring nuclear weapons which will not threaten the US homeland directly (but US bases in the region) and may make a US reprisal less likely.[75] To come to some conclusions on this matter we have to look at Japan's military power and the various constraints mechanisms surrounding it.

JAPAN'S MILITARY POWER

During the 1980s Japan considerably expanded its military expenditures and armaments, driven by the perception of a Soviet threat and by American demands for more burden sharing. Japan has today 237 700 people under arms, of which about 150 000 are in the army, 43 000 in the navy and 44 500 in the air force.[76] The army strength is about equivalent to that of Britain's army. Manpower numbers, however, do not directly translate into fighting power, particularly compared with the British army which has had considerable combat experience. Moreover, the reservist basis is very narrow with 47 900 (of which 46 000 are army) and would be considered unacceptable by most Western military forces. It is therefore a recurrent demand of the Defence Agency and defence specialists to upgrade the reservist basis. The Self Defence Forces (SDF) suffer from difficulties in recruiting volunteers in a very competitive job market. Although unemployment is presently running at a comparatively high level, this has not much improved the recruiting situation. The SDF is not a very desirable nor fashionable career for most Japanese. A stronger Japanese involvement in PKO may possibly ease this problem.

In terms of hardware the SDF dispose of an impressive range of weapon systems, including some 1160 main battle tanks, 15 tactical submarines, 62 principal surface combatants, 100 P-3C anti-submarine warfare aeroplanes, 170 F-15 and 110 F-4 aircraft. The weapons are constantly upgraded and modernized and the lifespan of individual systems is very short in comparison with most other military forces. A submarine is retired after only 15 years.

The hardware, as the manpower, suffers from the lack of combat experience. High technology weapons are extremely vulnerable and sensitive and exercises do not provide sufficient testing. Moreover, exercises are made difficult because of land constraints and the high residential density of Japan.

The aim of the Japanese government is to foster a strong and independent arms production capability and to become less reliant on the US for arms in view of the difficulties in the economic relationship which are affecting technological cooperation, and the uncertainties in the post-Cold War era. The private sector is interested in benefiting from the growing amount of funding provided by the government for defence-related research, and from the opportunity of an additional market. The Technical Research and Development Institute (TRDI) of the Defence Agency is the most important government institution to achieve the goal of greater technological self-sufficiency. It uses funding to multiply R&D in the defence sector or the dual-technology sector by private companies. The TRDI selects companies that have technology of potential use for military applications or companies approach the TRDI in order to find an additional application for a technology and to expand their R&D funding base. The aims of the government and private enterprise have been summarized in the following way:

– obtaining and indigenizing foreign civilian and military design, development, and manufacturing capabilities
– diffusing these capabilities as widely as possible throughout the economy
– nurturing and sustaining the primes and subcontractors to which commercial and military technologies could be diffused and from which indigenous development could be generated.[77]

Japan has the third highest military budget in the world with expenditures of $47 billion (¥4720 billion) in Fiscal Year 1995–96. Although this is only 0.95 per cent of Japan's estimated GNP for that period it is in absolute and comparative terms very high. In the Asia Pacific the size of Japan's military expenditures can only be compared to those of the US. However, as a volunteer armed force, personnel expenditures are over 45 per cent and the increase over the previous year is only 0.86 per cent. Moreover, the defence budget contains considerable expenditures for the stationing of US troops in Japan. In order to squeeze more out of the budget, the SDF relies on rolling payments for individual weapons over several years. The committed expenditures are higher than the annual defence budget. In FY 1991 78.8 per cent of Japan's annual budget was occupied by obligatory expenses determined at the beginning of the budget planning, such as personnel expenses, food and other overhead expenses, and payment for the procurements already ordered in past years.[78]

In regional terms Japan's defence expenditures and hardware appear very impressive, albeit not in quantitative terms. The most important factors are related to the evaluation of Japan's future intentions. They include the distrust of Japan in view of its insincere attitude towards the past, the gradual erosion of self-imposed limitations (for example, the lifting of the ceiling of 1 per cent of GNP in 1987), the constant upgrading and modernization of Japan's weapon systems even during budget cuts, the enormous 'surge capability' and technological capability of the Japanese economy, and the doubts hanging over the sustainability of the Japanese–American alliance against a background of rising competition and strife.

In regional terms Japan is a towering technological giant who can offset other Asian forces by its technological ability although the Japanese forces suffer from severe logistical and organizational shortcomings. Japanese arms production is driven by technological considerations, but the motives behind these efforts are more varied and have led Michael Chinworth to conclude in the case of Japan's efforts to co-produce the American Patriot missile:

> The Patriot case demonstrates a long-term thinking in Japanese defense planning by both industry and government, often in conjunction with one another, that belies the image of a Japan obsessed with its postwar pacifist legacy. The country is not about to embark on revived militarism, but plans and steps made throughout the period examined in this paper demonstrate that government officials and industrial players both are looking to the future for serious expansion of Japanese domestic production and defense capabilities despite the significant political and economic constraints on policy makers that remain even today. . . . Both groups of decision makers are enhancing the future of a strong Japanese military power by their shared perception of a need and desirability for developing domestic weapon systems for both political and economic reasons.[79]

Formal domestic restraints on more defence efforts have been subject at times to either elimination, reinterpretation or softening. Public opinion overwhelmingly accepts the SDF and the Security Treaty. It understands the necessity to contribute to Japan's own defence and a global balance. Former Prime Minister Takeshita stated several times the necessity to build up Japan's defence capabilities 'commensurate with its economic power'. This phrase had been used by American leaders in the past, but never by a Japanese Prime Minister. The PKO debate (see Chapter 3) has shown that the government prefers to dilute the Constitution through increasingly 'liberal' interpretations rather than making clear and limited revisions to it, thus eroding the value of the Constitution as the enshrinement of Japanese pacifism. It is this constant erosion of principles, and the ambiguity created by the pursuit of open-ended, ill-defined or even contradictory goals (for example, an independent arms production ability vs. a ban on arms exports) which makes the incantation of Japan's long-term peaceful intentions somewhat less convincing to many people. One often-used phrase is the promise that Japan will never become a big military power, a standard phrase used by Japanese prime ministers and politicians. But how credible is such a promise if we consider that Japan is at least in regional if not in global terms already a big military power in view of its defence budget, and the quality and quantity of its armament? The real meaning of 'not becoming a big military power' is, however, different and could be expressed much better: Japan will not use its growing military power as a means to further its political and economic interests and instead will use it only for purely defensive purposes, or in addition, as one may add now, for peace-keeping purposes under stringent conditions.

A. Political Inhibitions

Apart from the already mentioned limiting factors on the numerical indicators, however, there are considerable political circumstances which militate against a 'strategic breakout' of Japan. The weight of the past may raise fears with Japan's former enemies, but it is also a strong dam against the revival of militarism in Japan because it discredited the military leaders and proved to many Japanese the futility of military power. Added to this comes Japan's economic self-confidence – why attack Pearl Harbour if we can buy it? The failed experience of militarism and the long American protection has fostered a very naïve pacifism (see Chapter 1).

The most important factor militating for a militarily non-ambitious Japan is probably the decline of military power as a means to attain or protect national interests. Keohane and Nye came in their book on 'Power and interdependence' to the conclusion that 'trends in the role of force is to erode hierarchy based on military power'.[80] They estimated that four conditions made the use of military force by major countries less likely: (1) risk of nuclear escalation; (2) resistance by people in poor or weak countries; (3) the possibility of negative effects on economic performance; and (4) negative domestic public opinion. The argument is strengthened in Japan's case by the success of economic power as well as America's security guarantee. Owada Hisashi, one of Japan's top diplomats, put it this way:

> Military power no longer has the decisive weight even though the Gulf Crisis proved that it is still a very important component. But there are now other kinds of power – economic, scientific, technological, along with the ability to analyse information, and the power of people to take collective action in a sense of solidarity, and what will be at stake as the power of a nation will be the sum-total of all these elements. In that sense, Japan must play a role commensurate with its power, as has been said for these several years.[81]

The proof for this shift from military power to economic power has been for most Japanese the failure of the US in Vietnam, and on an even greater scale the demise of the Soviet Union. Although the Soviet threat was consistently used by the Japanese government for the justification of its security policy, notably the existence of the SDF and the Japanese–American security alliance, even conservative Japanese politicians have never believed in the immediacy of a Soviet threat to the same extent as did the Europeans or the Americans. Paul Kennedy's hypothesis of 'imperial overstretch' has been readily accepted in Japan, but the Japanese apply it also to the economic fate of the US.

B. Does Japan have Nuclear Ambitions?

Japan's very strong civilian nuclear industry is often mentioned when evaluating the country's future security policy. Japan has been successful in achieving an indigenous nuclear fuel cycle. It is general knowledge that Japan has the technological ability to develop nuclear weapons and the necessary delivery systems. Observers are particularly concerned with Japan's growing plutonium stockpile which according to some cannot be fully justified on the grounds of using it in Fast Breeder Reactors (FBR) or in mixed fuel rods (MOX). This does not prevent Japan from arguing that other states, notably North and South Korea, should not engage in enrichment. A full evaluation of the civilian nuclear industry leads, however, to the conclusion that Japan's nuclear industry is entirely technology driven and the underlying motivation is to counteract the high dependence on oil even if some commentators, industrialists or politicians emphasize or add to this motivation that military security options have to be maintained. The government and the parliament support the Three Non-Nuclear Principles of not manufacturing, not possessing and not introducing nuclear weapons although the latter principle was certainly flouted many times by the US as a consequence of the nuclear umbrella extended over Japan. The nuclear allergy in Japan is very strong since the use of nuclear bombs over Hiroshima and Nagasaki. By domestic law (for example, the Atomic Power Basic Law) and international agreements (NPT, IAEA Safeguard Agreement) Japan has committed itself not to go nuclear.

Although Japan has become very active in promoting nuclear arms control (see below) this will not stop questions about the possibility of a 'strategic nuclear breakout' in case external circumstances (that is, the end of the US nuclear deterrent or nuclear weapons on the Korean peninsula) change dramatically. But there is also a very strong prestige factor involved which could weigh heavily on Japan's decision to go nuclear in case of a complex borderline situation involving domestic as well as external difficulties. There is considerable dissatisfaction among more nationalistically inclined people that Japan deserves to have nuclear weapons as the ultimate accolade of its new power status, notably in view of middle powers like France and Britain. There is a feeling that these two countries would not have been able to preserve their present international status and prestige while their economic power has declined had it not been for their nuclear power status. This feeling is particularly strongly linked to Britain's and France's permanent seat on the UN Security Council while Japan is kept outside. In addition, there is a feeling that Japan cannot take on international responsibilities with real success without nuclear weapons. The Japanese Ambassador to the European Communities, Kobayashi Tomohiko, said in 1993 that

> ... everybody knows that nuclear weapons are a powerful 'political' weapon in international politics in the real world. Without nuclear weapons, today, any Japanese international political initiatives or involvements will lack *real political clout* [underlined in the original text]. What should be done about this? It is a big question, and a delicate one which I am not entitled to discuss officially.[82]

On the other hand, most nationalists may take sufficient consolation from the fact that Japan *could* acquire them because of its technological ability.

C. Japan's Involvement in Arms Control

In order to create a more peaceful international environment, to reduce regional and global suspicions towards its future security policy and to project itself as a responsible global power, Japan has increasingly become vocal in arms control and disarmament issues.[83] At the same time it is in this area, as well as in the promotion of a regional security dialogue, where we can observe a translation of its military power, or rather its potential for a more forceful and independent security policy, into political power.

The Japanese government has been increasingly bold in pushing nuclear arms control which has strong popular support because of the experience of Hiroshima and Nagasaki. On 2 November 1994 Japan introduced a resolution in the UN General Assembly's First Committee (dealing with disarmament and arms control) urging nuclear weapon states 'to further pursue negotiations on progressive and balanced reductions of nuclear weapons in the light of Article 6 of the NPT, with a view to the ultimate objectives of the cessation of the manufacture of nuclear weapons, the liquidation of their existing stockpiles and the elimination from national arsenals of nuclear weapons and the means of their delivery'. The US was concerned about the effect of such a resolution on the chances of the unlimited extension of the NPT to be negotiated in 1995, while the Japanese side pointed out that such a resolution could actually help and prevent the passing of an even more demanding resolution by the Non-Aligned countries. Japan had finally to settle for a resolution which did not mention Article 6 of the NPT. Still, France, the US and the UK abstained together with Cuba, India, Israel, Brazil and North Korea from voting on the Japanese resolution.[84]

However, in 1993 the Japanese government was even discussing whether it should support the indefinite extension of the NPT. The motives for this wavering attitude were probably manifold. On the one hand there are those who wanted to put pressure on the US and other recognized nuclear weapon states to fulfil their obligations towards nuclear disarmament, but there were also those who did not like to continue the inequality between nuclear and non-nuclear weapon states. The earlier quote by the Japanese diplomat Kobayashi Tomohiko illustrates the latter point, which is not an official position but reflects a widespread discontent with the NPT's inequality which led also to the long delay between Japan's signature and ratification of the treaty in the 1970s. In the end Prime Minister Hosokawa set an end to the debate in August 1993 and from then on the official position was in favour of an indefinite extension. Japan also used its influence with other countries to get a majority for this position at the NPT Review conference in May 1995.

Japan has been a long-time advocate of a step-by-step approach to a comprehensive nuclear test ban. This is obviously a delicate position for a country relying on the nuclear umbrella of the US, but also in view of

China as an important neighbour (which still tests nuclear weapons), economic partner and potential security threat. Japan was instrumental in making China accept the NPT regime and finally in moving the country to sign the Treaty in 1992. Control over the flow of high technology to China, together with American pressure, has played a major role.[85] Japan has been instrumental in working on scientific measurements for the detection of nuclear tests in the Geneva Conference on Disarmament.

Japan is also supporting various measures in the area of conventional arms control. In 1991 Japan initiated in cooperation with some EU countries the creation of a UN Register of Conventional Weapons with a view to improve the transparency of armament procurements and arms transfers. The first registration took place in 1993, with 83 countries reporting the total volume of exports and imports in 1992 of seven types of offensive weapons. This register is a natural extension of Japan's efforts in Asia to enhance military transparence. Even MITI has joined the effort by promoting its Asian Export Control Initiative which conducted bilateral working-level consultations with South Korea and Taiwan, as well as hosting an Asian Export Control Seminar in January 1995 to help set up more effective arms export control regimes in Asia after the demise of the Coordinating Committee for Export Control (COCOM). Apart from conferences and training Japan holds out the easing of control over its own high technology exports to Asia as a lever to make other Asian countries adhere to a new control regime.[86]

D. Japan's Growing Support for a Regional Security Dialogue

Japan's motivation to encourage a regional security dialogue is similar to that which determines its attitude to arms control. In addition, the weakening of the global power balance is encouraging the move towards security discussions in Asia. However, while this is a development which the Liberal school of international relations would emphasize, it has also to be recognized that any cooperative approach to regional security in Asia is difficult because of the region's diversity and complexity, and it is only the fear about the future direction of American and Japanese security policy towards the region as well as the fear that other major regional powers may fill a potential power vacuum which has finally led to more willingness to discuss common security interests on a regional level. We can observe on this issue a greater Japanese assertiveness as well as a willingness to give more credence to the non-military pillar of the country's security policy and to mutual assurance.

Until the end of the Bush administration, Japan's political leaders opposed discussions of security at a regional level. The reason was the opposition of the US to such an approach. The US preferred to rely on its bilateral security arrangements with several Asian states and was concerned about the possibility of regional security discussions leading to limits on its freedom of navigation of its nuclear-armed fleet in Asia. Japan was not interested in upsetting its only military alliance partner and was also not much moved by any practical impact of the end of the Cold War in Asia. The security situation in Asia was considered too complex and different from Europe to allow any process which might have looked like the beginning of the Conference on Security and Cooperation in Europe (CSCE). In addition, Japan was concerned about a negative political backlash if it took a leading role in view of its past behaviour towards Asia and because of its present economic domination of the region.

At the end of the Bush administration American officials started to change their opposition to a regional security dialogue due to increased pressure from Asian countries, Canada, Australia and the loss of the military bases in the Philippines.

In 1990 the Australian and Canadian foreign ministers had suggested the establishment of some sort of Asian equivalent to the CSCE.[87] In July 1991 Foreign Minister Nakayama proposed that security issues should be on the agenda of the ASEAN Post-Ministerial Conference (PMC) and he even proposed setting up a preparatory meeting of Senior Officials. He did not think of including China and Russia.[88] At the time the ASEAN member states rejected the idea but later in February 1993 agreed to it. The then Secretary of State Baker was rather dismissive of this proposal and complained about the lack of prior consultation by Japan. Satoh Yukio, however, who was involved in the Japanese proposal, writes that the MFA had been consulting with the US on this for one year.[89] In June 1992 Prime Minister Miyazawa established his own Advisory Committee (Committee on Asia and the Pacific and Japan in the 21st Century) and he mentioned when launching it that Asia had now, like Europe, to look for a multilateral security framework, which had to include the US.[90] It is therefore not surprising that in December the Committee came to the conclusion that for the time being Japan's participation in a regional security dialogue should be effected through the ASEAN PMC, but that this forum could evolve into a more formal structure resembling the CSCE.[91] In July 1992 Miyazawa suggested at the Washington National Press Club using the ASEAN PMC and APEC for a 'two-track approach' to security issues like Cambodia and the Korean peninsula. This approach was later explained by a MFA official as efforts on a subregional level to address issues like Cambodia, Korea and the South China Sea, the other track being the promotion of a region-wide security dialogue centred on ASEAN.[92] In summer 1992 at the Munich G-7 Summit the final declaration contained at Japanese insistence a statement that the already existing organizations of the ASEAN PMC and APEC can make contribution towards peace and stability in Asia. In September of the same year Japan and Indonesia hosted a dinner in New York on the occasion of the UN General Assembly which included the ASEAN countries and Vietnam, Laos and Russia. In October 1992 Miyazawa called on the US and other Asia Pacific nations to consider establishing a framework for handling regional security issues. 'I believe it is about time for Japan, the US and other Asia Pacific countries to further contemplate a framework of such Asia–Pacific regional cooperation'. He added that such a framework would not replace Japan's security arrangements with the US.[93]

By 1993 the lukewarm attitude of ASEAN towards Japan's proposals had changed, and the new American administration started to see in regional security discussions a valuable addition to its bilateral security agreements with Asian countries. In August 1993 ASEAN and its seven dialogue partners (Australia, US, EU, Canada, Japan, South Korea, New Zealand, but this time also including two guests, Russia and China, as well as three observers, Laos, PNG and Vietnam), finally decided to set up the ASEAN Regional Forum (ARF) for political and security discussions. The first meeting took place in 1994 in Bangkok. A variety of subjects was proposed for study such as confidence and security-building measures, nuclear proliferation, PKO, exchanges of non-classified military information, maritime security issues and preventive diplomacy. As can be seen from the calendar of events leading to this, Japan played an important catalytic role and was instrumental in overcoming American resistance.

Although the above chronology may give the impression of a very proactive Japanese attitude (after a long time of ignoring the security dialogue), the government is rather wary of projecting a high political posture because it may otherwise arouse latent suspicions among Japan's Asian neighbours about Japan's hegemony. The Japanese warming for a regional security dialogue does not imply a wish to reduce the bilateral security treaty with the US. Public opinion would not support it, and it would be counterproductive for Japan's relations with Asia. This regional dialogue is considered as an important process of reassurance rather than confidence building.[94] This careful and low-key approach is also formulated in the following quote by the Parliamentary Foreign Vice Minister, Hirata Yoneo:

> . . . it is of primary importance to maintain the existing bilateral security regimes such as the one between Japan and the US and the one between the US and the Republic of Korea. On top of that, we need to

work parallelly on the establishing of frameworks with two or more countries concerned for solving individual conflicts and confrontations, on the developing of a loose framework of the entire region for discussions and cooperation which would supplement the bilateral security regimes in the long run, as well as on the promoting of economic development that is going to play a vital role for security in this region.[95]

It is also interesting to note that the Defence Agency has now embraced regional security dialogue. While the Agency is not responsible for Japan's security policy which is the prerogative of the MFA, it has more than a bureaucratic power-motivated interest in supporting such dialogue. It has now officially recognized that dialogue among Asian nations is an important means to improve the security environment in Asia and to reduce uncertainties. As a result it wants to expand an already existing programme of dialogue with ministers, bureaucrats and defence officers and even introduce the exchange of military observers for military exercises. In addition it proposes to conclude agreements with Asian nations on the prevention of sea and air accidents in the region. This is the first time that the Agency officially supports CBMs although the word itself is not used.[96]

E. A Nascent Security Dialogue with Europe

Japan's widening interest in global security and wish to appear as a responsible and non-threatening military power is also reflected in its growing security dialogue with Europe on a bilateral as well as multilateral basis. Japan is obviously interested in European views on what is happening in Russia and the successor states of the former Soviet Union, whereas European countries benefit from Japanese views on the Siberian part of Russia, China and East Asia in general. The security field is an underdeveloped area in Japanese–European relations which reflects the weak political relationship. Expanding the security dialogue with Europe is also a way for Japan to enhance its prestige and to show to its Western partners that it has become a power with global concerns.

Both sides have in the last years stepped up exchanges of information on a bilateral level, notably involving Britain, France and Germany. In addition the Japanese government meets the European members of the G-7 on the occasion of the annual summit meetings. The security dialogue reached a climax at the beginning of the 1980s during the SS-20 debate which culminated in the G-7 summit meeting in Williamsburg in 1983. At that time then Prime Minister Nakasone signed the final communiqué which spoke of the 'indivisibility of Western security', the first time Japan linked its security in such a public way with the West as a whole. However, in reality the SS-20 debate showed that the US as much as the European partners were willing to conclude an agreement with the Soviet Union even if this meant the transfer of Europe-based SS-20s to East Asia where they would still threaten a member of the West.[97]

Since the July 1991 Joint Declaration between Japan and the EU, strengthened by an even more politically interested position paper of the European Commission in 1995 (Europe and Japan: The next steps), the European Commission and the Council of Ministers have found several items of security cooperation.[98] The above-mentioned arms register of the UN was co-sponsored by Japan and several EU members. There are now joint efforts to explore how to improve the efficiency of removing landmines and a proposal was made by the European side to put up a joint satellite to track ships movements in the South China Sea as a confidence-building measure.

The Director of the Defence Agency is occasionally visiting NATO, and Japan has been sending parliamentarians to the North Atlantic Assembly since 1980. Japan and NATO organized in October 1994 for the third time since 1990 a NATO–Japan Security Conference in which government officials and academics from both sides take part.[99] At the first meeting in 1990 in Knokke, France refused to attend because it felt that NATO was violating its charter by organizing such a conference.[100] Since the end of the Cold War, Japan has become more interested in security dialogue with Europe and to confront together global security issues such as nuclear proliferation, nuclear disarmament safety and environmental matters and peace-keeping. This is also seen as a demonstration of the country's eligibility for a permanent UN Security Council seat since it proves that Japan takes interest in global issues. In 1991 Japan started to show interest in seeking observer status in the Conference on Security and Cooperation in Europe although Japan had been so far rather negative towards regional security approaches. The Japanese government sees membership as a means to strengthen relations with the 51-member CSCE, but it realizes also the importance of a regional security forum which reaches within less than two miles of Japan's northern border. In addition it is a matter of prestige, since all member states of the Group of Seven industrialized democracies but Japan belong to the CSCE. Were Japan a less important country it would have no chance of becoming a member, since it is not a European country nor is it militarily present in Europe. One security specialist even proposed that Japan becomes a full member because the differences between the security frameworks of Europe and Asia were to him no longer as stark as before.[101]

A variety of factors has pushed the Japanese government also to take interest in the situation in the Balkans. The UN Secretary General's special representative in the Balkans, Akashi Yasushi, is a Japanese who is lobbying the government very strongly for political and economic support of the region. In addition Japanese interest in the region, as shown by Foreign Minister Kono's visit to Croatia and Hungary in April, is a positive nod to the Europeans to acknowledge Japan's new global role. As of April 1995 Japan had pledged a total of $140 million in aid to states that once formed Yugoslavia.[102] Whereas any military role of Japan (for example, PKO) is difficult to imagine, the donation of aid, that is the use of economic power, can have a significant impact.

CONCLUSIONS

Japan's regional security environment has considerably changed and the Japanese government is slowly and incrementally responding to these changes by adjusting its military alliance with the US and its own military force. In addition Japan is becoming more involved in arms control and security dialogue to improve its security environment, reduce suspicion concerning its military power and intentions, and to loosen its reliance on the security treaty and the SDF.

Japan's military power is considerable, notably if considered in its regional context and when taking into account Japan's economic and technological potential. Its economic and technological power plays a crucial complementary and enabling role in its hard power. Japan can exert considerable influence on arms control issues and the enhancement of the regional security dialogue because it is in the interest of everybody else that Japan does not become an independent and even bigger military power.

On the basis of the above analysis the question of where Japan's hard power is going (including where is it already today) has to be broken down into five separate, albeit related, points. The first is Japan's military capability. This capability is that of a major military power despite the many caveats one has to add to the impressive numerical, technological and other indicators. Arms production and nuclear power are primarily driven by considerations of technology and autonomy. The security alliance with the US, however, also provides Japan indirectly with offensive and power projection capabilities. This is particularly important for China's perception of its security environment and its debatable perception of its rightful position in the Asian balance of power.

The second point relates to Japan's security policy and its intentions. This

intention is entirely defensive although Japan's superior military technology may have an ambiguous impact on the perception of other countries.
Advanced surveillance technology can provide an additional deterrent,
but if this one appears to break down Japan will have to decide whether
to launch a preventive attack or not. Theatre missile defence is a purely
defensive weapon but can be seen as highly destabilizing by countries like
China and North Korea, particularly in conjunction with a global American protective missile umbrella.

The third point is about the relationship between economic power and
military power. In view of the first two points this one cannot be answered
easily and we agree with Peter Katzenstein and Okawara Nobuo who wrote:

> The case for the inevitability of a nuclear-armed, militarist Japan is just
> as implausible in the light of all we know about contemporary Japan as
> the notion that Japan will be the first and only example in history of a
> state wielding huge economic and technological power without corre-
> sponding military might.[103]

What does 'corresponding' or what American politicians have often
called 'commensurate' military might mean? Japan certainly could have
more military might than it has, in terms of manpower (for example, introduction of the military draft which is cheaper) and hardware (for example,
simply by keeping weapon systems longer).

The fourth point has to deal with the issue whether the build-up of
power potentials in and around Japan does not risk creating a momentum
of its own. In a thoughtful article Andrew Hanami asks:

> Though war may be avoidable, raising power levels may yet demand a
> heavy price from its participants. US establishment of a cost-effective
> sentry (Japan) at the Northeast Asian gate may have unleashed forces
> that will lead to the multiplication of Asian sentries of varying stripes
> across the region as they interact at an increasingly lethal level of force.
> This result could be inevitable in the long run, and be in part fuelled by
> a kind of technological determinism, in which case the question becomes
> both pace and substance.[104]

Such a momentum can only be avoided by expanding regional and
bilateral security dialogue and creating more confidence and assurances on
all sides. It has to go with restraint on building up military power. The end
of the Cold War and the domestic political constellation in Japan is cur-
rently supporting such restraint.

This leads immediately to the final point about the reversibility of Japan's
present security policy which is related to the interaction between Japan's

security policy and the regional environment. It is clear that most elements of Japan's security policy can be reversed, and it is likely that they will be reversed if there is a dramatic deterioration in Japan's security environment which goes beyond a mere withering of the American military presence and support. Apart from an American withdrawal or dramatic weakening, events on the Korean peninsula can strengthen those Japanese opinions who want to reverse the present course. The build-up of military potential by Japan's neighbours serves as a dam against a possible Japanese 'strategic breakout', but at the same time can also trigger such a breakout. More difficult is to judge whether there is anything inherent in the presently pursued defence policy which can develop a pull factor towards a Japanese 'strategic breakout'. An insufficient security policy can contribute to a reversal. When suddenly faced with an unprecedented security challenge which cannot be met by the available military means, options may appear inescapably to lead to a 'strategic breakout' because of the weight of the challenge (appropriately presented in a hysterical climate) and that of the latent options developed over time (for example, the quick development of some nuclear weapons due to an advanced civilian nuclear programme or the opportunities offered by advanced weapon technology). An insufficient security policy could also mean the pursuit of military security without regard to the security interests and perceptions of one's neighbours, thus setting off or encouraging an arms race. As we have seen, however, Japan has recognized this danger and the government is now actively involved in cooperative security efforts, promoting greater military transparency and encouraging a regional security dialogue. Finally an insufficient security policy could also mean destroying the military alliance with the US as the most important factor militating against a reversal by letting economic or technological interests take so much precedence that populist American perceptions of Japan being the more immediate threat to America's security may carry the day. However, such an outcome depends not only on Japan but to the same extent on the US.

3 The Use of Soft Power in Japan's Foreign Relations

INTRODUCTION

Japan's soft power derives from its economic, financial and technological power. Its structural power in the world economy is, for example, illustrated by its status as one of the world's major importer of raw materials and energy resources, which gives Japan considerable influence on the options and bargaining powers of other countries which are vulnerable to Japan either because they are competing with Japan for the same resources or because they are dependent on the export of these resources. Increasingly Japan is translating this structural power into influence on the shape of the international regimes which are important for free trade and the availability of these resources. So far Japan had relied on the US and other Western powers to secure appropriate regimes, and in the first instance relied on economic measures such as aid and investment to achieve access and secure supply.

This chapter will evaluate how far Japan has now moved towards influencing these international rules, using its economic power, as a means to maintain the integrity of its political economic system and to pursue its national interests. The end of the Cold War has taken away the relatively simple framework consisting of reliance on the US, but it has also increased Japan's range of alternatives. The shift of importance from military to soft power has been to Japan's advantage as the world's second largest economy. Foreign Minister Kono Yohei wrote in 1995 that the end of the Cold War had enhanced Japan's options and Japan was no longer to base its decisions on the demands of the East–West confrontation and on the fact that it is a 'member of the West'.[1]

In this chapter we will therefore look at how Japan's involvement in world trade and world investment leads not only to influencing the international regimes which rule them, but how this takes Japan to even exert influence on the way other countries run their economies and foreign policies. For the former we chose the GATT negotiations which led to the establishment of the World Trade Organization (WTO), contrasting it with Japan's almost non-existent influence over the international regime of global finances. The latter is best illustrated by Japan's foreign direct investment (FDI) and development aid where its power ranges from influencing economic development patterns to influencing the political options of other countries, developed and developing countries alike.

On the multilateral level Japan has become an indispensable member of most international organizations and influences their activities as the second biggest financial contributor. Japan is increasingly using this power for goals which are beyond narrow economic confines, including peace-keeping operations and the request for a permanent Security Council seat.

While looking at Japan's soft power we will contrast the country's relations with the developed world, mainly Europe and the US on the one hand, and with the developing world, mainly Asia, on the other hand. It is natural that Japan's influence is more significant on economically weaker countries, and reflecting its geographical position and relative strength, the range of Japan's influence is strongest in Asia. It is here where the transition from influence on economic outcomes to political outcomes is most visible and tangible.

INFLUENCING THE RULES OF INTERNATIONAL ECONOMIC INTERACTIONS

Japan 'arrived' on the world scene twice – in 1868 and again in 1952 – to find the ground rules for international economic interaction established by others who had more power and influence. These ground rules, as for example embodied in GATT, have to be adjusted from time to time to keep pace with the greater sophistication of world trade and the complexities resulting from a vastly increased number of very different participants. As one of the most important trading powers and a member of all relevant international organizations, Japan has naturally become involved in taking part in this constant adjustment and its economic stature provides it with considerable influence. Moreover, Japan now increasingly feels that the ground rules should better reflect Japan's interest. One of Japan's leading spokesmen, Okita Saburo, a former minister and economist, put it this way: 'The world economy is gradually formulating new rules of behaviour. . . . But it is crucial that the process not be one of any single country's demanding that others be "the same as me" or "do what I say"; it should be a give-and-take process, with everyone borrowing the best the others have to offer.'[2] This statement was clearly aimed at the US, which so far has been most vocal and influential in forming the rules of economic interaction. The former Vice-Minister for International Affairs in MITI, Hatekayama Noboru, put Japan's claim more bluntly: 'Japan has been the recipient of rules which have been made by others. From now on we would like to contribute to the formulation of new rules.'[3]

In practice Japan's approach to the international rules of economic inter-action is more sophisticated than just insisting on the change of rules, if it acts at all. It is aware of the considerable opportunities resulting from the significant differences between its own political economic system and that of its major Western partners while these differences are not covered by international regimes. Japan's leaders have in fact discovered that insist-ing on the strict adherence to such rules may now often be more beneficial than changing them. Whereas in the past the ban on exclusionist practices, dumping and other illiberal economic measures was often a problem for Japan's exporters and invoked condemnation and countermeasures, Japan can now rightly claim that many indicators of a liberal economic regime are positive in Japan and such countermeasures therefore are no longer justifiable under GATT rules. By demanding the stricter adherence to and conformity with GATT rules (or now those of the World Trade Organ-ization, WTO), Japan is projecting itself as a model GATT member while using GATT rules to refute attempts by other countries to use measures incompatible with GATT to counter Japanese advantages related to its political economic system which are outside of GATT regulations (for example, the cumbersome distribution system, the bias against foreign products and services, high entrance costs for newcomers). During the Uruguay Round, Japan benefited also from the fact that rules for the circumvention of anti-dumping duties (for example, through transship-ment, re-exporting) could not be agreed on. Japan has become increasingly vocal in propagating the values of free trade and liberalization and has gone on the offensive in trying to prove that those who accuse it of being a protectionist and an unfair trading partner are either not much better or even worse. The remark of Charles Kindleberger comes to mind when he said that 'free trade is the hypocrisy of the export interest, the clever device of the climber who kicks the ladder away when he has attained the summit of greatness'.[4]

The main targets of Japan's countercharges are the US and the Euro-pean Union. Japanese representatives are quoted as suggesting for the GATT successor organization, the World Trade Organization (WTO), subjects like 'legal harassment' in world trade (referring to anti-dumping measures and Washington's Super 301 legislation), regionalism and trade (referring to exclusive economic organizations like possibly the EU or NAFTA) and competition policy (referring to anti-trust policies in the US and the EU).[5] As part of this pro-active strategy, the Japanese government has begun to disclose measures by trading partners which it considers not to conform with GATT. In 1991 the Japanese Fair Trade Centre, an independent research institution, published a report criticizing US and EC trade practices, notably their anti-dumping measures.[6] In MITI's White Paper of May 1992 the Japanese government strongly criticized the United States for having departed from GATT regulations in deploying various protective trade policies and agreements on certain products since the 1970s. The government announced that it would play a more assertive role in GATT to penalize countries that violate international trading rules. Economic aid would be withheld from Third World countries that violate free trade.[7] In May 1992, the Industrial Structure Council, an advisory panel of MITI, said in a draft report that the US was the most questionable among Japan's ten major trading partners.[8] As criteria the panel used import restrictions, government procurement, unilateral actions against other countries, extension of domestic anti-trust policy to foreign countries, anti-dumping measures, origin rules, product standards, tariffs, protection of intellectual properties, regulation on foreign investment and regulations on services. The US was named questionable in ten of these 11 areas.[9] The final report came out in May 1993 and explained that the purpose of such a report was to refute the assumption of a clear linkage between trade balances and inadequate market access, and that the use of multilateral forums would be better than the unilateral approach which often impeded the settlement of problems.[10]

The GATT rules also help Japan to successfully resist American demands for guaranteed trade performance targets to change the American trade deficit with Japan. From an American perspective one can argue that Japan only wants to benefit from a position of advantage, as for example expressed in its trade surplus with the US which was facilitated by a long-lasting flouting of GATT rules (for example, protecting its domestic market from outside competitors) by withholding from the American side the means (that is, guaranteed trade targets) to narrow the gap thus created over time. From a Japanese perspective the American demands amount to the abandoning of a fundamental GATT rule just at the moment when Japan tries to become more GATT-conformable. One can also argue that the US could offset Japan's economic advantage by 'putting its economic house into order' as even promised by the US in the Japanese–American Strategic Impediment Initiative (SII) agreement at Japan's insistence as a condition for accepting the agreement. Japan's resistance against trade targets is very much supported by other major trading partners such as the European Union. It is clear that giving in to American demands on trade improvement targets could globally open the gate to managed trade. Technically the strength of the argument is on the Japanese side, but because its advantageous position is based on flouting the ground rules in the first place, the Japanese policy is far from easily acceptable without some compromise to be found elsewhere. It is these circumstances which led to a new height in the Japanese–American trade conflict when the US invoked its own Super 301 trade legislation and threatened in May 1995 sanctions against over $5 billion worth of Japanese car exports to the US without going first through the dispute settlement mechanism of the WTO, thus allowing Japan to sue the US in the WTO for breaching the rules of the new trade organization only five months after its establishment.

Japan's new stance on applying the rules of GATT, and now the WTO, has also not prevented Japan from increasingly invoking trade sanctions against Asian countries, using the same arguments as used traditionally against Japan by its trading partners in Europe and North America. Japan imposed in January 1993 anti-dumping penalties on 103 Chinese companies for alleged predatory pricing of their exports of ferrosilicon manganese, used in steel production. China's share in the Japanese market increased from 17 per cent in 1989 to 39 per cent in 1992. The Japanese government had previously threatened to impose similar duties on South Korean knitwear exporters but refrained from it after the Korean side had agreed to 'voluntary export restraints' as Japan had done itself in many cases when confronted with similar dumping charges. In 1992 Japanese cotton spinners warned Pakistan and Indonesia about anti-dumping action.[11] The point here is that Japan may be more cautious in invoking such trade sanctions than its other industrialized partners because of its past, but feels now strong enough to do it when there is sufficient domestic pressure to do so. Japanese companies are not shying from using anti-dumping procedures either, as the example of Komatsu has proved when it joined in May 1995 more than ten European excavator makers in supporting a request to the European Commission to investigate alleged dumping in Europe by several Korean companies. Komatsu is producing excavators in the Northeast of England.[12]

A. Japan's Use of GATT/WTO Conciliation Mechanisms

The change to a more proactive attitude in GATT is also illustrated by a more active use of the reconciliation mechanisms of GATT and the refusal to accept any more the role of the accused when it comes to the invocation of these mechanisms as has been the case in the past. In 1990 Japan secured for the first time since joining GATT in 1955 a panel ruling against EU anti-dumping duties on mainly electronic goods assembled in the European Union (then called the European Community) by Japanese 'screwdriver' plants and won the case.[13] In 1992, after having failed to win a GATT conciliation attempt against EC anti-dumping duties on Japanese audio-cassette tapes, the government took the matter up to the next stage but the GATT panel ruled against Japan, accepting only one argument out of 40 put forward by Japan to substantiate its case. According to the European Commission, Japan has not yet complied with another GATT panel ruling on Japan's discriminatory taxation system concerning alcoholic beverages which discriminates against foreign spirits. Japan argues that it has complied with the panel's ruling after having made several tax reductions. Since the basic discrimination still persists in the eyes of the European Commission, it expressed its intention to take the matter up with the WTO in 1995. With the improvement and streamlining of reconciliation mechanisms in the WTO for which Japan lobbied very actively, we can expect more Japanese use of these mechanisms and American unilateralism in the car trade dispute has given Japan a good opportunity to win.

The Japanese changed strategy will add a new dimension to the Japanese–American trade conflict and have a major influence on the fate of the new rules which were created for the new WTO. Although the US has agreed to the streamlined dispute settlement process of the WTO, Washington is very much torn between a bilateral and a multilateral approach towards settling disputes, particularly if the WTO settlement process is not seen as helping the US to reduce its trade deficit in certain sectors because the settlement does not cover the true causes of the deficit. In addition, the settlement process still takes a long time despite streamlining, and time is not on the side of the Clinton administration as it goes into a new round of presidential elections and has to show results. By tightening the rules of the WTO the Japanese government has made sure that many features of its economic system which undermine imports or give it a special advantage fall outside the international rules. It hopes that it will have a better chance of avoiding condemnation on such multilateral panels than in bilateral negotiations because the panels will be international and look only at narrow technical rules, thus excluding the possibility of political pressure as well as the consideration of trade barriers which are outside of WTO rules but are very much at the heart of Japan's trade disputes with other countries. An impatient US, trying to reduce the car parts imbalance which accounts for the biggest share of the bilateral trade, is therefore very tempted to take refuge in unilateral and punitive actions, even at the risk of undermining the WTO. Under the WTO a dispute settlement process still takes considerable time, allowing Japan to gain from the length of the settlement process and the fact that the recession and the appreciation of the yen is leading to structural changes along the lines demanded by its trading partners. At the same time it can take the moral high ground against unilateral and punitive measures. Moreover, American retaliatory measures of a regulatory kind and thus outside of the WTO (for example, holding back licences or shipping and telecommunication permits) may be contested by American companies who would suffer from them because of the increased interdependence with Japan.

B. Japan's Fight for a Special Rice Regime

The maintenance of its exclusionist rice regime is one of the best known examples of Japan's power to prevent or delay change of a particular manifestation of Japan's political economic system. Nowhere else are economic and political interests so closely interwoven, even after the change of power in July 1993. The maintenance of the rice regime is closely related to the maintenance of Japan's political economic system. The LDP, but also the SDPJ, have traditionally been dependent on the vote of farmers as a result of the electoral system and the unchanged constituency borders which have not taken into consideration the shift of population to urban areas. Subsidies to farmers have therefore been very important for maintaining the favour of this disproportionately big voting block.[14] Until 1994 the rice market was totally closed off to imports. American pressure to open the Japanese rice market increased during the multilateral Uruguay Round. The reasons given by the proponents of the rice import ban were the following:

– Japan's already high dependence on imported food (over 50 per cent)
– Rice-based family farms and village culture being the basis of rural life in Japan and being threatened by the import of much cheaper foreign rice
– Concern of Japanese consumers about lower food safety and pesticide controls in case of foreign imports.

The Japanese Diet had voted over the past decades for three different resolutions to preserve Japan's costly self-sufficient rice economy. The revision of the Staple Food Control Act in order to allow rice imports would therefore have been very difficult. Due to agricultural protectionism and the strong financial support given to the Japanese rice economy in the 1950s in response to a shortage of rice at that time, a very powerful agricultural cooperative (*Nokyo*) had come into being with considerable financial clout.[15] While the power of *Nokyo* over the political establishment has grown, rice farming has continuously declined and since 1991 rice is no longer the number one farm product. Since the Uruguay Round took place, when the LDP was gradually losing power as a coherent party, there has therefore not been much political will to risk votes by making any changes. But the Japanese government finally agreed to the deferment of tariffication for six years, starting in 1995, with the option of renegotiation at the end of it. During this six-year period Japan will allow initially 4 per cent of domestic consumption, rising finally to 8 per cent, to be covered by exports, and import quotas will be allocated on a country-by-country quota, giving the US as a major rice exporter the chance to get a particularly high quota through direct negotiations. As a result of a poor harvest in 1993, the government allowed foreign rice imports in 1994, but through various controls and directives managed to make a huge profit from these imports. In order to keep farmers sweet about the GATT round compromise, the Murayama government agreed in October 1994 to offer ¥6 trillion over six years (compared with expenditures for agriculture of ¥3.41 trillion in FY 1994) to farmers, including expenditures for rural public works, integration of farmlands, low-cost loans and other measures.[16] Moreover, the government succeeded in avoiding a change in the over-50-years-old Food Control Act and in reducing the bureaucratic power of the Ministry of Agriculture. The conclusion is that the 'weak' Japanese government was successful in forcing the other GATT partners to accept an extremely limited and conditional opening of the Japanese rice economy. The Japanese government could muster this strength because the famous landslide election in July 1993 has been an unprecedented victory of conservative forces in Japan, leading to the SDPJ not only losing half of its seats in the Lower House, but having to accept a radical shift in its posture to the right in order to take part in government. Moreover, it shares the same agricultural interests as the conservative parties. Finally this minimal Japanese concession proved again Japan's power towards the US which was pushing hardest for an opening of Japan's rice market, but had to consider other trade disputes with Japan and hopes to expect to recoup some points by getting a bigger share from the import quota system than other rice exporters.

The rice issue had a considerable impact on Japan's effectiveness and contribution to the Uruguay Round and stands in contrast to Japan's increasingly proactive stance as observed above. While being quite successful in tightening certain rules during the Uruguay Round, Japan's government used very sparingly its political power as an economic superpower during the Round. It proposed major tariff reductions in sectors like textiles and clothing, non-ferrous metals, fisheries, transportation equipment and chemicals and worked behind the scene on new rules. Although Japan was very interested in the Uruguay Round and from early on joined forces with other countries to get the Round started in the first place, the attention given to the agricultural agenda, one of only 15 areas covered by the Round, was very visible.[17] Because of the Japanese resistance to a change in its rice import ban, it missed an important opportunity to make an impact on the negotiations befitting its economic stature and the gains it derives from an open international trade regime. Instead Japan was seen as hiding behind the disputes of other countries in order to avoid a difficult compromise and made a token compromise only at the last minute.[18]

C. International Finances: More Relational than Structural Power

As the largest creditor nation in the world, Japan is interested in the major issues determining the international regime affecting the international financial market. In contrast to the US and even Britain, its structural power is still relatively weak. This is due to the fact that its status as the largest creditor nation is very recent, and its financial system is much less internationalized and still very inward looking. Still, Japan's financial system weighs heavily on the stability of the global financial system. Helleiner argues that because of deregulation and internationalization Japan acquired considerable structural power in the international financial system, for the Japanese banks as well as for the Japanese government.[19] He agrees with the interpretation that the October 1987 Wall Street crash started in Japan because of the action of Japanese banks in the US, and was stopped by the Japanese government when the reverberations threatened to engulf Japan.[20] The Wall Street crash thus illustrates that the Japanese financial market has become a major player.

Despite its financial woes, Japan stays the largest creditor nation and its ability to influence the global financial markets remains. Withdrawing money from abroad as a result of the current recession means, of course, less money for other economies, less reinvestment in already existing Japanese foreign investment projects like overseas subsidiaries, and less funds available for support of the American budget deficit. Japan's government is conscious of its financial power as shown by the rather unguarded comment of the former Vice-Minister of Finance for International Affairs in the Ministry of Finance, Utsumi Makoto. He is reported to have told his American counterparts when faced with the threat of sanctions to promote Japan's opening of financial markets that Japan would slash Japanese credit to the US.[21]

However, with the exception of deregulation which is closely linked to the stability of the financial markets, there are not many signs of Japan trying to shape the international financial system. Its influence on other players is of a more indirect nature. Its financial institutions are, for example, said to have less political inhibitions (such as trading with outcasts like former

South Africa) because of the absence of historical or religious links (former colonies, Middle East) and this may push other players to ease their inhibitions.[22] Japan's major influence on the international financial regime may be more exerted through its reluctance towards deregulation. In view of the Japanese trigger of the Wall Street crisis in 1987, and recently the steep appreciation of the yen with its unsettling influence on global financial markets, one wonders whether the Japanese government has any incentives to loosen these controls which would moreover diminish the power of the Ministry of Finance, one of the major pillars of Japan's political economic system.

Despite the traditional caution of the Japanese government, or sometimes even because of it, the Japanese financial system is vulnerable to crises and the government's reluctance/inability to reform it could have a serious impact on the international financial system. The three main aspects are the price risks which result from currency fluctuations, risks which result from new financial instruments, notably the trade in derivatives, and risks which are inherent in the international payment modi.[23] The yen has been subjected to a high appreciation several times in recent years. Moreover, the Japanese currency is, like the dollar, not linked to any multilateral currency arrangement which would put a brake on fluctuations. The Barings security scandal in February 1995 was closely linked to speculations with the Nikkei index in Japan. If even an experienced institution like Barings was unable to control its derivatives activities, Japanese financial institutions can be assumed to be even less able to control them because of their much more recent experience with these financial instruments. In the case of payment modi Japan is for a variety of reasons more exposed than other markets. The possible combination and coincidence of risks makes the Japanese financial system particularly dangerous not only for Japan itself, but for the global financial system as a whole. Regulation and informal influence by the government does not necessarily reduce these risks because some measures may actually enhance risks by decreasing transparency and lowering liquidity. The Bank of Japan is still much more subject to political pressure (and thus bureaucratic mistakes) than, for example, the German Bundesbank. Whereas the major banks can weather the loan crisis, regional and long-term credit banks are in much worse condition and the collapse of one or of several at the same time could become the start of a chain reaction.

After the Great Hanshin earthquake on 17 January 1995 another possible catalyst for a crisis may be an earthquake hitting Tokyo, which is the political as well as economic and financial heart of Japan's over-centralized political economy. Despite the warning from the Kobe earthquake, the political and economic world seems to be unable to prepare the country better for such a crisis. However, the international repercussions from such a natural catastrophe alone may not lead to a meltdown of the global financial system because the role of insurances is surprisingly low, as the Kobe earthquake has shown, and the withdrawal of liquidity from abroad as a result of the recession has been substantial without engendering a global liquidity crisis. It is rather the confluence of various other risk factors which may be triggered by a Tokyo earthquake.

This short overview raises serious questions about Japan's ability and willingness to contribute to the maintenance of a stable global financial system. Moreover, international cooperation among central banks is limited and their regime still weak and untested. The present Japanese financial system is vulnerable to crises, but so would be a totally open financial system without experienced players. Either way, Japan is exerting power and influencing the options and material circumstances of others.

FROM FOREIGN INVESTOR TO ECONOMIC MODEL

As the world's largest creditor nation which wants to sustain its trading power, Japan has become within a very short time one of the world's biggest investors. The total amounted in Fiscal Year 1994/95 alone to $41.1 billion, an increase of 14 per cent over the previous year.[24] The US, as Japan's main trading partner, is attracting the country's largest share of investment. The US financial markets are particularly attractive for Japanese companies which are very limited in their overregulated home market. Moreover, Japan's chronic trade surpluses need to be invested and the US with its sophisticated financial instruments and attractive state bonds offers a good haven. Investment in subsidiaries helps to overcome American protectionist measures. From 1988 to the end of 1990, Japanese investors exported about $52 billion into the US.[25] In Fiscal Year 1994/95 investment to North America rose by 16 per cent to $17.8 billion, accounting for 43 per cent of Japan's total foreign investment. In 1991 Japanese investors held $49.8 billion in US debt, which was nearly five times the $8.3 billion of Japanese debt held by all foreign companies combined in 1990.[26] According to American statistics the UK is the biggest investor in the US, but these figures may hide the fact that a substantial amount of money is actually only channelled through London as a convenient money market. Since Japanese companies also use London, the share of Japanese funds into the US may be higher than the statistics indicate.

Japanese capital flows into the US have attracted particular attention for various reasons. In the 1980s Japan was the world's principal exporter of portfolio capital and thus the principal source of financing for the US current account deficit. During the late 1980s the composition of Japan's outward investment shifted to direct investment which manifested itself in the US in a series of highly publicized purchases of American companies and real estate.[27] The Japanese investment also attracted attention because of its rapid rise from a very low level and because it constituted the most visible face of a greater role of foreign direct investment in the US, which was until the 1970s lower than in Europe. Japan's FDI is dominating in banking in contrast to manufacturing and other sectors. At least in 1990, Japanese banks accounted for 55.3 per cent of US banking assets held by foreign banks which amounted to 11.8 per cent of total US banking assets.

A. Japan's Foreign Direct Investment in Europe

Europe has also benefited to a great extent from Japanese financial flows which go beyond the more visible investments in the manufacturing sector. In Fiscal Year 1994/95, however, Asia overtook Europe as Japan's second biggest investment destination after the US. Investment in Europe fell by 22 per cent to $6.2 billion, compared with an increase of 53 per cent or $5.2 billion of Japanese investment to Latin America.[28] The greater interest in Asia is explained by its fast growth, the lower level of emotional and traditional ties with Europe compared with Asia, as well as the low degree of control over European subsidiaries compared with that enjoyed in Asia.[29] By the end of 1994 there were 720 manufacturers affiliated to Japanese companies in Europe, an increase of 19 over the previous year. This was the smallest increase this decade, compared with the new arrival of 95 companies during the peak in 1989–90. In view of the yen's appreciation, however, the rate of investment is to increase again.[30]

The role of the Japanese financial institutions in Europe is substantial because of the country's huge liquidities. In Europe, London has become the favourite place for Japanese financial institutions which can enjoy there a more deregulated environment. As of March 1995 there were 37 banks (nine subsidiaries and 28 branches) in London which held 14.6 per cent of Britain's total assets. The next biggest foreign asset holder is the US with 8 per cent.[31] In June 1991, at the height of the Japanese economic bubble, the share of the then 31 Japanese banks in the UK in total British assets was 19.2 per cent (£252.8 billion out of £1317 billion). This compared with a share of 42 per cent for British banks and 9.8 per cent for American banks.[32] Only 20 per cent of the lending by London-based Japanese banks goes to Japanese clients in Europe, the rest is linked to international syndicated loans. In 1994 ¥1 trillion ($11.6 billion) worth of yen issues were floated in the Euro-markets although the yen is more a transit currency.[33] Japanese banks have with 23 per cent contributed more to Eurotunnel's loan finance, the consortium which built a tunnel under the Channel, than those from any other country.[34] When Eurotunnel needed a final injection of vital funds amounting to £700 million, the Japanese banks nearly jeopardized the survival of the project which had been finished by then because they were reluctant to put up more money.[35]

Japan is a founding member of the European Bank of Reconstruction and Development. Established in 1991 Japan has a share of 8.5 per cent, equal to that of the UK, France, Germany and Italy and only surpassed by the American share of 10 per cent. Recently the Japanese Export–Import Bank has decided to no longer limit its lending to developing countries but to expand it to industrialized countries as well. The Bank decided to provide an untied loan facility of up to £125 million for the financing of a private railway link between London and Heathrow airport. This is the Bank's first untied loan for a European infrastructure project.[36] While the prime motive for lending is the need to invest liquidities, there are also political interests involved. Prime Minister Thatcher was known to encourage Japanese banks to contribute to the Channel tunnel project in recognition of the opening of the London financial market and Britain's free trade attitude towards Japanese economic activities in Europe. The new role of the Export–Import Bank, which is controlled by the Japanese government, is also certainly linked to improving relations with Britain as a champion of Japanese commercial interests in Europe. The Bank has also invested in the US and signed in April 1993 a shareholders agreement to take 10 per cent in the Los Angeles maritime harbour to facilitate coal exports to Japan. It was the Bank's first equity investment which became possible through the 1989 revision of the Export–Import Bank of Japan Law.[37] While this equity investment is helpful to secure Japan's coal imports and to diversify away from imports from Australia (around 70 per cent of Japan's coal comes from there at present), the move certainly has political motives too in view of the economic friction between Japan and the US.

Most in the public eye is Japan's investment in manufacturing in Europe. Britain is with a total of 205 cases (as of 1994) the preferred location for Japanese direct investment in Europe in the manufacturing sector, followed by France (111) and Germany (107). More than 40 per cent of Japan's cumulative investment into the EU has come to Britain, amounting to £17 billion as of 1994. Over 200 Japanese firms operate as many as 270 manufacturing plants in Britain (28 per cent of the total in the EU and EFTA at the beginning of 1994), which has resulted in the creation of 70 000 jobs. The government is keen that the manufacturing capacity is supplemented by research and development facilities and over 30 Japanese companies are involved in R&D.[38] For Britain Japanese investment is a welcome input into an economy which has been buffeted by the decline of its traditional industry, labour problems and insufficient investment in education. The benefit is also appreciated by the Labour Party because Japanese manufacturing investment is concentrated in strongholds of the party in Wales, Northeast of England and Derbyshire.[39] Thanks to Japanese investment, Britain has become a net exporter of TVs and is increasing its car exports to the European continent. Nissan Motor's factory in the Northeast of England is exporting 80 per cent of its output to the European continent. The positive influence on upgrading product and management quality of subcontracted companies, or companies which aim to become subcontractors or just want to stay competitive, is also substantial. One has to keep in mind, however, that despite the great visibility and recent spectacular growth of Japanese manufacturing investment in Europe and the US, most investment is from other countries, such as from the US and the European continent in the case of Britain, or from Britain and the Netherlands in the case of the US.

The importance of Japanese manufacturing investment and of Japan as a market has considerably contributed to a lessening of frictions between Japan and Europe despite Japan's continuing trade surplus. The federal structure of the US, the geographic concentration of Japanese manufacturing in the US and the accessibility of the US administration to particular interests has not generated the same sanitizing effect on trade frictions despite the considerable economic benefit for many states and industries. Within the EU Britain has been instrumental in changing the mood in the trade area from confrontation to cooperation when its Department of Trade, in cooperation with business, created in 1988 the 'Opportunity Japan' campaign (1988–91), which is said to have succeeded in doubling British exports to Japan and the adoption of many Japanese ways of management. The campaign was then followed by 'Priority Japan' (1991–94) and later 'Action Japan' (1994–97). In France this change was emulated with an official campaign 'Le Japon . . . c'est possible'. However, the overall trade deficit of Europe and the US with Japan seems to be hardly touched by these efforts.

B. Japan's Foreign Direct Investment in Asia

Although the cumulative amount of Japanese investment is still lower in Asia than in the US and Europe, the Japanese investment in Asia has to be seen in relation to and in the context of the size of Asia's economies, their developmental stage, and their link to other Japanese flows such as trade, ODA and technology. First, Japan is the most important trading partner of most Asian countries. Japan's total trade in 1993 amounted to $602 billion, of which $177 billion was with Asia's most important subregion, that is, Southeast Asia. The comparative figures for the other two most important trading partners of Japan, US and EU, were $160 billion and $86 billion respectively.[40] The biggest trading partner for Japan after the US and the EU in 1993 had become China with a total trade of $37.7 billion (a rise of 31 per cent over the previous year), followed by Taiwan with $31.6 billion, Korea with $30.6 billion and Hong Kong $24.6 billion. In 1994 Japan's trade with China had risen to $46.24 billion, amounting to a 22.2 per cent increase and a Chinese trade surplus of $8.88 billion.

Secondly, Japan's trade with Asia is intimately linked with its investment pattern in the region. East Asia has generally become very attractive to foreign investment and it more than doubled its share of global investment stock from 6.2 per cent to 13.6 per cent during the 1980s.[41] The cumulative amount of Japanese investment in Asia in 1993 was $66.5 billion, compared with $177 billion in the US and $83 billion in Europe. As we have seen, Japanese new investment in Asia has now overtaken that in Europe, and instead of falling as in Europe it rose by 24 per cent.[42] In 1993 China became Japan's second largest destination for its exports, with a rise of 45 per cent over the previous year. China is now Japan's biggest new investment location, although with $6 billion of investment in 1994, Japan ranks as third biggest foreign investor in China after Hong Kong and Taiwan. Japanese investment in Asia has thus also overcome the fall of investments in the years after the level of 1989 when it was $8.2 billion. Since 1989 it had gone down to $7 billion in 1990 and to $5.9 billion in 1991. A similar fall occurred in Japanese investments in other countries as a result of the recession and the banking crisis.[43] Investment in manufacturing amounted in the period 1981–94 in Asia to $28.3 billion, compared with $37 billion in the non-manufacturing sector. In the US and in Europe the manufacturing share in Japan's total investment is much less during the same period (see Table 3.1).

The reason for Japan's continuing interest in investing in Asia and greater shift to Asia in its global investment pattern is to cope with the appreciation of the yen and the rising production costs in Japan. Asia provides the best opportunities, as mentioned before. In addition, the average return on Japanese investment in Asia is 3 per cent, compared to 1 per cent in Europe and −0.1 per cent in the US. The differences are even starker when looking only at the return on manufacturing investment, which is

Table 3.1   Japanese manufacturers' direct overseas investment (in $ million)

Region	Financial year			
	1986	1990	1992	1993
US	2 138	6 386	3 784	4 039
Europe	370	4 593	2 101	2 039
NIEs	573	805	439	736
ASEAN	193	1 553	1 808	1 474
China	23	161	659	1 377
Total	3 806	15 486	10 057	11 131

Source: Ministry of Finance, Japan

reckoned to be 5 per cent in Asia, 3 per cent in Europe and −0.9 per cent in the US.[44]

The trade and investment position in East Asia gives Japan considerable power to shape the trade relationship to its maximum benefit. While tariff rates on non-agricultural goods are on the whole similar to those of the EU and the US, tariff rates on raw and processed agricultural commodities are higher. The more Asian products are processed, the higher Japanese tariffs move. This kind of tariff escalation has a negative impact on regional industrialization efforts. Asian agricultural products are also hurt by Japan's quantitative restrictions on agricultural products.[45] The practice of transfer pricing by Japanese multinational companies seems to be relatively widespread. This practice disguises capital outflows and therefore reduces tax revenue for the Asian hosts of Japanese investments.[46]

C.   The Political and Economic Benefits of FDI

The evaluation of the benefit of Japanese trade and investment for other countries is very difficult. In Asia it has been instrumental in pulling many countries out of poverty and helping South Korea, Taiwan, Singapore and Hong Kong to reach the status of Newly Industrialized Economies (NIEs). In many cases this has also gone hand in hand with a frightening degradation of the natural environment which obviously cannot be blamed only on Japanese companies. The investment in Asia, together with ODA to which we come later, has led to the acquisition by Japan of considerable power and influence over the perception, material circumstances and bargaining position of these countries. Since we will look at the political and economic influence of Japan on Asia after having dealt with ODA, we will concentrate here on the effect of FDI on Europe and the US.

For obvious reasons the impact of Japanese investment on Europe and the US is much more limited than on Asia. It can be measured in the impact on the survival of certain industrial sectors, employment in deprived regions, working and management practices, and technology. The investment has provided Japan with considerable influence over specific industrial sectors in Europe and the US, as well as with significant bargaining power, if not with central governments then at least with local authorities. In the case of Britain it has clearly influenced the British government to improve bilateral relations with Japan and this has had a certain effect on the relationship of the EU with Japan as a whole. In an age of chronic, if not structural, unemployment and need for modernization of economic structures, Japanese investment has been a boon to many local communities.

The impact of Japanese investment on national economies as a whole and certain sectors is, however, uneven. Japanese investment has led to more Japanese imports of high value-added parts for Japanese production abroad. Given that Japanese companies operate in the UK at significantly lower labour costs than their UK-owned competitors, suspicion has been raised about the 'crowding out' of traditional output, leading to an actual reduction in GDP and a worsening of the current account balance.[47] Looking at TV production, one may argue that Japanese exports, followed later by manufacturing investment, 'crowded out' British producers, but today Britain, thanks to Japanese investment, is a net exporter of TVs. A similar chain of events occurred in the American TV industry. Marcel van Marion, as an executive of Philips in Eindhoven an insider, has traced in his book the fate of colour television in Europe and the special British role in facilitating Japanese advances in colour television and electronics generally in the EU and the US.[48] He concludes that the Japanese were successful because of an illiberal economic regime at home and the use of dumping.

Special attention is now also devoted to the contribution of Japanese FDI to the technological base of the host nations. Growing R&D operations by Japanese companies in their major overseas markets are, however, still largely limited to the adaptation of Japanese technologies to local markets rather than developing new technologies. The aim is to develop a global network of production and R&D sites. Some argue that Japanese FDI is still too recent to have advanced to the stage of localized R&D, but a recent American government report comes to the conclusion that all multinationals tend to concentrate R&D in their country of origin, including American companies where the share of such activities abroad amounts to less than 13 per cent. In the US Japanese affiliates have by far the lowest level of R&D intensity which is measured as the ratio of R&D spending to sales. This may be due to the higher Japanese share of investment in wholesale trade rather than in manufacturing.[49] However, the same low R&D activity by Japanese affiliates has been found in Europe.[50] While Japanese R&D activities in host nations are still very low, Japanese companies have not been slow to use FDI (either through cooperative agreements or acquisitions of foreign companies) as a means of acquiring foreign technology. The share of cases of Japanese companies investing in US high-technology companies amounted between 1988 and 1993 to 438 cases (or 57 per cent of all identified cases, compared with 13 per cent by the second most active foreign investor, the UK). Compared with the investments by UK companies, Japanese investment showed a steep increase and was highly focused on a set of vertically integrated sectors, primarily electrical equipment, primary metals and motor vehicles.[51]

In this context it is also important to mention that Japan uses its financial might to enhance its R&D basis by becoming a funding agent of international research projects. It is motivated by the inadequacy of its own fundamental research, the difficulty in finding enough qualified staff in Japan (cooperation between industry and universities in Japan is difficult) and pressures by other developed countries urging Japan to contribute more to international research. As a result the Japanese government initiated several major research programmes to which foreign researchers are welcome, such as the 'Human Frontier Program' (research of the human brain), the 'Intelligent Manufacturing System' (robot and other production systems), fundamental research for computer technology of the fifth generation and 'Real World Computing' (user-focused computer technologies). These programmes have found considerable response in other countries, notably in Britain with its diminishing public funds for university research.

In an age of unemployment, the employment effect of Japanese investment is naturally the main focus of the public and thus the government. William Holsten suggests, however, that for the evaluation of Japanese investment of all kinds, we should look beyond the creation of jobs, and also take into consideration Japan's commitment to indigenization, the impact of Japanese investment on values, the *keiretsu* structure of some investments, the degree of technology transfer, local sourcing, trade impact and reciprocity.[52] Many of these issues are too recent, since a proper evaluation involves a long timespan, as Europeans know from the way American investment in Europe was perceived in the 1960s and is appreciated now. The situation is changing fast and differs from one industrial sector to another in the case of manufacturing investment. For the purpose of this book the question is rather to what extent these sites will be operated from

Tokyo, which is important in terms of level of transferred technology, indigenization of management and ultimately decisions about closure or expansion.[53] In a Japanese multinational company true decision-making rests with the headquarters in Japan. The problem is that decisions made very far from the branch plant may have a crucial bearing on the fate of the host community, and such decisions are made outside the host nation and its industrial and social context.[54] The greater the extent of foreign involvement in a local economy, the less can this economy be protected by the national government from the fluctuations in the economy of a particular important foreign company and from the world economy. From a liberal market economy point of view this is a normal phenomenon of free market forces at work which are credited with insuring a rational allocation of resources. According to this view, if one community or region suffers then it has to adapt. The social and political costs, however, can be considerable, and the effecting foreign company can thus exert considerable influence over the abilities and bargaining powers of host communities and host nations. The recession has proved for the first time that Japanese transplants are not immune from its effects and that Japanese management does not preclude redundancies. A survey found that in 1992, 51.2 per cent of responding companies reported a deficit in their European operations, compared with 23.7 per cent in 1989. More than a third of manufacturers had dismissed employees in Europe.[55]

D. Dependence or Interdependence?

The issue of the nature of players (Japanese government or Japanese companies) has an important bearing on the discussion of whether Japanese FDI creates dependence or contributes to interdependence. Whereas in the introduction we succeeded in bringing some clarity to the difference between dependence and interdependence, the nature of players complicates an evaluation because of the relatively close links between business and government/bureaucracy in Japan. Theodore Moran therefore makes no allowance in his definition of dependence: 'When foreign corporations (or their home governments) can threaten to issue orders to their US-based affiliates that would delay, place conditions on, exercise blackmail through, or ultimately withhold the goods, services, or technology upon which the US has become dependent.'[56] This definition would correspond to vulnerability dependence as defined in the Introduction.

According to Moran's definition there are sectors in the American economy which may have achieved dependence on Japan. He quotes an American government report sample of American companies in 1991 of which 42 per cent stated that Japanese suppliers had rejected their requests to purchase advanced goods, parts or technologies, or had delayed their delivery by more than six months.[57] Ross Young, in a study on the semi-conductor manufacturing industry in the US, gives concrete examples of several American companies which suffered damage because Japanese suppliers refused to sell them vital equipment in good time.[58] This with-holding or delaying of technologies or of parts is, however, the result of commercial competition, and is not aimed intentionally at weakening the US defence industrial base. However, this latter result may happen as a consequence if the foreign company has no subsidiary in the US or if the foreign control of a US-based foreign-controlled subsidiary is considered a security risk.

The issue of dependence is considered most crucial in the important and future-oriented industrial sectors such as electronics which are also closely related to most advanced weapon systems. The share of semiconductors in any new weapon system is now close to 50 per cent.[59] Young compares the electronics industry to a food chain where the competitiveness of one industry is closely linked to that of other related industries. The fear is understandable that foreign competitors may withhold critical equipment which can be crippling in industries with very short life-cycles such as the semiconductor industry. This fear is enhanced by the circumstance that Japan's semiconductor equipment producers are linked to Japanese semi-conductor producers through debt, equity or other affiliations. Dependence on foreign supplies also weakens the US negotiating position in trade talks or dumping investigations because American buyers will not risk their busi-ness with a foreign supplier by making statements contrary to the interests of that foreign supplier.[60]

In a dispassionate treatment of national security implications of foreign-controlled suppliers to the US military, Graham and Krugman come to the conclusion that the implications during a war between the US and the for-eign country from where the company originates are far from conclusive in light of the past, and that various laws for wartime production fur-ther reduce the likelihood of foreign ownership doing any harm.[61] Their conclusions on the ability of the US to maintain a defence industrial base are less clear. On the question whether FDI has been the cause of the erosion of America's defence industrial base or rather the symptom, they are more inclined to assume the former, finding fault for any erosion with the government as well as industry. In view of Ross Young's book an answer depends very much on the specific sector. The erosion of Amer-ica's defence industrial base is taking place with the relative erosion of the overall technological ability of the US, and not all reasons for this can be put to 'predatory Japanese trading' or 'predatory Japanese FDI'.[62]

In Europe there seems to be hardly any awareness of these issues.[63] However, even without special consideration for the defence sector, the reliance on fewer and fewer suppliers of strategically important industrial products as a result of increasing industrial concentration, whether they are produced in Japan or not, can be risky. The 1993 destruction by fire of a Sumitomo plant holding a world market share of 55 per cent of the world's production of epoxy resin, a key material used to package semiconductor devices, as well as the impact of the Great Hanshin earthquake of 17 January 1995 on the delivery of parts for Malaysia's Proton car, was a reminder of the possible impact of natural catastrophes, let alone human intervention. The high-rising yen has also affected the supply of products on which Japan has a particular hold, such as semiconductors where it has a world share of 42 per cent.

Also we face again the contradiction that Japan demands or implicitly assumes that all other players accept a growing degree of interdependence while for itself it tries to fend off dependence. Although the ability and economic viability of such a contradictory strategy is diminishing, Japan is still very strong in the control over technology, transplants, financial flows, and so on. Techno-nationalism is a strong feature in Japan's political economic system as Yoda Naoya confirms:

> Techno-nationalism has deeply penetrated Japanese culture and society. This penetration is a paradigm of Japanese politics and society. Techno-nationalism did not suddenly appear: it is deeply rooted in Japan, much more so than in Europe and the US. Globalism on the economic side and nationalism on the political side coexist in Japan, where they are negative and positive poles.[64]

In the 1991 World Investment Report, Japan ranks next to last among the industrial nations (ahead of only South Africa) according to its measure of FDI as a share of gross domestic capital formation.[65] The role of foreign direct investment is extremely low whether measured in sales, manufacturing employment or in assets.

This discussion of Japanese FDI shows that the Japanese government as well as Japanese business gain considerable leverage over the options and bargaining power of others. Without its significant FDI in the US and in Europe, the Japanese–American trade conflict may have turned nastier and Japanese–European relations may not have improved as much as they have. For Japanese business, FDI has allowed it to overcome protectionist barriers erected by the EU and the US and to create a favourable climate in many local communities towards Japanese business activities. Even without any political (security) considerations, Japanese FDI and exports have created dependence (measured by vulnerability) and above all interdependence (measured by sensitivity).

E. Japan as an Economic Model

Leading beyond the issue of dependence vs. interdependence is the development of Japan becoming an economic model for other economies. Japan's FDI in the manufacturing sector has been playing a crucial role in transferring production and managerial skills, either directly or indirectly. 'Learning from Japan' has in many countries become a motto to overcome industrial decline and to cope with Japanese competition. The economic model function is also an important part of the formation of a consensus between Japan and others because if Japan influences other countries/ companies to perceive Japanese production and managerial skills, and later possibly also some aspects of Japan's political economic system (for example, 'industrial policy') as worthwhile to emulate, then Japan will have reduced the strain deriving from the systemic differences which now bedevil some of its bilateral relationships. Although according to our definition of power this is power exertion, it would not be perceived as such.

It is obvious that other countries which want to compete with Japan will have to adopt to a certain degree the Japanese economic system, notably the system of production. As the discussion on 'lean production' has shown, the Japanese system is more competitive because of its organization. Organization, however, has not only to do with the organization of material factors, but also with human beings and their condition of life. Be it the physical shape of the environment which has to bow to economic needs, or the effect of a Japanese-style relationship between subcontractor and contractor on the workers and the independence of the subcontractor, the quality of life of people will be influenced which may be contrary not only to the tradition and values of a non-Japanese people, but those concerned may also not be given a vote in such a shift.

The transfer of the relationship between contractor and subcontractor as well as the role of labour unions in Japanese transplants has attracted particular attention. Not only is the contractor–subcontractor relationship recreated abroad by some Japanese affiliates, but also preferential trading.[66]

Japanese-type management is attractive for British employers and their unions because some 'Japanese production and personnel systems appeal to them, particularly skill-building, abolishing status distinctions, emphasising quality and pushing creativity and responsibility to the shopfloor'.[67] Many Japanese companies in Britain are also more willing to work with trade unions than are British companies. When Toyota established its British factory at the beginning of the 1990s some labour unions in Britain condemned the 'alien approach' of some Japanese investors, particularly the proposed 'no disruption' clause which meant 'no strike deal'.[68] Similar 'no strike' deals had, however, been worked out in many other Japanese transplants, and some had even excluded labour unions. British labour unions had the choice of not only losing workers in closing British (or rather British-based) factories, but also being excluded from the new Japanese car factories set up by Nissan, Honda and Toyota if they did not accept the Japanese demand of single union and no-strike deals. It is well known that single union factories are the norm in Japan.

The transfer of Japanese labour and management practices varies from company to company, from sector to sector, and from region to region. It is therefore difficult to speak of 'one Japanese model'.[69] Although there is generally praise for Japanese management practices, there has also been some criticism. Philip Garrahan and Paul Stewart observed at the Nissan car factory in the Northeast of England a 'management-by-stress strategy' and they are critical of the strong corporate consciousness fostered by the Nissan management.[70] The 'Nissan Way' rests in their eyes 'upon control through quality, exploitation via flexibility, and surveillance via teamworking'.[71] Sue Milsome concludes that there 'is little evidence that Japanese-style international competitiveness can be achieved in Britain by copying some, or even most, Japanese working methods' and she observes controversy in the literature 'whether or not Japanese-style working practices, namely total flexibility and greatly increased operator responsibility, represent an improved or reduced quality of working life'.[72]

On the other hand, in view of the successful transfer of many Japanese production and managerial skills to Japanese and non-Japanese companies abroad, Japanese commentators, business and politicians have become much more assertive in praising the Japanese system and offering it actively as a model. In an already cited report which was commissioned by the Ministry of Foreign Affairs and written by business leaders, it is stated: 'In particular, the Japanese practice of treating workers as colleagues, rather than treating them mechanically as the elements and means of production, is clearly a more human form of capitalism.'[73] In the context of Japan's cultural diplomacy and cultural emanation in Chapter 4 we will look at this issue again from the broader perspective of Japan as a societal model and how this is being propagated abroad.

AID GIVING: THE JAPANESE WAY

A very common approach in the literature to Japan's aid is to praise the fact that the Japanese contribution is the highest in absolute terms, but then to qualify it by pointing out various shortcomings such as its geographical concentration on Asia, the low grant element, and so on. While this criticism has its justification, the basis of it is changing and it fails to detect other important features. Instead we suggest focusing on Japan's efforts to influence the basic aid philosophy and to use aid as a means of exerting influence on various sectors in recipient countries.

Japan's power as an international financier and investor is enhanced by its position as the world's biggest donor of ODA. In 1992 Japan provided 18 per cent of all ODA in the world. This allows Japan to satisfy to some extent the outside demands for more international burden sharing, but also provides opportunities to influence economically as well as politically the fate of the Third World. The following will give an overview of Japan's ODA in general, investigate how Japan influences aid giving worldwide and find out how aid leads to political influence. We will focus on Asia which receives two-thirds of Japan's aid and where the economic and political influence of Japan is felt most strongly.

In 1989 Japan became for the first time the number one aid donor, ahead of the US.[74] In 1993 it disbursed $11.2 billion compared with $9 billion for the US although there is a certain inflationary effect in dollar terms due to the appreciation of the yen. In addition, the share of ODA in Japan's GNP has actually been declining since 1991. From the 1980s the ODA budget was given preferential treatment within Japan's national budgeting process (as was the defence budget). Real average annual growth exceeded 7 per cent for the period of FY 1985/86 to FY 1990/91. In 1994 Japan gave $13.34 billion (£8.5 billion).[75] For FY 1995/96, however, ODA will increase by only 4 per cent. Although Japan's absolute ODA amount is now the highest in the world, in terms of GNP to ODA it ranks only 18th (in 1993) among the 21 member countries of the OECD's Development Assistance Committee (DAC).[76] The ratio has been vacillating between 0.3 per cent and 0.32 per cent since 1987 but amounted to only 0.29 per cent in 1994. Japan's grant element is also, at 77 per cent, much lower than that of the DAC average of 93 per cent. Whereas the share of loan aid for infrastructure projects is very high, this is not the case with aid for social capital projects and technical aid which are also both below DAC average although both percentages are increasing. However, in view of the decreasing aid from other developed countries due to the end of the Cold War and the recession, Japan's aid is becoming even more important. In 1993 out of a total of $11.26 billion, loan aid accounted for 31.5 per cent, contributions and subscriptions to international organizations 28.6 per cent, technical cooperation 22.8 per cent, and grant aid 17.1 per cent. In line with the predilection for using the term 'big power' (*taikoku*) in various contexts, the Japanese speak therefore with justification of '*enjo taikoku*' (development aid big power).[77]

The main institution deciding ODA is the Ministry of Foreign Affairs, and the three bodies carrying out ODA are the Japan International Cooperation Agency (JICA) which is controlled by the MFA, the Export–Import Bank of Japan and the Overseas Economic Cooperation Fund (OECF). Apart from these bodies, other ministries and agencies are also involved, making the decision-making process very cumbersome and non transparent. The Ministry of Foreign Affairs is in charge of grant aid and some of the contributions to international organizations, JICA is responsible for technical cooperation and the OECF and Export–Import Bank handle yen credits. The Ministry of Finance is in charge of contributions to the World Bank, the International Development Association, the Asian Development Bank and other regional development banks. The ODA budget is funded from three sources: the General Account, the Fiscal Investment and Loan Programme, and notes for capital subscriptions appropriated for contributions to international financial institutions. Until recently the privileged situation of ODA in the general budget went unquestioned, but with the recession also hitting Japan the proposed increase of 4.8 per cent of ODA for the budget of FY 1994 was for the first time criticized by the media.[78]

Japan has become very good at publicizing its ODA contribution. One of the main tools has been the announcement of ODA doubling plans. In 1978 a three-year plan was announced with the aim of doubling ODA by 1980. This was followed in 1981 by a five-year plan designed to double ODA by 1985. On 9 June 1987, at the Venice Summit of the G-7, then Prime Minister Nakasone Yasuhiro announced a scheme to recycle extra funds totalling more than $20 billion to developing countries.[79] At present the Fifth Medium-Term Target is valid, which is for the period 1993 to 1997 and which is to bring Japan's total ODA to $70–75 billion.[80]

A. Asia as Japan's First Aid Recipient

Asia is the biggest aid recipient of Japan's ODA with a share of around 60 per cent. Out of a total of 155 countries worldwide receiving Japanese aid, 27 countries are in Asia. This circumstance significantly strengthens Japan's economic power in Asia. In 1992, 63.3 per cent of ODA yen loans went to Asia (the largest item being economic infrastructure), 45.5 per cent of its grant aid, and around half of its technical aid. In 1993 the top nine ODA recipients on a net disbursement basis were China ($1350 billion),

Indonesia ($1148 billion), the Philippines ($758 million), Thailand ($350 million), India ($295 million), Egypt ($275 million), Pakistan ($188 million), Bangladesh ($185 million) and Sri Lanka ($147 million).[81] This heavy focus on Asia is reflected in public opinion which supported Asia as a priority region with 56.7 per cent, while only 16.6 per cent were in favour of distributing aid equally to all regions, and Africa received with 7.3 per cent the highest other single region support.[82] About 30 to 50 per cent of capital flows to ASEAN countries in the 1980s were ODA funds, of which Japanese ODA alone accounted for 15 per cent in the case of Indonesia and Malaysia, and about 25 per cent in the Philippines and Thailand.[83]

Within Asia, China enjoys a special position as Japan's largest aid recipient and as the receiver of particularly favourable conditions. Since 1979 China has borrowed from Japan ¥1.6 trillion in the form of low-interest loans.[84] China is the only country which receives from Japan multi-year aid rather than support for specific projects. In December 1994 Japan announced a further loan package for China of ¥580 billion ($5.8 billion) for the period 1996–98 although China had asked for a five-year period loan as in the past.

This official aid to China (as well as ODA to other Asian countries) has to be considered in conjunction with Japan's increase of private investment flows into China which are at present increasing rapidly. In 1992 private investments amounted to slightly over $2 billion on a contracted basis, increasing to almost $3 billion in 1993 and $3.5 billion in 1994. The recently declining number of projects indicates a growing hesitation in the face of mounting obstacles to foreign investment in China: 1805, 3488 and 2228.[85] There are also several factors which may lead to a decline of Japanese loans to China, such as the stage of development already achieved by China, the concern about China's military build-up (see Chapter 2), the link between yen loans and environmental destruction, the negative impact of the yen's rise on China's repayment ability, the Japanese doubts about the degree of true appreciation of the Japanese aid by the Chinese people, and the doubts which at least some Japanese harbour about the effect of this aid on the improvement of Japanese–Chinese relations.[86] The issue of a smooth transfer of Hong Kong in 1997 is also a concern of Japanese investors and the Japanese government has been taking it up in talks with the Chinese.[87]

B. Increasing Aid to Other Developing Countries

Despite the heavy emphasis on aid to Asia, however, the sheer size of Japan's aid budget against the background of decreasing aid funds from other industrialized countries enhances the global importance of Japan's aid. Responding to political pressure from the US to expand aid to other areas than Asia, Japan gave for example in 1992 $860 million to sub-Saharan Africa. It is now the fourth biggest ODA provider of Africa. In October 1993 the Japanese government organized an international conference in Tokyo on development of Africa which was the first such conference organized by Japan. This cannot be interpreted in immediate economic interest terms because the trade with Africa represents only 1.5 per cent of Japan's foreign trade and half of this is realized with South Africa.[88] The aid involvement goes back to the time when the Japanese government tried to balance its strong trade relationship with South Africa, despite international sanctions against that country, by providing aid to other African countries. This growing global reach is also reflected in the membership in regional development organizations: In 1973 Japan became a member of the African Development Fund, in 1983 of the African Development Bank, in 1976 of the Inter-American Bank, and in 1991 of the Multilateral Investment Fund for Latin America and the Caribbean.

Japan is now with the United States the biggest contributor of ODA to multilateral agencies, which amounts to around 25 per cent of its total ODA (31.6 per cent in 1992). Japan is now the second-largest shareholder in the International Monetary Fund, rising in November 1992 to the second rank (from 4.34 per cent voting shares to 5.64 per cent) which it occupies together with Germany. Britain's voting share declined from 6.36 per cent to 5.08 per cent.[89] Japan was a partner in 55.4 per cent of the total $19.15 billion co-financing loans by the World Bank between 1987 and 1991.[90]

Japan's aid is also enhanced by joining forces with Britain and the US, complementing Japan's lack of aid personnel and aid experience. In recent years Britain's Crown Agents have implemented roughly half of Japan's non-project grant aid, mainly for Africa, totalling ¥82.6 billion, or more than £500 million. Other examples of Japanese–British aid coordination include projects in Russia and the New Independent States (NIS), Sri Lanka, Nigeria, Zambia, Tanzania and Bangladesh. Other British organizations such as the British Council have also been involved. Japan and the UK are also cooperating in the privatization programme of Poland. In the latter case Japan paid for the visits of Polish entrepreneurs and union leaders to British institutions and companies.[91] The procedure is far more cost-efficient and probably makes it also socially easier to help Polish privatization than sending these leaders to Japan.

An agreement on Japanese–American joint aid efforts was achieved in May 1991 and strengthened in January 1992 during President Bush's visit to Tokyo as part of Japan–US Global Partnership Action Plan. There had been, however, joint projects before. MITI offered to hike to $5 billion its initial co-financing commitment of $1 billion in trade insurance over several years. In March 1992 the export–import banks of both countries and MITI decided to support American and Japanese companies with joint export financing for five development projects worth more than $1 billion (three in Southeast Asia, two in Latin America).[92]

In contrast to the governmental and corporate sector, the private sector, which relies mainly on contributions from individuals and Non-Governmental Organizations (NGO), is still very small in contrast to other Western countries. In 1992 there were 270 non-profit organizations dealing with Third World issues, constituting 1.3 per cent of the total number of private foundations in Japan. Most of the outside funding for these NGOs comes from the Voluntary Deposit for International Aid (a postal deposit system) and the Ministry of Foreign Affairs.[93] Many of these NGOs are critical towards Japan's official aid, arguing that it is too much oriented to industrial projects of benefit to Japanese industry rather than developing grass-root development projects.

C. The Role of Business in Aid Giving

Like any other industrialized country, aid giving is linked to the interests of private enterprise. Thanks to the close unofficial and official links between government bureaucracy and industry, corporate sector interests are reflected in the way aid is distributed. However, the complex bureaucracy of Japan's aid administration and distribution has not always worked for the benefit of Japanese companies. Moreover, the degree to which private business interests can influence aid giving depends also on the nature of aid and is therefore constantly changing. Multilateral aid is less accessible for the private sector than grant aid. The most important aspects facilitating the influence of private business have been the very low number of aid officials, the aid-on-request basis and the insufficiencies of the recipients' bureaucracies. The new ODA Charter of June 1992 (see below) contains a paragraph which says: 'A close relationship will be maintained between ODA, direct investment and trade, so that those three can organically promote the development of developing countries.'[94]

Although most of Japan's aid is non-tied, the 'on request' basis (*yosei shugi*) gives private business the possibility to 'help' developing countries to make applications for ODA because they very often lack the manpower to do so on their own. Trading companies and consulting companies are most closely involved in such attempts.

Grant aid is particularly vulnerable to private sector manipulations. It has been confirmed even by a MFA report that grant aid is more likely to be misguided and abused than loans which may further reduce Japan's interest in bringing into line with other donors the low grant element of its aid as demanded by other Western countries.[95] In 1994 the Fair Trade Commission investigated 37 major trading firms for rigging bids related to the purchase of equipment and materials for ODA projects.[96] These grant aid projects occupy, however, only a very small part of Japan's ODA. The accusations apply to less than 20 per cent of Japan's ODA, involving grants and technical cooperation which is tied to Japanese companies.

Justifying the high share of loan aid, the Japanese government claims that the payment of interest and repayment of the principal serves to enhance the recipients' self-help efforts and fosters better economic discipline. Japan's desire to focus on loans and thus to teach aid recipients 'good housekeeping' is also reflected in the strong attitude which the government took on debt relief to those Asian countries protesting about the effect of the steep appreciation of the yen on their yen repayment obligations. Although most of the funding borrowed from commercial banks is in dollars, the funds from the Japanese government are denominated in yen. Between 1985 and 1993 the total debt owed to official Japanese lenders among the five leading economies of the Asian region more than doubled to nearly ¥7000 billion (£45.2 billion). Most of the Asian currencies are tied to the dollar and have therefore in the last decade steeply depreciated against the yen. The exchange advantages enjoyed by Asian exporters due to the yen's rise are increasingly failing to offset the mounting yen debts. The share of the yen loans in total debt has risen in the last ten years from 27 per cent to over 35 per cent.[97] China and other Asian borrowers have therefore started to press Japan on debt relief. While Japan is fighting the consequences of the yen's appreciation at home it is not easy for it to muster enough political will to help those Asian countries. The government has therefore not surprisingly so far shown the cold shoulder to requests for debt relief.

Most of Japan's ODA is allocated to economic infrastructure, in particular to transport and communication. A high proportion goes to industry, mining and construction. The official explanation is that adequate infrastructure is the foundation for development.[98] On the other hand, this kind of priority is clearly benefiting Japanese private industry in terms of involvement in the creation of such infrastructure and in terms of using it for Japanese trade and investment. As Yanagihara and Emig put it politely:

It raises the question of whether the philosophical preference for 'real economic ingredients' results from a well-studied analysis of competing development approaches or represents rather an ex post facto justification for the program as it developed in the 1950s and has served Japanese interests well ever since.[99]

In general, however, the direct benefit of ODA for Japanese companies is decreasing because of the growing tendency to 'untie' aid and to make it open to non-Japanese suppliers.[100] The increasingly developed level of the East Asian economies reduces opportunities to link Japanese private sector interests in these countries with ODA. A good indicator of this tendency are the complaints by business federations and their loss of interest in ODA.[101] In addition, the recent publication of rigging procurement for grant aid will make business even more cautious to get involved, thus opening at least this sector to genuine international tendering.

D. Changing the World Bank's Aid Approach

The most important multilateral development bank is the World Bank in Washington. Japan became a member of the World Bank in 1952. From then until 1966 Japan was able to finance 37 projects through loans, receiving a total of $862.9 million. In 1970 the country became a creditor nation for the first time and joined the ranks of contributors to the World Bank, paying back its last loan in 1990. Japan's capital share in the World Bank is 7.43 per cent and its voting share is 7.22 per cent (US 17.9 per cent and 17.37 per cent; Germany 5.74 per cent and 5.58 per cent, UK 5.5 per cent and 5.35 per cent, respectively).[102]

Increasingly Japan is now using its position in the World Bank to influence the aid philosophy of the developed countries. Japan's criticism is directed against the aid philosophy of the US, which in Japanese eyes over-emphasizes free-market reforms for poorer countries while neglecting the useful role government intervention can play in economic development.[103]

In October 1991 the Japanese Overseas Economic Cooperation Fund submitted the document 'Implications of the World Bank's focus on structural adjustment' to the World Bank.[104] The World Bank strongly opposed the publication of this document, but the Executive Directors, led by the Japanese, allowed it.[105] In the report the authors point out that although 'the efficient allotment of resources through market mechanisms is an important aspect of economic policy . . . other factors besides efficiency have to be taken into account.' It recommends the protection of domestic industries to some degree for a certain period to permit the development of a viable export industry. It also criticizes the World Bank's policy towards the financial sector as putting an excessive emphasis on market mechanisms. It casts doubts on the assumption that the introduction of market mechanisms and the elimination of restrictions on the private sector alone will generate sufficient investment.

These thoughts are clearly based on Japan's experience with 'controlled capitalism' and express a fundamental doubt that free market forces alone or at all stages of economic development can generate economic success. The document refers to a dispute between Japanese aid agencies, that is, ASEAN/Japan Development Fund (AJDF) and the World Bank on loan interests to the Philippines because the World Bank expressed concern that interest rates at below the prevailing market rates would hinder the development of a financial market.

Also in October 1991 Bank of Japan Governor Mieno Yasushi reminded the annual meeting of the World Bank and the IMF that 'Experience in Asia has shown that although development strategies require a healthy respect for market mechanisms, the role of government cannot be forgotten.'[106] In 1992 the Japanese government was successful in having the World Bank set up a study which positively evaluated the role of governments in stimulating economic growth through public policy instruments in eight high-flying economies in East Asia (Japan, South Korea, Taiwan, Hong Kong, Singapore, Indonesia, Malaysia, Thailand) and which it financed with $1.2 million.[107] The Japanese government eventually paid a total of $3.5 million to fund this and other minor studies by the World Bank.[108] The major report, referred to as the 'Miracle Study', was a strong message to the World Bank that Japan wanted acknowledgement of the success of different development strategies, as exemplified by the eight Asian economies. In October 1994 the Overseas Economic Cooperation Fund (OECF) and the Japan International Cooperation Agency (JICA) jointly organized a conference which also provided a platform to explain Japan's message to the world on how aid should be given and the role of the state in development appreciated.[109]

Many more studies have been conducted since then by various Japanese ministries and agencies to spread the message about Japan's development policies. The MFA is reported to run a three-year study through its affiliate, the Foundation for Advanced Studies on International Development (FASID), and the Economic Planning Agency and the Ministry of Finance's Institute of Fiscal and Monetary Policy are also conducting similar studies. All these organizations are in addition actively organizing conferences on East Asian lessons for developing countries, involving also American institutions.[110]

Japan's influence on the World Bank and other multilateral aid institutions should, however, not be overestimated. What is impressive so far is that Japan is making its influence felt in contrast to the past, rather than the degree of influence. A major impediment to Japan's influence on aid policies of multilateral aid has been the limitation of voting shares by other donors, notably the US which wants to protect its traditionally highest voting share. Although Japan has been willing to contribute more money, this was several times turned down because of its accompanying effect on voting share. Japan manages to circumvent these restraints to some extent by stepping up its contributions to development projects which are co-financed by international organizations and where individual national contributions are not capped. In this way Japan provides more than half of the financing of co-financed projects of the World Bank and around a third of those co-financed by the Asian Development Bank.[111] Co-financed projects allow then Japan to exert greater influence on projects. Another means of influencing the aid strategy of the World Bank is, for example, the sending of an own investigation team in addition to that of the World Bank, as happened in the case of a bridge project in Bangladesh which resulted in the delaying of the decision on the project. In the case of World Bank aid to Cambodia and Mongolia, Japan could exert more influence because of shared chairmanship with the World Bank.[112]

However, compared with the US, Japan's influence is rather limited, albeit growing. Alan Rix concludes in his book that despite Japan's hearty defence of its aid philosophy and approaches to development, this does not make Japan an international leader in development aid. He acknowledges Japan's enormous influence over the economic policies of less developed countries and potential influence over policies of multilateral agencies, but he has doubts about the general applicability of Japan's aid model, its motives and its aid practices. He sees the domestic, political and administrative aid structures as one of the greatest obstacles to Japan's effective aid leadership.[113]

E. Influencing Environmental Politics

The status of the biggest aid donor has given Japan the opportunity to influence global environmental politics as well as the environmental conditions and policies of developing countries. Japan initiated the foundation of the UN World Committee on Environment and Development and it had a share in the propagation of the 'sustainable development' strategy.[114] At the UN Conference on Environment and Development held in Rio in June 1992, Japan announced the goal to expand bilateral and multilateral aid on the environment to around $7–7.7 billion over a five-year period from FY 1992. However, reflecting the general structure of Japan's ODA, over two-thirds of the 'environmental aid' in FY 1992 consisted of government loans, whereas only 11.1 per cent and 5.9 per cent was for grant aid and technical cooperation, respectively.[115]

The government has domestically launched a series of programmes and institutional measures related to domestic and global environmental issues. These actions were to a large extent a reaction to foreign criticism of the ecological consequences of Japanese economic activities, but also the realization of an alarming increase of trans-boundary pollution from China and South Korea (acid rain).

Japan has been singled out because of its impact on tropical timber. It imports 30 per cent of all tropical timber in the world, and half of all tropical hardwood logs traded internationally. The country is also the largest market for tropical plywood.[116] Japan has come under intense criticism from conservationists because of the ecological impact of this position on tropical forests in East Asia, notably Malaysia and Indonesia. In this context Japan's ODA is also negatively implicated in aiding deforestation rather than establishing the basis for a sustainable exploitation of timber resources. One major Japanese reaction to defuse this criticism is the support of the office of the 1985 established International Tropical Timber Agreement in Yokohama. Japan has also become the largest financial contributor to the organization.

Japan's reaction to its environmental catastrophes in the 1960s has proved that radical policy changes and generous funding can remedy short-term environmental damage. In addition Japan developed since then a very successful industry of environmental equipment where it has become the world's largest exporter. It has been argued that Japan is an example that massive ecological problems can be solved without abandoning steep economic growth rates.[117] The Japanese strategy of 'getting dirty, getting rich, cleaning up' is therefore very attractive for developing countries and more likely to be followed than the more fundamentalist and moralizing Western approach to 'sustainable development'. Japan's leadership is also supported by the fact that most of these countries are in Japan's direct economic sphere where also over 50 per cent of Japan's environmental equipment goes.

In view of the direct threat to Japan by China's environmental degradation, the Japanese government has now also embarked on linking ODA to more concern for the environment. China's pollution as a result of reckless industrialization is a serious concern for the future of East Asia. In the case of China, Japan could achieve greater stress on projects in China's less developed interior rather than in the industrialized coastal regions. For the first time Japan's loan programme to China is now linked to environmental concerns. Japan insisted that thermal power stations built with yen loans will from now on include equipment to control sulphur dioxide emissions which are not only harming China's environment, but also that of Korea and Japan.[118] As a result of Japan's pressure, both countries signed in December 1993 an agreement for the protection of the environment. This is the first agreement in which China admits the existence of acid rain and other air pollution in China.[119]

Japan's successful domestic environmental policies and its growing activism in international environmental issues have led to the question whether Japan may become an international leader in environmental issues.[120] Although Maddock establishes a good case of Japan's model character and structural ability to provide financial and technological incentives for a more sustainable global environment, he doubts that Japan can do much at present. He faults conservative political and economic forces, the weakness of the relevant bureaucracy (for example, the Environment Agency), and the domestic political process of compromise and compacts which cannot provide leadership needed to propagate a Japanese environmental vision. Even this critical conclusion is based on taking many Japanese declaratory efforts too much at face value (for example, the dressing up of certain ODA projects as 'environmental aid') and underestimating the gap between the consequences of Japanese manufacturing investment in many Asian countries on environmental degradation and the efficiency (and time-lag effect) of Japanese environmental technology exports. Maddock is, however, right in pointing out that Japan is able to exercise structural power in the form of rewarding cooperation or penalizing non-cooperation, denying or opening access to markets, aid, technology or innovation, but it cannot mobilize the political resources needed for the supply of an important public good such as the environment.

F. Influence on Aid Policy and Development Strategies in Asia

Japan's influence on aid policy and economic development strategies is naturally strongest in Asia. The regional development bank, the Asian Development Bank (ADB), is dominated by Japan.[121] The Manila-based bank was established in 1966 and its President has traditionally been a Japanese. Although Japan would be able to contribute more funds and does so to ADB institutions which do not affect voting shares (for example, the soft loan window), the US has so far insisted that both countries stay the two largest capital shareholders with each holding 16 per cent. The US has difficulty in increasing its capital stake in the ADB because of domestic financial constraints. Parity between the two shareholders has actually slipped, due to American arrears on capital payments. In the 1980s the ADB moved from being a lender for public-sector projects to more involvement in private industry. In 1993 a conflict arose between on the one hand the US, and on the other hand Japan and other donors concerning a steep increase of the Bank's capital in order to accommodate greater borrowing demands from its two largest members, China and India.[122] In the previous year the US had also successfully resisted an increase in the Bank's capital, as well as slowed the flow of funds to Vietnam because of its own foreign policy requirements.[123] On the other hand, the performance of the ADB has been criticized for being too lax in administering projects and checking its own performance.[124] The confrontation between Japan and the US is, however, not simply about Japan's willingness to increase funding and the US being against it because of voting share implications and a tight domestic budget, but has also to do with the fact that Japan is now so much more affluent and willing to take more risks, whereas the US administration is coming under congressional pressure to be less generous, more strict on procedures and able to prove to Congress that it gets something out of it for its foreign policy goals. As a result of increased emphasis on the quality of individual projects and a reassessment of the capacity of some members to absorb new loans, new loan and equity commitments fell in 1994 by 29 per cent to $3.7 billion (from $5.3 billion in 1993) although actual loan disbursements rose by 25 per cent to $3.7 billion. The situation for recipients is still better than that for World Bank recipients: While the World Bank is now receiving net payments from its members as loans are repaid, ADB net transfers to members are increasing.[125]

Other efforts to bring Japan's development strategies closer to Asian countries are on a bilateral level. For several years now Japanese ministries and agencies have been running courses for mostly Asian officials. The Institute for Developing Economies, a government-funded institution, the Finance Ministry's Institute of Fiscal and Monetary Policy and the Bank of Japan run courses to train foreign officials in Japan while Japanese officials are seconded to foreign ministries in the region.[126] Other means of spreading the Japanese way of developing a national economy are conferences and the exchange of delegations. Such activities are also very important to foster a pro-Japanese network in Asia.

An interesting development is Japan's so-called 'partnership programmes' which aim at enhancing South–South development aid. Japan has concluded such programme agreements with Singapore and Thailand by helping them train people from third countries. A similar programme is run with ASEAN for Egypt and Central and South American countries.[127] The Tokyo International Conference on African Development recommended an

Asia–Africa Forum which led in December 1994 to a conference in Indonesia. In 1992, JICA supported 1079 participants from 101 countries taking part in training courses in 22 host countries.[128] This not only helps to multiply Japan's aid efforts by benefiting from the development experience of 'just developed' countries but it is also very cost efficient since costs in these countries are lower than in Japan. Another example is Japan's assistance to South Korea in setting up its new development aid agency.

Japan's investment and ODA have an important bearing on the way the affected Asian countries are developing economically. The successful Asian countries are attempting to emulate Japan's export-led development, and support an autochthonous development system which Chalmers Johnson calls the 'capitalist developmental state' system.[129]

When Japan started in 1954 to give aid to developing countries, the recipients were all Asian countries and aid consisted mostly of payment of reparations and facilitation of Japanese export industry in Asia. Today Japanese yen loans are mostly given for infrastructure development projects which support the development of export-led development strategies in Asia while at the same time benefiting Japan's trade and investment in the region. Yen loans, which occupied 41.2 per cent of Japan's aid in 1992, contributed to 31 per cent of Indonesia's electric power and 12 per cent of its railways, 20 per cent of Thailand's electric power, 5 per cent of the Philippines' electric power and drinking water, 51 per cent of the electric power on the Malaysian peninsula and 20 per cent of its expressways.[130]

Japan is often accused of having no overarching principles or ideology, but the success of its economic development is considered by an increasing number of Japanese and Asians as more tangible and appropriate than, for example, American insistence on democracy and human rights. Edward Lincoln concludes from this circumstance that because 'Japanese emphasis is on efficiency and pragmatism rather than political ideology, developing countries may be more comfortable relating to it and thereby attracted to closer relations with Japan'.[131]

Several countries in East Asia have in the past launched official policies of taking Japan as an economic model. Singapore adopted in 1978 an official policy of 'Learn from Japan'. In 1987 a Filipino cabinet minister stated he wanted the Philippines to be like 'Japan Incorporated'.[132] An example of the positive acceptance of Japan as a model is the Malaysian Prime Minister's campaign 'Look East' in 1981 which referred to Japan. Although the movement had also an anti-Western overtone (notably against Britain) it is indicative of the above observation.[133] Malaysia is in other ways an interesting example because it is the first non-sinicized country to have now achieved NIEs status, having a Muslim majority although also a substantial Chinese minority. Malaysia is, thanks to Japanese investment, now the world's biggest manufacturer of air conditioners and has built up a substantial manufacturing capacity in electronics and car making, based on Japan's investments, ODA and transfer of technology.[134]

G.   Using Aid for Political Goals

The use of aid for the pursuit of not only economic but also political interests has clearly been prompted originally by outside, notably American, pressure. Japan felt therefore that it had to counter Western criticism of Japan for not contributing to the maintenance of the international system commensurate with its economic power and to use aid giving as a means to offset American pressure for more defence efforts.

In the 1980s the US started to demand that Japan should take security interests into aid giving considerations. Since the Japanese government was unwilling and unable to increase its defence expenditures as demanded by the US, it seemed easier to link aid with security concerns. As a result in the early 1980s the Japanese government used the expression 'aid to strategically located areas' or 'aid to countries bordering areas of conflict' in referring to aid given to certain areas like Indochina or the Middle East. This is as far as Japan could go according to the Japanese government because it interprets the Constitution as not allowing Japan to give military aid.

This aid with strategic connotations has also to be understood against the background of the government's concept of Comprehensive Security developed at the beginning of the 1980s.[135] The concept was prompted by the 1973 oil crisis and the weakening of American power. As a result wider economic and political–military considerations entered Japanese policies. In the former case strategic refers more or less to countries which are strategically important to Japan as sources for raw materials. The latter type of political–military considerations was related to outside demands for more burden sharing. Countries concerned by strategic aid were initially Thailand, Pakistan and Turkey. Due to American pressure Egypt, Oman, North Yemen, Sudan and Jamaica followed later.[136] The US-initiated mini-Marshall plan for the Philippines in 1989, the Multilateral Assistance Initiative, was directly aimed at helping the stabilization of the Aquino government as well as to provide the economic incentives to allow the Philippine government to accept a continuation of American bases, since the American government could not provide more aid as demanded by the Philippines as a quid pro quo.[137] Due to American pressure, Japan started to use aid as a leverage to pressure China, North Korea and Iran to practise self-restraint in exporting weapons.[138]

These developments towards political and strategic linkages led the Kaifu cabinet in April 1991 to state its four ODA guidelines which became in June 1992 part of the 'Official Development Assistance Charter of Japan'.[139] In it the Japanese government clarified its position towards the recipients further and introduced clear political, economic and military standards. The guidelines were more immediately prompted by concern that the parliamentary opposition (the Upper House was controlled by the opposition) and some NGOs might demand stricter control of ODA and force the hands of government by setting guidelines into law. It was also to counter the accusations of Japan having no clear policy (*'kao ga nai seisaku'*). Moreover, the Administrative Reform Council had started to look at ODA in January 1991 and was thought to be considering the proposal of a new agency to streamline ODA administration by incorporating all other agencies involved so far in ODA.[140] The government under Prime Minister Kaifu announced that decisions on ODA would be made after reviewing the recipients' performance in four areas: military spending, promotion of democracy, moves toward market economies and human rights.[141] The guidelines call to consider:

1. the relationship between environment and development
2. the avoidance of aid being used for military purposes or the aggravation of international disputes
3. the defence expenditures, the development and production of weapons of mass destruction and missiles; attitude towards export and imports of weapons
4. the promotion of democracy and a market-oriented economy, fundamental human rights, protection of freedom.[142]

The principles were, for example, applied in suspending aid to Haiti after the coup in 1991 and in suspending aid to Zaire following the political deterioration there.[143] In 1994 Japan stopped assistance to Nigeria because of the military's intervention in the process of democratization. The use of aid suspension to exert influence, however, predates the 1992 ODA principles. In 1984 Prime Minister Nakasone visited Pakistan and more aid to Pakistan was promised. He stated, however, that Japan should apply economic power more effectively in its diplomacy and that Japan 'cannot refuse to use economic cooperation for the purpose of mitigating tensions'.[144] Japan completely suspended its aid to Vietnam when the latter invaded Cambodia. The most well-known case of Japanese aid suspension happened probably after the Tiananmen massacre in June 1989 when the government 'subjected new aid to China to judicious diplomatic considerations' which did not prove very long-lasting.[145]

The political linkage of aid through the means of withholding or resumption has naturally led to difficult political decisions and even to conflict with Japan's main allies, which the government so far had always tried to avoid for good business reasons as well as temperamental inclinations. One example is the resumption of aid to Iran which is opposed by the US and Britain.[146] In May 1993 Tokyo lifted a 17-year freeze on yen loans to Iran, offering a first instalment of ¥38.6 billion ($394 million) to help with the financing of a power station. Tokyo thinks that economic aid to Iran will be more productive than sanctions in steering Iran away from terrorism. Despite American and British assertion of Iranian terrorism and the state-sponsored death threat over Salman Rushdie, a Japanese diplomat went on record that there is no solid evidence for Iranian involvement in terrorism.[147] Later, however, the Japanese government suspended the second instalment but did not agree to suspend economic relations with Iran despite Washington's trade embargo. Nearly 70 per cent of Japan's oil imports pass through the Strait of Hormuz although only 8.4 per cent of Japan's crude oil comes from Iran, which makes Iran the third largest source of oil supplies.[148] In addition, Japan runs a very high trade deficit with Iran. Against the background of these commercial interests it is therefore difficult to believe the government's official line that aid will be more useful in affecting Iran's terrorist policies. A similar line of argument was used for abandoning sanctions against China in 1990.

The application of the guidelines is therefore clearly very much dependent on other considerations.[149] Japanese government spokesmen make it clear that these principles are not to be applied in a 'uniform or mechanical way' but rather that the tendency towards fulfilling these principles is to be judged and that there should be 'friendly persuasion' and 'quiet diplomacy'.[150] Foreign Minister Kono Yohei qualified the application of these principles in the following way:

> It is necessary, in this regard, to take account of the trends in individual countries when deciding its assistance, since there are some cases in which it is not realistic in the short term to link aid directly with specific policies by the recipients.[151]

One of the earliest examples of foreign aid being used for political purposes in Asia is the case of Myanmar (Burma). It has been argued that after 1962 the Ne Win regime would have probably fallen had it not been for Japan's economic support. Despite a strong right-wing Burma lobby (mainly former Japanese army soldiers who served in Burma) in Japan, which all the way supported a repressive Burmese regime and had been instrumental in the success of Japanese companies gaining access to the otherwise isolated country, it was in March 1988 that the Japanese government decided to use its aid power the other way round and – for the first time – unilaterally warned Burma that it would reconsider its relations with Burma unless fundamental economic reforms were introduced. Several months later Japan cut off its aid in response to the killing of pro-democracy demonstrators. Until then Japan had been Burma's main aid donor since the middle of the 1950s. However, on 17 February 1990 Japan partially resumed financial assistance and recognized Burma's new regime, thus saving the new regime on the verge of bankruptcy.[152] In 1995 Japan gave Burma ODA (fertilizer and agricultural equipment for minority communities) and drew criticism from the US for breaking the international freeze on large-scale ODA.[153]

Japan's PKO involvement in Cambodia has been accompanied by a considerable aid programme. In January 1994 Japan resumed yen loans to Cambodia after a lapse of 25 years. In March 1994 the Japanese government hosted the International Conference on the Reconstruction of Cambodia and pledged $91.8 million in new grant aid to Cambodia. It helped the Indochinese countries to clear their arrears with international financial institutions to make them eligible for new loans from regional aid organizations. In November 1992 Japan resumed loan aid to Vietnam by providing a ¥45.5 billion loan.[154] This move was a challenge to the US because the latter had its sanctions still in place at the time of resumption of Japan's loans and Japan's policy put the US under pressure to do the same.

Japan's growing political overtones in aid giving have also led to involvement in geographic areas which have traditionally been areas of concern for Europe and the US. We mentioned already sub-Saharan Africa, but in spring 1995 Tokyo also gave emergency aid to the countries of former Yugoslavia through the World Food Programme, the World Health Organization (WHO) and United Nations International Children's Emergency Fund (UNICEF), as well as around $3 million to the Mine Information Coordination Centre under the UN Protection Force.[155] The Japanese government is also active in aid towards the New Independent States (NIS) of the former Soviet Union. Such aid serves at the same time to prove Japan's willingness to join Western support of that region, as well as a reminder to Russia what Japan could do for Russia if relations were better. In October 1992 the government hosted the Tokyo Conference for Assistance to the NIS and decided to provide $100 million in humanitarian aid. At Japan's suggestion the five central Asian republics of the former Soviet Union were added in February 1993 to the DAC list of aid recipients.[156] As a result of Japan's request, Kazakhstan and Kyrgyzstan formally joined the ADB and the admission of Uzbekistan was formally approved (as of May 1995). For Japan the Asian republics are the soft underbelly of Russia and the Asian character of these republics makes them particularly attractive.

There have also been reports of the use of more narrow political goals. In 1982 Japan was said to have used the threat of cancellations of agricultural purchases and investment contracts to Jamaica if their delegation continued to oppose the Japanese interests at the International Whaling Commission (IWC) meeting.[157] Brazil found a $400 million contract for agricultural investment tied to its IWC vote. Even industrialized countries were reported to have been threatened with economic consequences if they persisted in an attitude inimical to Japan's whaling policy.[158] When the Japanese Director-General of the World Health Organization (WHO) won his battle for re-election by the 31-member executive board of WHO, there were very strong allegations that Japan used its economic power to win votes on the board. His re-election against the candidature of an Algerian candidate was opposed by the major Western countries and there were allegations of mismanagement and excessive travel by him. It was notably alleged that there were threats to cut off fish imports from the Maldives and coffee purchases from Jamaica, both board members, if Japan's candidate were to be spurned.[159] Japan in the end achieved the re-election of the Director-General.

H. Aid and Japan's Russia Policy

The use of aid in Japan's relations with Russia deserves special attention in the context of using aid for political purposes. In this case Japan uses aid in order to press its claim for the return of the Northern Territories from Russia. From 1988 onwards Tokyo took initiatives to attract support from allies and major partners, including the annual summit meetings of the Group of Seven. Without the usual diplomatic politeness the government made it very clear in 1991 that Russia could not expect any economic aid beyond humanitarian aid until it had returned the disputed Kuril islands. One of the aims of the government has been to get support from the members of the G-7 for its strong stance. Using discussions of the Russian debt rescheduling as a lever, the Japanese side managed in 1992 to make the other members of the G-7 summit meeting in Munich accept a position which said that the dispute is not only a bilateral problem between Japan and Russia, but is one of global concern.[160] In April 1993 Japan, due to the G-7 rotation mechanism, was in the chair of the G-7 Joint Ministerial Meeting on Assistance to the Russian Federation and announced new support measures amounting to approximately $1.82 billion.

However, the funds have hardly been spent and a considerable part of it is in export insurance for Japanese exporters. Although Russia's foreign minister Kozyrev promised in March 1995 to support Japan's candidature for a permanent seat on the UN Security Council, the Japanese government is still withholding support for Russia's desire to attend the annual summit meetings of the Group of Seven as a full member.

An interesting example of the use of Japan's financial power was given by the very tentative offer to trade the islands for a massive financial package. In April 1991, Ozawa Ichiro, then Secretary-General of the LDP and still today a major power-broker, went to Moscow to offer informally an economic package of $26 billion in exchange for a Soviet return of the two smaller islands and a recognition of 'residual sovereignty' over the other two islands.[161] Nothing came about because Gorbachov was already too weak to accept such an offer and it is not clear whether the Japanese side would have been able to follow it through. The offer has never been repeated since then.

JAPAN IN INTERNATIONAL ORGANIZATIONS

International organizations have become a new arena for the assertion of Japanese interests and the influence over other countries. As a major power Japan's interests are like those of other countries affected by the wide range of international organizations which regulate and set frameworks, as we have seen in the case of the World Bank and other development-oriented international organizations. It is natural therefore that the Japanese government and Japanese companies have become active in influencing the activities of these organizations. The Japanese government recognizes that international organizations can make useful contributions to creating a more peaceful and prosperous international environment on which Japan depends for its own prosperity. Today most international organizations depend on Japanese financial support and any major programme needs therefore Japanese backing. For Japan support of international organizations counteracts unilateral tendencies which can often be observed in the case of the US, but which may also occur in future with potential regional hegemons like China in Asia. At the same time, without the US, as history has shown, an international organization is less capable and keeping the US interested has therefore become part of Japan's agenda in international organizations. In addition, a more pro-active attitude towards international organizations is also a way of responding to outside demands for more burden sharing. This has resulted in Japan finally sending personnel to Peace

Keeping Operations (PKO). This decision has more than any other decision awoken the Japanese to the post-Cold War era and started a fundamental debate about Japan's role in the world.

At the same time, Japan's growing contributions are prompted by a desire to receive international recognition and prestige, leading in turn to a greater eagerness on the Japanese side as well as demands by the outside for more involvement. Finally, international organizations provide an environment where Japan can take on certain leadership functions without being perceived as an obvious leader and without sacrificing too much political capital.

Membership in the UN responded very much to the aspirations of most Japanese when Japan finally joined in 1956, symbolizing the re-admission of their country to the civilized world. Many thought that UN membership would prevent a recurrence of past Japanese aggression in the Asia Pacific and that the UN with its peace-keeping functions would eventually provide for Japan's security and make rearmament unnecessary. The initially announced UN-centred diplomacy (*kokuren chushin shugi*) soon gave way to the realities of Japan's US-centred diplomacy, and Japan's UN diplomacy turned out to be very quiet and uninspired. This changed in the 1980s when more issues dealt with in UN organizations started to impinge on Japan's interests and there were calls on Japan to contribute more to the maintenance of the international system.

While Japan's financial contributions to international organizations have significantly increased, its staffing presence in these organizations is still low. On the basis of its financial clout Japan has become the number two financial contributor to many international organizations, and is often number one in voluntary contributions to special action programmes. In 1995 Japan's contribution to the UN budget was 13.95 per cent, second to that of the US with 25 per cent, and is to increase to 15.65 per cent in 1997. In staff terms Japan has still not achieved parity with its allotted quota.[162] Two organizations, the World Health Organization and the UNHCR, are now headed by a Japanese. Professor Ogata Sadako was appointed High Commissioner for Refugees in 1990. In 1993 Dr Nakayama was re-elected Director-General of the WHO although not without heavy Japanese lobbying as mentioned before. In 1993 Akashi Yasushi became the head of the UN operation in Cambodia and is now directing the UN activities in former Yugoslavia. Joining the UN relatively late has contributed to Japanese occupying few top positions. The highest posts have become more or less national hereditary fiefs. In 1992 the staff quota for Japanese at the UN was 165, but only 89 Japanese actually held posts. As of December 1991 there were 253 Japanese professional staff out of a total of 8709 in 23 major UN-related organizations. The highest numbers were in the UN General Secretariat, UNDP, FAO, UNESCO and WHO.[163] Increasing Japanese staff is now hampered by a policy of curtailing staff in some international organizations which have come under attack for over-staffing. In the IMF Japan had 25 staff out of a total of 1199 (as of March 1991).[164]

One of the main reasons for low Japanese staffing is the seniority system in Japan which makes secondment to international organizations very difficult and even more so switching jobs and returning later to Japan. In the case of the low Japanese staffing level in the World Bank (70 Japanese, or 1.7 per cent of total staff as of March 1991), some of the blame may have to go to the Ministry of Finance, which is reluctant to release high ranking staff to the Bank but at the same time is opposed to other ministries sending staff.[165] As a result there is still no Japanese occupying one of the most senior executive positions within the World Bank. It is interesting to note that such inter-ministerial rivalry can thus work against the competing interest of influencing the policies of international organizations.

Foreign posts are also not very popular because of the need to live abroad, which causes problems with family and the education of children. Although these problems affect everybody working abroad, the rigid Japanese educational system makes it worse. This is slowly changing with internationalization and deregulation, and international posts are becoming particularly sought after by Japanese women who see in international organizations promotion opportunities which are often denied to them in Japan itself. As of June 1992, 42 out of 89 professional staff at the UN were women.[166]

A. Reactive Protection of National Interests

Given the scarce resources available to Japan's MFA, priorities have to be set and sometimes Japanese participation in international forums only takes place when some national interest is directly affected. One early example is that of the Commission for Human Rights (CHR) in Geneva. Japan put up its candidature for the first time in 1981 and was admitted at the same time as the People's Republic of China. It is reported that the Japanese government's interest in joining the CHR was finally aroused when it was accused in the Commission of violating the human rights of the Korean minority in Japan. The government does not consider the Korean minority an object of Article 27 of the relevant human rights Covenant since these Koreans don't have Japanese nationality.[167] In later years there were several more issues where Japan had to defend itself against foreign accusations, such as Japan's large-scale bacteriological weapon experiments, the human rights situation of the Burakumin, finger printing of foreigners in Japan, and the compensation of the wartime army prostitutes. In 1993 the CHR criticized Japan's discrimination of nationality in paying war compensation. Being a member of the Committee Japan can now much better defend itself. The Japanese delegation apparently exerted considerable pressure on members of the UN Sub-commission on Human Rights to drop compensation claims by Asian women who were army prostitutes.[168]

Rather than seeing a mission in human rights, the Japanese government is more concerned with the disturbing effects the raising of human rights issues can have on bilateral relations. There is a dislike towards direct and visible interference into what is often considered the exclusive domain of the sovereign state as became obvious again in Japan's reaction to the Tiananmen massacre.[169] Another factor, at least in the 1980s, was the fact that Japan was a latecomer to human rights conventions and still has not ratified the majority of them. On the other hand, it has also to be appreciated that the government wants first to prepare the domestic legal framework for accession to human rights covenants before joining them.

Japan's heavy financial involvement in helping refugees started with the end of the Vietnam War in 1975. It was unwilling to accept Indochinese refugees to the same extent as other Asian countries did because of social reasons. Instead it became a major financial contributor and the Japanese head has been extremely active in raising the profile of the UNHCR in Japan in order to create greater awareness of the refugee crises worldwide. Japan paid in 1992 one-third ($35 million) of the total cost of $116 million needed for the UNHCR's Cambodian refugee repatriation programme.[170]

B. Longing for Prestige and Recognition

With Japan's greater self-assertiveness in international relations, and as the second highest financial contributor to the UN, it is not surprising that considerations of prestige have entered Japan's UN diplomacy. One way of enhancing prestige and influence is to occupy top posts as mentioned before.[171] While all major countries are keen on such positions and deploy considerable efforts for them, foreign observers seem to be surprised that Japan is now doing the same. It is this fact, rather than Japan deploying any unusual means, that may account for the publicity which the re-election of the Japanese head of the WHO attracted.

Since Japan had no headquarters of any UN organization, it actively promoted the establishment of the United Nations University (UNU) in Tokyo in 1975. Preceded by a fierce competition between several other countries, including Canada, Switzerland and Australia, Japan won because it offered $100 million initial funding for an endowment fund which now amounts to $211 million.[172] It was hoped at the time that the presence of the UNU could help to dissociate the country from its image as an 'economic animal'. What appealed also to Japan was the fact that the UNU was conceived as a university which would be neither Western-centred nor nation-centred as are universities in Japan.[173] Other Western countries have been doubtful about the justification and quality of the UNU and Japan is therefore still the most important financial backer. Japan's contribution in 1994–95 for the operating budget of the UNU was $16.7 million out of a total of $47.5. The UNU is not a university in the conventional sense but is a centre which coordinates, guides and finances international research. The research itself is taking place in already existing research facilities all over the world.

The ultimate international accolade is, however, a permanent seat on the United Nations Security Council (UNSC). Most attention and efforts are presently spent on achieving this goal. So far Japan has been elected seven times as a non-permanent member of the Security Council (most recently 1991–93) which reflects not only its intention to raise Japan's international profile, but also the fact that the Asian bloc voting for Japan shows it values Japan's ability and willingness to speak on its behalf.

In order to create a new permanent Security Council seat for Japan a revision of the UN Charter is necessary. For this reason, but also to use a Charter revision to delete the so-called 'enemy clauses' Articles 53 and 107, Japan has supported a review of the Charter and was successful in 1969 in having a review adopted as an agenda item. As a result an ad hoc committee was established in 1975 in which Japan actively participated. In addition, Japan has tried to improve its credentials as a good UN member by supporting efforts to make the UN stem more efficient, particularly in view of strong US dissatisfaction with certain agencies like UNESCO. In the 1980s US UN diplomacy turned rather confrontational and American contributions to the UN budget were withheld. In September 1985 Foreign Minister Abe Shintaro proposed the establishment of a 'Wisemen's Group' to recommend reform of the UN's administrative and budgetary process. Japan played an active role in this group and Robert Immerman even called it Japan's most notable UN initiative.[174]

A permanent UNSC seat is widely supported by the Japanese public although there is concern that Japan will then have to openly declare its position on all issues reaching the UNSC which would result in very much disliked confrontations with other countries. Some argue that Japan can only claim a permanent UNSC seat if it is willing to become a full participant in

PKO, while others explicitly exclude such a link.[175] In 1994, 56 per cent of respondents to an opinion poll expressed agreement with Japan becoming a permanent member of the Security Council and only 18 per cent disagreed. Of those disagreeing, 31 per cent explained their opposition by saying that Japan would have to take an active part in UN military activities if it became a permanent UNSC member.[176]

The Japanese government pressed its case also by pointing out its financial contribution to the UN. At least as early as 1976 Japan made it clear in the discussions of the country's UN financial contribution that the decision on this would have to take into consideration the privileges enjoyed by the permanent members in the Security Council.[177] A senior Japanese diplomat was even quoted as saying: 'The UN question is basically a question of money. We'll be raising our contribution soon from 12.4 per cent to 15 per cent – and that should give us a right of entry.'[178]

It was only in 1993 that the Japanese government clearly suggested that as part of a restructuring of the UNSC, the body should be enlarged from 15 (including the non-permanent members in addition to the five permanent members) to about 20 members. An unpublished MFA study suggested that Tokyo would be willing to exclude a veto right to the new members. The veto exclusion was firmly rejected by Germany which had already made clear its intention to seek a permanent UNSC seat.[179] Before, in 1992, Prime Minister Miyazawa had veiled his country's request in the demand for reforms of the UN which should take the new international circumstances into account. At the same time the Japanese ambassador to the UN, Hatano Yoshio, had told interviewers that Japan hoped to have a permanent seat on the UNSC in five years' time while the Prime Minister's spokesman, Hanabusa Masamichi, was quoted as hoping to achieve this goal by 1995, the UN's 50th anniversary.[180] Foreign Minister Kono justified Japan's request this way in 1995:

> ... In the maintenance of international order, it is not the overwhelming military might of some countries that is playing a major role, but concerted international action towards such destabilizing factors as nuclear proliferation and various conflicts which threaten peace. Therefore it is inappropriate that a country like Japan, which is playing a prominent role in such international cooperation, is not permanently engaged in the UNSC, which makes decisions regarding concerted international action.[181]

Japan did not receive wide support for its 'application' except from the United States. The main reason for the reluctance of other countries is the fact that changing the UN Charter and the Security Council membership would open a can of worms in terms of other countries (for example, India and Brazil) demanding a seat as well. China and South Korea are very reluctant and seem to want to use the issue to get a clear Japanese apology for its past behaviour. The sensitivity of the issue again became apparent when the Security Council members quickly agreed to transfer the seat of the defunct Soviet Union to Russia although it would have been an appropriate opportunity to reconsider the composition and even the function of the UNSC in a very much changed international environment. Germany declared up to summer 1992 that it was officially not interested in a permanent Security Council seat, expressing publicly its intention to work with the allied members of the Security Council while hoping that Britain and France would abandon their seats in favour of a European Union seat. This hope has now been abandoned and Germany expressed in September 1992 its wish to become a permanent member of the UNSC.[182] The dissension among the member states of the European Union about Germany's application and the possible repercussions for France and Britain led in May 1995 to the refusal of a March 1995 proposal by the European Commission to support Japan's bid for a permanent Security Council seat.[183]

A compromise may be found in giving Japan and any other candidates a permanent seat, but not veto power, as mentioned in the previously quoted unpublished MFA study. A UN working group deliberating these and other issues suggested in an intermediary report in 1994 that seats should be increased from 20 to 25 seats.[184]

C. Peace Keeping Operations

The issue of Japan's involvement in Peace Keeping Operations (PKO) has become the focal point for Japan's ability and willingness to contribute to the maintenance of the international system, involving not just cheque book diplomacy but including ultimately the sacrifice of Japanese lives.

Before the Japanese Diet finally passed in June 1992 the International Peace Cooperation Law (IPCL) Japan had already become a major contributor to the funding of PKO in the UN (see Table 3.2). The major obstacles on the way to full participation in PKO were and are still today the Japanese Constitution, public opinion and the still widespread distrust in the ability of Japanese democracy to withstand militaristic temptations if the SDF's mandate were extended to include PKO.

The path to June 1992 is strewn with attempts to overcome these obstacles. As early as 1980 the government interpreted the Constitution as not allowing the participation of the SDF if the mission of a UN force would include the use of force but thus also leaving open the possibility of the

Table 3.2   UN and PKO contributions (in percentage) as of January 1994

	UN Budget share	PKO Special Contribution share
USA	25.0	31.7
Japan	12.4*	12.5
Germany	8.9	8.9
Russia	6.7	8.5
France	6.0	7.6
UK	5.0	6.3
China	0.7	0.9

* To be increased to 13.95 in 1995, to 15.43 per cent in 1996 and to 15.65 per cent in 1997
Source: Ministry of Foreign Affairs, Japan

SDF participating in some ways in PKO although the SDF Law does not include such missions.[185] In 1983 the government had to drop a planned proposal for greater Japanese participation in PKO activities which was to be contained in a MFA document for the UN General Assembly on strengthening UN peace-keeping capabilities. In 1984 Prime Minister Nakasone asked the MFA to study Japan's participation in PKO, but clarified later that he had no intention of seeking an amendment of the SDF Law to allow SDF to take part in PKO.[186] In 1987 the Japanese government declared for the first time that the deployment of minesweepers abroad would not be against the Constitution when then Prime Minister Nakasone asserted that Japanese minesweepers could constitutionally operate in the Gulf but he ruled out deployment at that time because of the fear that Japan might be drawn into the Gulf crisis.[187] In 1989 then Prime Minister Kaifu promised that the government would begin studying plans to dispatch the SDF 'for purposes of fostering international cooperation, fulfilling the protection of Japanese abroad and contributing to peace'.[188]

The catalyst for progress on PKO was finally a conflict again in the Middle East when the US assembled in 1991 an allied force to drive Iraq out of Kuwait. Due to the lack of preparation in the bureaucracy and government as well as clumsy handling of the issue by both, the government did not succeed in sending any personnel to this force, but provided a total of $13 billion towards its costs, the highest amount from any outside party to the conflict. Despite this considerable feat, proving Japan's financial power, Japan did not receive much gratitude because it was seen as a contribution which compared poorly with the sacrifice of lives by other countries, and in addition seemed to have come reluctantly and late because of Japan's political process, indecision and bureaucratic blundering. In 1991 the Japanese government sent a minesweeping flotilla consisting of six ships to the Gulf, arguing in a rather imaginative way on the basis of Article 99 of the SDF Law that this did not amount to sending troops abroad.

The war against Iraq and the negative reaction to Japan's contribution, however, gave the impetus to pass in June 1992 the International Peace Cooperation Law against the votes of the SDPJ which took resort in a futile 'cow walk' in order to delay the law. An earlier draft had been dropped by the LDP in November 1990. The law had, however, to incorporate the following restrictions in order to garner the support of the moderate opposition parties:

1. Agreement on a cease-fire shall have been reached among the parties in the conflict.
2. The parties in the conflict, including the territorial state(s), shall have given their consent to deployment of the peace-keeping forces and Japan's participation in the Force.
3. The peace-keeping force shall strictly maintain impartiality, not favouring any party in the conflict.
4. Should any of the above guideline requirements cease to be satisfied, the Government of Japan may withdraw its contingent.
5. Use of weapons shall be limited to the minimum necessary to protect the lives of the personnel.[189]

In addition, the participation of the SDF in the 'main part' of peace keeping (observation of armistice, disarming of combatants, exchange of prisoners) was frozen, pending the passage of another law. The SDF is not allowed to participate in any missions entailing the use of weapons, and weapons can only be used for direct self-defence. The Law has also to be reviewed in 1995. A participation in an allied force like that mobilized by the US in 1991 is not possible under the International Peace Cooperation Law.

In view of all the previous obstacles and the restraints accompanying the IPCL as well as the present political paralysis in Japan it is not to be expected that Japan will become in the near future a fully fledged participant in PKO or even peace-enforcing ventures. In his speech before the UN General Assembly in September 1994, Foreign Minister Kono declared that 'Japan does not, nor will it, resort to the use of force prohibited by its Constitution', but he did not make clear what sort of force is then allowed.[190] A general international disillusionment with PKO after the international experience in Somalia and Rwanda and the lack of funding will help Japan to confront future international criticism. A clear constitutional anchorage of PKO has not been achieved, and Japan's politicians have again gone the easy way by reinterpreting the Constitution. The SDF are not undivided in their attitude towards PKO because they are concerned about political controversy which has traditionally made their life difficult, and they are worried about being sent abroad without sufficient preparation and equipment for activities which hitherto did not belong to their brief. On the other hand, the SDPJ has since summer 1993 taken part in forming two cabinets and is now accepting the constitutionality of the SDF and accepts the Japanese–American security treaty which they refused to do until recently. This has considerably weakened the camp of those opposing PKO participation.

The debate in Japan on PKO is taking place between three positions which may be characterized as nationalist, realist and anti-militarist.[191] The nationalist position claims greater independence in foreign and security policy and an abandonment of the subordinate relationship with the US. The realist position has sympathy for the former, but does not want to sacrifice Japan's economic interests and prefers cooperative relations with the US and other Western partners. The anti-militarist position can be found among left-leaning Socialists, the media and the peace movement. The PKO debate has, however, shown that there is still widespread suspicion about Japan's democracy being able to withstand the resurgence of militarism, and in this context the IPCL was seen as a dangerous attack on the dam holding back the militarists of the past. Even prominent conservative politicians echoed this feeling.

Since the International Peace Cooperation Law was passed in 1992, Japan has dispatched the SDF from October 1992 to September 1993 (civil engineering troops) to Cambodia, from March 1993 to December 1994 (about 50 soldiers for logistical tasks) to Mozambique and from October to December 1994 to Zaire/Kenya to help refugees from Rwanda (378 soldiers). During the deployment to Cambodia one election monitor and a policeman were killed, but no one from the SDF which was deployed far away from any potential danger zone. The Japanese government did not sent any SDF to the UN action in Somalia because of the absence of an armistice and of an official invitation from the Somalian government (which did not exist).

Public opinion is still very passive about PKO and does not want to expand Japan's contribution to operations which entail the use of arms. In a survey in 1994, when respondents were asked whether they thought that Japan should continue to participate in those operations undertaken so far, 15.5 per cent replied that Japan 'should participate even more actively than so far', 43.4 per cent that Japan 'should continue participating at the present level', 25 per cent that Japan 'should participate but as little as possible' and 8.6 per cent that Japan 'should not participate'.[192]

The PKO debate will continue to have a prominent place in Japan's foreign policy debate because of the continuous need of personnel contributions to an ever-growing list of conflicts calling for UN intervention. In addition, the IPCL of 1992 has not clarified once and for all the legality and limits of Japan's involvement in PKO. The issue will continue to serve as a litmus test for Japan's debate about its place in world politics as well as about its contribution to the maintenance of a peaceful international environment which goes beyond the use of soft power.

D. Representing Asia in International Forums

Japan's role in international organizations is enhanced by its leading role in the Asian region. As a result of its towering economic position in Asia and close links to the Western industrialized nations, Japan has become a natural spokesman for Asia in international organizations and forums. Other Asian countries, except China, have come to rely on Japan to take up their causes in global forums such as the G-7 summit meeting or in the UN. At the same time Japan acts as a political mediator between East Asia on the one hand and Europe and the US on the other. It is now customary that Japan collects the viewpoints of its major Asian partners before a G-7 meeting. Since November 1975 Japan has been a participant in the summit meetings of the advanced industrialized nations. In June 1979 the first G-7 meeting took place in Tokyo and the government used the occasion to raise the issues concerning the Asia Pacific, which was until then taken up only by the US, if at all. This has not always been easy because other issues diverted the attention of the summit members. At the 1980 Venice meeting the leaders were more interested in the Teheran American hostage crisis and the invasion of Afghanistan, whereas Prime Minister Ohira tried to raise the Cambodian conflict. In 1988 at the Toronto summit Prime Minister Takeshita argued for international aid to the Philippines and support for the Seoul Olympic Games, and recalled the need for a peace settlement in Cambodia.[193] In 1994 Japan supported the candidature of a South Korean as new head of the WTO.

While raising issues of concern to Asia, Japan has also grown into the role of explaining differences appearing between Asian and Western approaches to certain political topics, ranging from human rights to the Malaysian initiative for the creation of the East Asian Economic Caucus. Concerning Western, notably American and European, pressures for more attention to human rights and in particular more humane working conditions, Japan has grown into the role of helping to insulate East Asian countries against outside pressures.[194] One example given by David Arase is the UN-sponsored Asia Regional Preparatory Meeting for the World Conference on Human Rights held in Bangkok in March 1993. Japan signed the declaration with reservations because of the contradictions between its 1991/92 new principles on aid which link human rights to ODA, and the Declaration which calls for a separation of the two issues. On this matter the Japanese government came under strong pressure not only from East Asian governments, but also from a group of influential politicians, academics and business people who oppose the Western-sponsored link between human rights and aid.[195] Other examples of Japan's soft approach towards human rights in Asia were the mild official reaction to the Tiananmen massacre and the disregard for political asylum of Chinese in Japan.

Japan has become a key actor in regional economic organizations.[196] On the one hand, Japan can help Asia through such organizations to promote a counterweight or rather a deterrence against the development of exclusionist tendencies of economic groupings elsewhere such as NAFTA and the EU, but, on the other hand, the other Asian countries fear that any Asia-based organization may become dominated by Japan and reduce the importance of Asian organizations like ASEAN. The Japanese government is very aware of these concerns. Inter-ministerial competition is sometimes for Asian countries a welcome barrier against too strong Japanese leadership. An illustration was the plan of MITI to have an annual Asia–Pacific conference of trade ministers which in 1989 was opposed by the MFA and by some ASEAN members.[197] Due to competition between the MFA and MITI, Japan took a rather passive role in the 17-nation Asia–Pacific Economic Cooperation forum until 1994 when the annual summit took place in Indonesia. Another complication with APEC has been the strong American role since the Seattle summit in 1993. ASEAN member states were concerned about being overshadowed by a new US-led organization, and Malaysia's prime minister boycotted the summit. Japan did not want to be seen to be tilting too much towards the American agenda. APEC is seen by Japan now as a framework for dialogue to promote regional economic development. The most important task for Japan is presently to mediate between the US and the other Asian countries, notably on the kind and speed of the US-proposed free trade area. While the US wants to have formal and binding decisions to force the issue, Japan prefers agreement on general principles and wants to rely on the power of self-interest and the effect of good examples given by the more advanced Asian countries.

E. Is Japan Forming a Separate Economic Bloc in Asia?

These growing political links between Japan and the rest of Asia, in addition to its close economic linkages, raise naturally the question about Japan's intention to form a separate Asian bloc. Japan's active or passive attitude towards such regional integration would be decisive for the success of such an enterprise.

The drive of East Asia towards regionalization cannot be separated from a simultaneous drive towards globalization, and both developments are created and sustained by the same economic forces. References to regionalization often amount merely to the enumeration of features which East Asian countries share, like high growth rates, export orientation, an ill-defined 'common culture' and growing trade and investment flows. Regionalization specifically refers to the coordination of production and markets in East Asia through market forces. Japan plays in these developments and driving features a key role as the main provider of investment, aid and technology. Japan also helps to maintain its strong trade position in Asia by still maintaining the Generalized System of Preferences (GSP) with South Korea, Hong Kong and Singapore although their advanced economic development prompted the US to abolish them and the EU to phase them out.

One development taken as a major symbol of Japan trying to create a separate economic bloc is the increased use of the yen in the region. In 1991 the share of Japan's exports to Asia settled in yen increased to 41.9 per cent, compared with 37.5 per cent in 1990 and 33.4 per cent in 1987 according to MITI. The yen is increasingly used because Japanese companies can force the foreign exchange risk on others and many Japanese exporters are selling to their own subsidiaries in Asia.[198] However, the dollar is still more widely used than the yen in settling trading accounts. The share of global reserves that is denominated in yen was only 8.7 per cent in 1993. Only in April 1995 did the Japanese government for the first time state that it was in favour of greater use of the yen in Japan's international trade.[199] The volatility of the Asian currencies against the yen is a major factor in restraining the use of yen as an international currency. Only a proportion of regional external debts denominated in yen has surpassed those denominated in dollars.[200] Reflecting the strong Japanese economic presence in Asia, the yen has acquired a dominant influence over interest rates in Singapore and Taiwan; the holdings of the yen in Asian central banks have increased to 17.5 per cent of their foreign exchange reserve portfolios, overtaking the Deutschmark's 15.2 per cent.[201] The overall picture does not therefore justify speaking of a 'yen bloc'.

The distribution of world trade shares is also not supporting a Japanese economic bloc. The share of East Asia's exports in world exports moved from 20 per cent in 1985 to 19 per cent in 1990 and to 24 per cent in 1993.[202] The intraregional share of East Asian exports moved during the same three years from 32 per cent to 30 per cent and finally to 31 per cent. This compares with a much higher intraregional share for the EU (56 per cent, 61 per cent and 56 per cent, respectively) or NAFTA (35 per cent, 37 per cent and 47 per cent, respectively). It is also worthwhile to remember that Japan's trade ratio with the US is 29.2 per cent for exports, and 23 per cent for imports (the American trade ratio with Japan is 10.3 per cent for exports and 18.5 per cent for imports).[203] The reason for low intraregional trade is not only that Japan and other East Asian countries export so much more to the US and Europe, but also that East Asian intraregional trade is heavily restrained by high tariff barriers. There are still formidable barriers to more intraregional links which go beyond Japan–Other Asian Countries links, and even here the Asian countries complain like the Western countries about the difficult access to the Japanese market. Japan has thus become a catalyst for the economic integration of East Asia although it is still more an integration oriented towards Japan rather than one among the East Asian countries themselves. Japan's position in Asia can be compared to that of the hub of a wheel from where spokes go to many Asian countries. Still, as a result of its economic activities in Asia Japan has done more for Asian integration than any single Asian country. Increasingly the NIEs form their own hubs with spokes to the less developed Asian countries, as is demonstrated by Korean, Taiwanese and Thai investment in Vietnam, the Philippines, mainland China and so on.

One of the main questions of economic regionalization – does it promote or hinder global trade expansion? – cannot yet be answered at this stage. Due to its character, economic regionalization in Asia has not yet led to a strong political institution, nor has it created similar political forces to eliminate intra-group trade barriers as in the EU. There is the temptation for Japan to use Asia's much slower progress in opening its markets to the outside world as a defensive shield for its own reluctance to open. While Japan is obviously more open than other Asian markets (except Hong Kong), defending Asia's slow pace by referring to an Asian way of development (which means Japan's own development strategy) also rationalizes Japan's opening speed and at the same time reinforces the appearance of a grouping of Asian economies with distinct features.

In view of the simultaneous development of regionalization and globalization as well as political considerations, Japan has been very cautious in participating in any further development from regionalization to institutional integration like the OECD or the EU, let alone translating it into a policy of regionalism, particularly if such a move would entail any exclusive features which would ultimately hurt Japan's much more important economic interests outside of Asia. Any economic integration along the lines of the OECD or the EU is faced with problems like different economic and political systems in East Asia, different stages of economic development and Japan's past policy of military conquest and domination (see Chapter 4 on the latter point). Japan's East Asian neighbours see also the danger of an Asian bloc excluding them from their two biggest non-Asian markets as is illustrated by the following statement by Lee Kuan Yew, then Prime Minister of Singapore, at the opening of the APEC group meeting in July 1990, when he observed that the world was becoming divided into three separate trading blocs, dominated respectively by the dollar, the yen and the German mark:

> Asians will feel that they have been quarantined into the Japanese yen bloc so that they can be excluded from the markets of prosperous Europeans and Americans, that the Whites have changed the rules just as Asians have learnt to compete and win under those rules.[204]

Although the Japanese government has so far resisted supporting Mahathir's proposal for the EAEC which would exclude the US, there is a certain degree of sympathy with some political leaders and opinion leaders in Japan for the proposal.[205] This is partly the result of the ongoing trade frictions with the US, but also part of the present Asia fever in Japan and the perceived need to respect East Asian wishes and sensitivities (see Chapter 4). Mahathir has attracted huge media attention in Japan, and a book 'The Asia which can say No' has been published with Ishihara Shintaro, the author of 'The Japan which can say No'. Mahathir was even quoted saying that Japan's membership in such an exclusively Asian group would be 'much more meaningful than a thousand apologies for the events which took place more than half a century ago'.[206] Some people accept the principle of the EAEC but want to discuss whether it should exclude the United States and, second, how exclusive or rather inclusive it should be. One compromise proposal is, for example, to have such a grouping under the wings of APEC, OECD or GATT which then would exclude the United States.[207] At present the strongest political forces are backing institutional integration under the loose umbrella of APEC.

On the other hand, the Japanese government is convinced that an EAEC which excludes the US would economically not make much sense and would offend the US which everybody wants to keep committed to Asia. But there is a feeling that Japan cannot simply ignore a regional initiative.

However, the longer the government leaves this ambiguity the more the EAEC idea will be kept alive and take a life of its own, later possibly forcing Japan to be more positive and allowing Japanese proponents of the proposals to garner more support in the meantime. In order to placate all sides the present Japanese policy is to advocate 'open regionalism' which reflects Japan's interests in open global markets everywhere because of its global economic interests while at the same time leaving it to Japanese business to strengthen its links with Asia without having to invest or sacrifice political capital in the creation of a Japanese bloc. As such the shadow of a more closed and Japan-led Asian bloc serves as a useful bargaining chip against temptations of closed regionalism in the EU or NAFTA.

CONCLUSIONS

This chapter has traced a clear development from using economic power not only for narrow economic aims, but also for wider political goals, including international prestige and recognition. In most cases Japan is still reactive, avoids sacrificing political capital, and is often initially prompted by outside pressure. Narrow economic interests, domestic political paralysis and concern about negative Asian reactions because of the country's historical legacy prevent the Japanese government from taking an open leadership role even there, where it would look relatively natural and easy. On the other hand, Japan is changing or reinforcing international regimes in ways which are increasingly benefiting its national interests. Its FDI and other collateral activities are having an impact on the way many countries (notably in Asia) develop and run their economies. Even in the industrialized countries Japan is influencing political and economic policies of governments and shaping the way companies are trying to compete in the international market-place. However, to gain a complete picture of Japan's foreign policy and power we will have to investigate how Japan transforms its economic power to exert influence on the third level, that is, influencing ideas, knowledge and truth.

4 Japan as a Cultural Superpower?

INTRODUCTION

Economic activity is very pervasive and demands permanent efforts to create the right environment for it to be most effective. The cultural sphere is part of this environment and can therefore not escape from becoming an object of these efforts. Economic activity based on free market principles is particularly effective in permeating culture in the widest sense to benefit from it while also being able to help it prosper. It should therefore not be a surprise that Japan's economic expansion is having an impact on the culture of those countries where it is most active. Some of this impact is incidental and not planned, particularly on the level of low culture and mass consumer culture because of the contrast between Japan's advanced economic level and that of other countries, notably in Asia. Increasingly, however, culture is perceived by political and economic leaders in Japan as a means to create an environment abroad conducive to Japanese economic activities and to become generally more accepted. In this chapter we will focus on the one hand on Europe and North America, where Japan's cultural power is being manifested in the dissemination of high-brow culture, notably the arts, and information and lobbying, and on the other hand on Asia where Japan's mass consumer culture with all the trappings of low-brow culture has become very pervasive, supported by Japanese investment and supplemented by official cultural diplomacy focusing on Japanese language teaching. Particular attention will be given to the historical and cultural factors influencing Japan's relationship with Asia.

Japan may seem an unlikely candidate for a cultural power. After all, culture is one of the very few areas where Japan suffers from a trade deficit if one considers solely cultural exchange in terms of translated books and exported films. In 1990 more than 3000 translations of English books were published in Japan. In contrast only 82 Japanese books were translated and published in the United States in that year. More than 100 feature-length American movies are released in Japan every year. Of Japan's 25 top-grossing films in 1991, 21 were American.[1] The takeover by Sony and Matsushita of American film studios during the boom economy resulted in a commercial failure although they provide both electronics consumer companies with software where they are still weak. While Matsushita had to sell 80 per cent of its share in MCA at a great loss, Sony wrote red figures for its acquisition of Columbia Pictures (now renamed Sony Pictures).[2] In 1991 Japan's national TV station NHK attempted the creation of a world-wide news network to rival the American Cable News Network. But its planned Global News Network in English language, to be based in New York with editorial responsibility delegated to different regional centres, failed to raise the necessary funds and partners.[3]

Moreover, Japan has not the same cultural emanation as the other major Western countries have, and Japan's language and geographic remoteness only aggravate these natural disadvantages. We will see in this chapter, however, that these cultural trade imbalances and natural disadvantages are becoming more relative and are less effective in hampering the development of Japan's cultural power in Asia than they are outside of that region.

CULTURAL DIPLOMACY

Shaping cultural relations through cultural diplomacy and the dissemination of information is an important means for governments and business to influence the perceptions of other people.[4] It is obvious that a country with the economic power of Japan can muster considerable resources for these purposes if and when it decides to do so.

Cultural diplomacy is the government-led shaping of cultural relations. It adds credibility and legitimacy to bilateral relations which are otherwise mostly in the hands of professionals such as politicians and government officials.[5] Cultural diplomacy is intimately related to economic power in the sense that it can underpin cultural emanation as well as economic expansion. The Japanese government started to pay more attention to cultural aspects of diplomacy in the 1960s and 1970s when Japan's economic expansion and success led to a rising level of conflict with many partners. Cultural diplomacy therefore came to be considered as a means of damage limitation and not so much as the means to spread a way of life as in the case of the US or the particular concept of civilization like France does. In 1972 the Japanese government established the Japan Foundation. The original endowment of ¥5 billion (and ¥6.1 billion from Keidanren) grew to ¥104.2 billion as of 1995. In addition, the Japan Foundation receives annual government subsidies which include funds from the ODA budget. The economic link is also expressed by the fact that business groups provide funds which amounted in FY 1990 to ¥5.2 billion (FY 1989 ¥3.9 billion) in addition to the other income from the government.[6] In contrast to the German Goethe Institut or the British Council, the Japan Foundation is an enabling body, supporting and funding other people of relevance to Japan's cultural diplomacy (notably Japanese studies and language programmes overseas), whereas the other two organizations own more staff and facilities at home and abroad to do it themselves. This allows the Japan Foundation to spread its cultural activities much wider and probably to achieve more value for money. In addition, the Japan Foundation can probably count more on financial support from Japanese companies than can its Western counterparts from Western companies. The example of the Japan Foundation seems to be very attractive since two East Asian NIEs, South Korea and Taiwan, have started to imitate the Japanese institution with the setting up of the Korea Foundation and the Chiang Ching Kuo Foundation, respectively.

While Japan is expanding its cultural diplomacy thanks to its economic strength, other countries have to cut back as we have seen in the context of ODA and contributions to multilateral organizations. The German centres abroad of the Goethe Institut receive almost 30 per cent less in 1995 than in 1992.[7] In 1991 the BBC cut its Japanese language service of the BBC World Service although it was relatively popular and cost only £279 000 annually to operate.[8]

The importance of cultural diplomacy can also be gauged from the fact that public information and cultural affairs have been brought into the Minister's Secretariat of the MFA, whose coordinating functions have been enhanced by the recent restructuring and streamlining of functions. The Cultural Affairs Division of the Minister's Secretariat supervises the Japan Foundation.

In 1988 one of the three pillars of Prime Minister Takeshita's Global Initiative was the expansion of cultural exchanges which he put into the framework of Japan's contribution to the international community: 'International cultural exchange serves to form an open global community in which cultural diversity is understood and accepted with tolerance, thereby contributing to international cooperation and world peace.'[9] The factors behind this interest in cultural diplomacy are manifold:

- a recognition that Japanese economic activities in Asia, including aid, has negative effects on local culture and tradition
- to counteract the image of Japan being a mere 'economical animal', thus facilitating Japan's economic activities, particularly in Asia
- support of Asian culture may help Japan to reassert its Asian identity in Japan as well as in the region and satisfy those who are concerned about too much 'Westernization'

– the expansion of help to preserve cultural artifacts can be interpreted as Japan sharing more global burdens
– to facilitate a more comprehensive understanding of Japan through the spread of information on Japan's politics and society.

According to a survey of the Japan Foundation's Japanese Language Institute, as of 1993 there were 1 620 000 people in 99 different countries and territories studying the Japanese language.[10] Japanese studies would not have flourished as much as they have in the last two decades without the generous financial backing of the Japan Foundation and Japanese business. Many foreign research institutes have to rely on Japanese support for their work on Japan, or have to make sure that their research is of interest to Japanese customers. William Wallace laments that even a research institution like the Royal Institute of International Affairs in London has to rely on Japanese money for the funding of its 'most strategic current project' on 'Changing paradigms of European order'.[11]

Japanese companies have considerably strengthened their sponsorship in order to become good 'corporate citizens'. The so-called 'Cones Europe' report on Europe 1992 had urged the Japanese companies to set about winning the hearts and minds of Europeans. It advised them to join every possible trade association and industrial body and to work diligently within them, hire lobbying and public relations firms to promote their interests and image, recruit senior establishment figures as non-executives to open doors for influencing government officials and politicians, set up a Europe-wide intelligence gathering network, and to go into sponsorship.[12] The Japanese companies have taken most of these recommendations on board and are now actively pursuing them.

Britain is the focus of Japanese cultural diplomacy in Europe because of the concentration of Japanese investment in this country and because of the facility of the English language. The activities of the Japan Foundation are strengthened by three private foundations which are the Daiwa Anglo-Japanese Foundation (capitalized at £20 million), the Great Britain Sasakawa Foundation (capitalized at £10 million) and the Japan Festival Fund (capitalized at slightly over £1 million).[13] The biggest cultural event was probably the Japan Festival in 1991 which was originally initiated by a professional British cultural promoter and cost around £20 million. In order to put this amount in perspective one has to realize that British industry spends annually £35 million on arts sponsorship. It was the biggest sponsored arts event ever and featured most arts. All Japanese companies who were present in Britain at the time contributed, as did many British companies which had some dealings with Japan.[14] Sponsorship by Japanese companies in Britain ranges now from concert series and museum galleries to league football and equestrian events.[15]

The Japan Exchange Teachers (JET) programme has been one of the greatest successes of Japan's cultural diplomacy and will probably have a most significant effect not only on the perception of Japan in the world, but also on the perception of the Japanese themselves of the rest of the world. The programme started in Britain, and has since then been expanded to all English-language speaking countries in the Western world, other European countries and includes now even a few people from Asian countries. It has allowed many young graduates to stay up to three years in Japan, either as language teacher assistants or as assistants in the international offices of cities and prefectures throughout Japan. The number of British students alone increased from 150 participants in 1987 to 733 in 1994 with the number of Americans being triple that. Many participants are staying on, others are coming back to work for Japanese or Japan-related companies or go into Japanese studies.

A. The Importance of Information Dissemination

Information is an essential part of influencing opinion abroad. Japan is probably the most information-soaked society in the world, where a very high literacy rate and high income allows ferociously competing media of all kinds to penetrate society in a way unknown in any other society. It is therefore useful to understand the Japanese concept and approach to information. Information is 'the raw material which enables us to assemble and transform scattered data in accordance with our particular purpose'.[16] Without it a capitalist economy cannot function. The Japanese have a very clear idea of information as a resource or transforming agent and have therefore in the 1960s developed the concept of 'Information Society'.[17]

First of all, there is a tendency in Japan to consider information as value-free or value-neutral.[18] This is particularly relevant at a time when technology and information has become crucial for the competitiveness of an advanced national economy. Moreover, the importance of information for creating consensus and control is recognized. The following statement in a Japanese study which offers Japan's societal model as an alternative for other societies has to be understood against the background of these two points:

> In the highly information-intensive society of the future, the Japanese type of control, through inducement and persuasion, is likely to come increasingly in demand. The more this method of control is adopted, the

stronger the possibility of people and organizations being bound together by relations of mutual trust.[19]

The relevance of this understanding of information for cultural diplomacy as a way to counteract negative foreign perceptions of Japan as a result of its economic activities is enhanced by the prevalent conviction in Japan that economic disputes are not so much created by different economic interests and procedures, but are based on the ignorance of foreigners about Japan and misunderstandings (*gokai*).[20]

In the last decade the Japanese government and Japanese industry (employers' federations as well as individual companies) have become very effective in disseminating information about Japan. No journalist or academic any longer does without the flood of available information from these sources. First, since this information is in foreign languages, mostly in English, it helps to overcome the language barrier and translations are often for many the only access to Japan. Secondly, the enormous amount of written material in Japan is very difficult to cover, and the difficulty of the Japanese language only enhances this problem. Finally, and this particularly concerns third-world countries but also educational institutions in Western countries with lack of adequate funding, Japanese commercial media products have often become too expensive. We have therefore on the one hand the phenomenon that Japan's prosperity enhances variety of opinion at home, while on the other hand the same factor leads to greater Japanese opportunities for 'image control' abroad by government and business.[21] At the same time, domestic variety leads also to a greater offer of interpretations of Japan for the outside world. An illustration may be the rapid increase of private organizations and voluntary groups engaged in international exchange activities in Japan which according to a survey by the Japan Foundation numbered 560 as of December 1985, that is, an increase of nearly three times compared with five years earlier.[22]

In view of its own limited resources and to multiply its own efforts, the government is encouraging cooperation with the private sector. The Advisory Group on International Cultural Exchange recommended in 1994 that efforts should be undertaken to 'allow private capital to play a larger role through the active and effective use of tax measures' and that 'serious consideration must also be given to measures which facilitate private-sector contributions to the Japan Foundation'.[23] In addition to the MFA various other major ministries are involved in their own information dissemination and try to involve business. The Ministry of Finance has initiated the Institute of Fiscal and Monetary Policy and the Foundation for Advanced Information and Research (FAIR) which have many overlapping functions and members. Both institutions work with foreign scholars, organize workshops and conferences, invite foreign bureaucrats and financial specialists, notably from East Asia, and collect and disseminate information. Japanese companies are members of these two and other affiliated institutions. It provides unique opportunities for financial circles to receive and disseminate information, as well as to influence foreign financial specialists, notably from developing countries in Asia, as we have seen in Chapter 3.

B. Lobbying in the US

As the most important partner for Japan, the US plays a central role in Japan's cultural diplomacy. In order to enhance the work of the Japan Foundation the government set up in April 1991 the Japan Foundation Center for Global Partnership devoted entirely to the relationship with the United States as a special branch of the Japan Foundation. The budget for this new institution amounted in FY 1990 to ¥369.99 million, generated from the interest of a ¥50 billion government endowment. This is in addition to the 12.4 per cent (¥104.81 million) in FY 1990 of the Japan Foundation's total budget which is devoted to the United States and Canada.[24] Moreover, the Center functions as a conduit for donations from private Japanese sources.[25]

The lobbying activity of Japan in the US has recently attracted particular attention. What Japan does is not intrinsically different from other countries, but it is the scale and the recent nature of these efforts which draws attention. In view of Japan's comprehensive and crucial relationship with the US, as well as its financial means, it should not be surprising although it does not correspond to the image of the quiet and ineloquent Japanese most people still harbour of the Japanese. Japanese agencies are represented in many ways all over the US to shape public opinion and nurture contacts. The MFA has 15 consulates throughout the US, more than any other nation. It can also use the Japan Society and the Japan Economic Institute who play a respected role in projecting a positive image of Japan.[26] MITI maintains a substantial presence through JETRO and there is a degree of cooperation with local Japanese Chambers of Commerce. Japanese companies have become major agents in endowing chairs, research and sponsoring events of all kinds.

Another level is the circle of American lobbyists working for Japanese causes as consultants or lawyers. Japan has the largest and most influential lobbying power in Washington. From 1988 to 1992 Japanese interests hired more than 125 law firms, consultants and public relations firms according to the US Justice Department.[27] This circle is assisted by the open nature of American business and government, the transfer of personnel from one to the other and regional differences.[28] A special case which illustrates the power one single company can wield in the US is Toshiba, which spent an estimated $30 million to oppose the threat of sanctions in 1987–88 in the wake of the illegal shipment of sensitive technology to the Soviet Union by one of its sister companies. Another example was the lobbying efforts by the Japanese side in relation to the car dispute in 1995. What is grating on many American as well as other foreign observers is the fact that the Japanese system is not as open to foreign lobbying although the American system is certainly at one end of the extreme in terms of openness. The Japanese lobbying power has had a considerable impact on shaping the agenda of Japanese–American relations. The Japanese side has been able to exploit the infighting of American government agencies and to expose the weak points in their postures. A major example is the issue of managed trade and the setting of numerical targets to reduce the American trade deficit. It was relatively easy to counter-attack the American position because the matter is extremely complex and the Japanese side could easily discredit the American side by making allegations deriving from the alleged choice of words by American officials which went against the principles of GATT (see Chapter 1).

IS JAPAN BECOMING ASIAN OR ASIA BECOMING JAPANESE OR BOTH BECOMING WESTERN?

Before investigating Japan's cultural influence on Asia it is necessary to understand Japan's relationship with Asia. Japan's attitude towards Asia and its perception of Asia is profoundly ambivalent, due to its cultural and historical experience as well as the diversity of Asia. The country is undoubtedly an 'Asian' country, not only by geography, but also culturally. Asia is, however, culturally so diverse that the cognitive value of this adjective is rather limited. In addition, history has tended to isolate and/ or alienate Japan from Asia, and has prevented the country from identifying with Asia.

Apart from the cultural and historical gap with Asia, Japan's posture towards the rest of Asia has to take many other inconsistencies and differences into account. There is, first of all, the size of Japan's economy in relation to the rest of Asia, including its most populous nations. In 1989 Japan's GDP was 1.7 times greater than that of all 12 leading East Asian nations combined, including India and China. Secondly, Japan's political system is a democracy although the differences from the political systems of some other East Asian countries are narrowing. Thirdly, its own political and economic development has brought Japan much closer to the other industrialized countries than to Asia. Fourthly, Japan's dependence on Asia bears no relation to the degree of dependence of Asia on Japan as a market as well as provider of investment, aid and technology. Fifthly, the legacy of past Japanese aggression against Asia has left deep marks, and the insincere attitude of Japan in general towards the past keeps the memory more alive than may have been the case otherwise. Finally, Japan has been closely allied with the US since regaining independence in 1952 and its foreign and security policy has been very much subordinated to the requirements of its much more powerful ally.

It is natural that Japan's posture towards Asia reflects these incongruencies. Japan's basic position (*kihon-teki tachiba*), as explained in the Ministry of Foreign Affairs's Blue Book, is based on the position of Japan being a member of the West (*Nishigawa no ichiin*) as well as a country in the Asia Pacific region. But what it means has never been clearly spelled out. Tanaka Akihiko interprets it as meaning:

> 'A member of the West' seemed to imply basic commonality of values and security interests with the other Western industrialised democracies; 'a country in the Asia-Pacific region' seemed to imply Japan's security interests in the peace and stability of its neighbourhood.[29]

An advisory panel on Asia and the Pacific, inaugurated in May 1992 under Prime Minister Miyazawa, submitted a report in December 1992 which was rather general and circumvented the critical issues by creating the two principles of 'Pursuit of the open door' and 'Respect for diversity'. The latter is a bow towards most Asian countries which pursue something less than the universal values of democracy, freedom and human rights, or at least maintain that they can be attained in different ways. The former is a bow to other Western countries and tries to assure them that Japan will not pursue an Asian exclusionist club.

A. Asianization of Japan?

Recently Japan seems to be gripped by a pro-Asian mood and many publications emphasize Japan's move towards Asia, its Asianization and a policy of regionalism.[30] This mood started in the 1980s with the increase of Asian imports into Japan as a result of Japanese investment in the region and the increase of Japanese tourists travelling to Asian destinations. While the surge of Asian imports has subsided, the interest in Asia has been enhanced by a variety of factors.

There is, first of all, interest and identification with Asia as a negative reaction. Sasae Kenichiro, a Japanese diplomat, writes about a tendency to pay more attention to Asia when relations with the West are in difficulty.[31] One extreme reaction to these difficulties is the 'return to Asia' (*Ajia kaiki*), whereas a more positive one is '*kyosei*' (economic symbiosis) which was mentioned in Chapter 1. There is also the feeling with some Japanese that relations with Asia and the US are mutually exclusive.[32] This sentimental and xenophobic form of Asianism is also related to dissatisfaction mostly with the American offensive on economic and value issues. A major illustration was the criticism heaped on Japan in the wake of Japan's mild approach to the Chinese government after the Tiananmen massacre although the US showed with its secret diplomacy a similar concern with keeping the dialogue with China open.[33]

Finally, the pro-Asian mood is the expression of a feeling that due to modernization (easily confounded with Westernization) Japan has lost at least part of its identity and by focusing on Asia it may regain this identity. Japanese tend 'to stress their [Asian countries'] similarity to the prewar culture and society of Japan'.[34] In this way, Asian cultures are utilized to satisfy a Japanese psychological complex, which grows out of the fact that, since the war, Japanese society has lost many of its traditional and diversified features. The pro-Asian mood is therefore also a reflection of the ignorance of the wider Japanese public about Asia. Looking at Asia as the 'lost paradise' ignores the fact that Asia is changing now even more rapidly than Japan in order to modernize. There is also a tendency to ignore in this context (and only here) the huge differences between Japan and Asia as well as among Asian countries.[35] This is all the more likely to happen if Asia is only seen in terms of economic dynamism and compared with the alleged decline of the other Western industrialized countries. Naturally this pro-Asian mood ignores also the economic realities of the different degrees of Japan's economic relationship with Asia compared with those relationships with the US or Europe.

The view that Japan has to rediscover its true Asian origins, after having followed the West for over a hundred years, also ignores the fact that we are now already in the middle of Japan's third turning to Asia since the Meiji Restoration, and that many Asians do not remember very fondly the last time Japan turned to Asia and subjugated it to allegedly free it from Western imperialism.[36]

The superficiality of the pro-Asian mood is also revealed by the persistence of racism in Japan against fellow Asians as observed in the treatment of Asian workers in Japan or the discrimination of Koreans. As a very homogeneous society Japan has great difficulties with accepting diversity, even if the 'others' are ethnic Japanese who have grown up in China as 'war orphans' and now try to reintegrate into Japanese society. Asia is also widely left out in the discussion about Japan's internationalization (*kokusaika*), which has more to do with Japan becoming like Western industrialized countries or speaking English than with the country's most immediate neighbours.

'Asianism' as a positive reaction is related to a growing consciousness of the importance of Asia to Japan in economic terms, but also increasingly in political and strategic terms. Japanese take pride in seeing that other Asians are successfully taking up the Japanese model of economic modernization.

On balance one can certainly not speak of the Asianization of Japan or the 'return to Asia' but rather of a greater awareness of Asia's importance for Japan if not a more positive attitude towards the area. It is disconcerting that this Asianism is based on so many emotions and mistaken perceptions of Asia. In addition, Tanaka Akihiko points out that this Asianism (*Ajia-shugi*) lacks a clear theory of international politics and it is therefore ambivalent in its policy implications:

Sino-Japanese joint responsibility may be an interesting idea from a culturalist viewpoint, but, from the realist's viewpoint, it is nothing but an attempt at condominium; from the liberal viewpoint, it is totally devoid of solid foundation because of differences of political values and institutions.[37]

B. Getting Away with the Legacy of the Past

The legacy of the past, and particularly the way this issue is handled by the Japanese, is what still weighs most heavily on Japan's relations with Asia. It casts a shadow over every positive aspect of Japan's relations with Asia, and it worsens every aspect of the relationship which is considered by the Asians as less welcome. It is thwarting Japan's natural political and economic leadership in Asia. The insincere and inconsistent way in which the issue is approached by Japan can also be regarded as another case of power exertion because Japan is seen as trying to make the Asians accept its own view of what happened in the past and to forget Japan's wrongdoing.

The issue again received a high level of attention in 1995 because of the celebrations of the 50th anniversary of the end of the war. Opinions on Japan's colonialism and the war in East Asia have many times led to the resignation of cabinet ministers, and the number of these incidents does not seem to decline but rather to increase. The contents of these opinions revolves around Japan's war guilt, the denial of certain incidents during the war (for example, the Nanjing massacre in 1937–38, the existence of brothels with Asian and some Western women organized by the Imperial Army), the evaluation of its colonial activities and the relativization of Japan's crimes by pointing at its unique status as the first and only country which suffered nuclear bombing.[38] Since an appropriate settlement of these issues has not been achieved within Japan, it has been impossible to show to the outside world an attitude which would reconcile the former enemies with the Japan of today to the extent as has happened between Germany and its wartime enemies.[39] Official apologies by Japan's leaders have been reluctant and half-hearted with the notable exception of Prime Minister Hosokawa in 1993 and Prime Minister Murayama in 1994. The Diet Resolution in June 1995 took great pains to relativize Japan's historical legacy by hinting at acts of aggressions by other countries. The public discussions of the extent and wording of official pronouncements before they are actually made, such as that of the Japanese Emperor before he visited China in October 1992 or the resolution about the war by the Diet in 1995, seem to undo whatever good could result from such pronouncements. Official critical pronouncements concerning the past will also have to be evaluated against the rampant historical revisionism in the Japanese mass media and literature. One new feature which may help revisionism and ignorance is the appearance of 'pulp fiction' which glorifies and rewrites the war.[40]

The historical revisionism is accompanied by clumsy reactions to demands arising from war and colonialism. Requests for compensation by the few remaining victims of Japan's forced army prostitution system are met by officials hiding behind legalistic positions because the government is concerned about creating a precedence for other demands. Instead of compensation for the former army prostitutes, Prime Minister Murayama announced in 1994 the Peace, Friendship and Exchange Initiative with a budgetary allocation of ¥100 billion for ten years from 1995 onwards. When China confronted Japan in February 1992 with the demand to pay for the destruction of about 2 million chemical weapons that the Japanese army had abandoned when they retreated from Northern China during the 1940s and made its agreement to the worldwide ban on chemical weapons conditional on a favourable response from Tokyo, the government tried to avoid taking responsibility by raising legalistic arguments concerning the sovereignty of China. Only after five months of mediation by Indonesia and Germany did Japan promise to help.[41]

Despite Japan's historical revisionism and legalistic approach, which is encouraged by the pride in its economic achievements, the long time which has passed since 1945 and the ignorance of the new generations which grew up after 1945, the country has achieved economic domination over Asia. The political costs of this insincere attitude towards the past are, however, considerable in terms of prestige, trust and acceptance. Japan's economic domination would be more acceptable to Asians if Japan confronted the legacy of the past. The issue of colonialism has sometimes been used by Asian countries to extract economic aid or favourable treatment. Political leadership by Japan in Asia can only be exerted indirectly or through other countries as we have seen in previous chapters. Nevertheless, Japan's economic and even cultural position is such that despite regular Asian outcries about the series of unrepentant and ahistorical Japanese statements, Asians have come to accept Japan's 'idiosyncratic' attitude towards the past for the day-to-day running of their political, economic and cultural relationship. Prime Minister Mahathir, keen on Japanese leadership in Asia for the support of his EAEC concept, even recommended Japan to stop apologizing for the past.[42] Generational change is also contributing towards a further erosion of Asian resentment towards Japan.

Asia is, however, divided about Japan playing a leading role in Asia, with China and South Korea being the most negative countries. In an opinion poll of business executives and academics in the Asia Pacific region (11 countries, including Taiwan and Hong Kong), it turned out that 70.2 per cent in all the 11 Asian countries agreed to a leading Japanese role, but only 16.2 per cent did so in China and 43.2 per cent in South Korea.[43] As we have seen in the previous chapter Japan cannot fully play a leadership role even when it comes to the promotion of regional forums. In the case of Asian violations of human rights, one of the reasons for Japan not daring to speak up is the legacy of the past, as became evident again in the government's reaction to the Tiananmen massacre.[44]

One of the most serious long-term costs of the way Japan deals with its past may be that it indirectly contributes to Japanese nationalism, which is on the rise for several other reasons as well, be it as a reaction to trade conflicts with Western partners or growing self-confidence based on the country's economic success. Younger Japanese leaders in particular are becoming impatient with a lack of political legitimacy of their country which denies them what they consider Japan's natural leadership role in Asia. Having to accept a low profile and take international initiatives by stealth or with the help of other countries only because of Japan's historical legacy is increasing their frustration with Asia, although by refusing to acknowledge the past they continue to maintain the vicious circle.

C. Influence on Asian Popular Culture

The very complex relationship with Asia has, however, not prevented Japan's success in the wide area of cultural diplomacy, dissemination of information and general cultural emanation. These cultural influences have a much greater impact on Japan's relations with Asia than with Europe or the US. The main reasons for this situation are Japan's advanced economic status compared with that of most Asian countries, its economic and increasingly political domination of Asia, and its economic role model function. In Asia Japan does not only rely on official cultural diplomacy but also on the emanation of its unique blend of Asian and Western way of life and popular culture.

Before we can evaluate Japan's official cultural diplomacy we have therefore to look at the emanation of Japanese culture and spread of popular culture in Asia. Japanese culture is attractive for Asians in the first place not as a result of government intervention but because of the expanded meaning of Japan as a successful model of economic development with all its accompanying trappings, mainly in the area of 'low-brow' culture such as fashion, lifestyle, business culture, golf, popular music, food and cartoons. The growing internationalization of Japan's economy has enhanced the accessibility, if not attractiveness, of Japanese culture. This can be most closely observed in East and Southeast Asia with its growing Japanese economic presence. The region is swamped with Japanese 'low-brow' culture.[45] It is also interesting to note how the import of Japanese culture can be separated from the Japanese language. Since 1989 there is among Korean students a Japanese comics boom of pirated comics which are found much more interesting than Korean ones which are tamer and less violent. The books are read even though most of the youngsters are hardly likely to be able to read Japanese.[46] On a more abstract level Japanese culture is attractive because of its thorough commodification of Japanese life, behind which is what has been called the most advanced postmodernism due to its 'combination of commodity reification, superficiality, simulacra, and the waning of affect'.[47]

Honda Shiro has further analysed the popularity of Japanese 'low-brow' culture in Asia. First, being based on US popular culture Japanese culture functions as a filter of the American version because the Japanese transformation has made it more palatable and acceptable for Asians.[48] Secondly, the rise of a new, rich middle class as a result of economic growth made Japan's popular culture attractive because it is urban-based, easy to consume, and without heavy cultural luggage compared to European and America culture. Thirdly, Japan's popular culture is the product of a very intense competition within Japan before it goes abroad. Fourthly, modern Japanese and Asian societies share similar themes, have no rigid value system attached and the values contained are closer to those of Asia.

The attraction of Japanese popular culture in Southeast Asia has been seized by powerful commercial interests from Japan which sustain and encourage it. Japanese retail business in East Asia and Southeast Asia is very strong (particularly in the more sophisticated markets of Hong Kong and Singapore) in the form of Japanese department stores. Their products and the accompanying publicity are very strong agents for this cultural import. Japanese manufacturers of consumer electronics provide, in the case of music, videos and films, both the hardware as well as the software. In contrast, Japanese software exports to Europe and the US are mostly limited to electronic video games and cartoons. As a result East Asia is a quickly growing huge entertainment market which offers tremendous opportunities for Japanese companies with their superior knowhow, software and hardware. In the case of records, Asia's $1 billion market is expected to grow threefold within the next seven years compared with a saturated $4 billion record market in Japan. Japanese entertainment companies are joining forces with Japanese hardware companies to find talents in Asia through sponsorships of talent search contests.[49] Another booming sector is publication, notably the publishing of Japanese cartoons (*manga*).[50]

The dissemination of Japanese popular culture in East Asia is to some extent reciprocated by the selective reception of certain Asian cultural phenomena like food, clothing and visual arts in Japan itself within the context of Japan's 'Asianization'. As Hohmann adds, however, this import is mostly organized by Japanese companies and economically does not benefit East Asian countries much.[51] The Japan Foundation is also an important funding agent for the popularization of Asian culture in Japan and uses it as a useful means to gain public support for its overseas activities.

D. Cultural Diplomacy in Asia

With the rise of economic and political disputes the Japanese government together with business started to use cultural diplomacy to make Japan's economic presence in Asia more acceptable to Asians. After all, imitating Japanese fashion or eating raw fish in Japanese restaurants does not make people automatically feel more positive towards Japan, as the high number of Japanese restaurants in Korea and the low level of appreciation of Japan may prove. The importance of Asia in the activities of the Japan Foundation can be seen from the distribution of its funds. The list of the top

20 recipient countries is topped in the period from 1986 to 1990 by the US (12.1 per cent), China (7.8 per cent) and Indonesia (6.4 per cent) whereas by region the Asia Pacific region tops the list with an annual share of around 37 per cent share, followed by Europe with around 17 per cent and North America with around 13 per cent.[52] In view of the much lower living costs compared with the United States or Europe such funding levels can achieve more in Asia.

This official support of Japanese culture is particularly directed at the teaching of the Japanese language. Of the amount to East Asia 66.4 per cent (54 per cent in the case of Southeast Asia) was devoted to the promotion of Japanese language and Japan-related study programmes.[53] The powerful presence of Japanese economic interests in the region and their vehicle function for the upward social mobility of the local people motivates an increasing number, particularly of young people, to learn the Japanese language in order to work with or for Japanese business.

The concentration on less developed countries enhances limited resources put into cultural diplomacy but can also have potentially damaging effects on those countries where indigenous culture has a weak economic base and cannot compete with Japanese imports and the technical support structure of popular culture. The Japanese donation of a cultural hall to Bangkok does not help indigenous culture if it is too far outside the capital and the technical infrastructure too expensive to maintain. The area of religious life is particularly sensitive because of the prosperity of Japanese religious organizations, allowing them to achieve considerable influence due to the economic disparity between Japan and most Asian countries.[54] Economic disparity is also an advantage for Japan when it comes to satellite broadcasting. A new stage of cultural power projection based on superior economic and financial power has been reached with this development although its full utilization has yet to come.

An interesting case is South Korea, which may not be a weak country but it is certainly very concerned about Japan's cultural power backed by economic power. In this case the memory of Japan's colonial past also plays a role when Japan forced Japanese high and low culture (including the adoption of Japanese names and the Emperor cult) upon Korea. Even today Japanese films, pop songs, Karaoke bars and even high culture imports are not allowed. In 1992 Seoul National University eliminated Japanese in the foreign language section of its 1994 entrance examinations, one of the arguments being that it is less worthy of academic research.[55] Japanese sports like Sumo are not permitted nor is the import of Hollywood movies starring Japanese actors. In September 1994 the Korean government slightly revised its restraints on Japanese culture. The Japanese side has apparently put pressure on Korea to lift the ban by linking it with South Korea's desire for more high-technology transfer to Korea. However, thanks to the spread of satellite TV, many Koreans have become able to surmount the official ban on Japanese mass culture.[56] Taiwan, another former Japanese colony, relaxed a three-decade-old ban on Japanese films only in August 1992.

CONCLUSIONS

The above analysis of Japan's cultural power in the widest sense certainly does not justify speaking of Japan as a cultural superpower, commensurate with its economic power. In the Western world Japan's efforts to disseminate its culture have been noted by very high profile events such as the Japan Festival in 1991 in Britain or Japanese weeks in various other European countries. Of a more lasting effect is most likely the JET programme, which not only enhances the attractiveness of Japan but also influences the understanding of the world with Japanese children. In addition, the support of Japanese studies in the tertiary sector of many countries has also a lasting effect. Nevertheless, Japan's cultural emanation will always be very limited outside Asia because of the geographical and cultural distances involved. The biggest hurdle is the Japanese language and the poor understanding of foreign languages by Japanese due to an examination-focused educational system. However, Japanese entertainment technology may have a lasting effect on the way we relate to our environment and to entertainment, or how we experience the increasingly blurred line between the real and the virtual (for example, virtual reality games) although the immediate cultural software may be Western (music, film, video).[57]

In the case of Asia, Japan's cultural emanation is much greater, distances shorter and the economic domination of Japan over the region gives an added motivation for Asians to adopt Japanese culture, be it karaoke, the Japanese language or attitudes towards work. But even by using Gramsci's definition of hegemony as a relationship, created by consent which is generated by ideological leadership (among other kinds of 'leaderships'), Japan's cultural emanation and influence does not yet go far enough to justify speaking of hegemony. Although the weight of the legacy of the past will continue to ease with new Asian generations attaining leadership functions or simply wanting to enjoy the material comfort accompanying Japan's presence in the region, it will still cast a shadow on Japan's political legitimacy and restrain its regional leadership. Japan is certainly not becoming more 'Asian', but Japan is contributing to the creation of a new universal culture based on Asian and Western elements. In view of China's rising power and the growing cultural competition from other economically successful Asian states it is also doubtful how dominant Japan's cultural influence can become and stay distinctly Japanese rather than Asian or Western. In the meantime, however, Japanese business is considerably benefiting from even a limited cultural penetration of other countries.

Conclusions

Faced with the paradox of a Japan which appears on the one hand unwilling and unable to take more international responsibilities and to become more 'normal', and on the other hand a Japan which tenaciously sticks to its national interests and is actually quite successful at protecting these interests, we chose to look at Japan's foreign policy from a perspective of 'outcomes' and to use a wider understanding of the concept of power.

An extended concept of power does better justice to the changing nature of Japan's political economic system and the regional/global environment. It allows one not only to understand visible exertions of influence and power by Japan, but also to discern outcomes which are causally related to Japan although there may have been no actor or no intention. The mere anticipation of any Japanese action can prevent other players from pursuing their national interests if they are seen as conflicting with Japan's. Japan's structural power may not yet be the same of that of the US, but its relative and even ideological/cultural power has grown considerably and is affecting the perceptions, alternatives, material circumstances and bargaining powers of more and more countries and players, irrespective of their geographical or cultural distance from Japan. Japan now matters so much that it does not actually have to do something in order to effect an outcome which is beneficial to its national interest. By refusing to take any action, as was illustrated by the case of the effect of the yen appreciation on Asian yen loan recipients or the case of the long-held ban on rice imports, the material circumstances of other countries are affected.

Japan's foreign policy in the 1990s emerges as the outcome of the contest between the requirements, results and constraints of Japan's political economic system and social structure on the one hand, and the challenges of a changing international environment on the other. The country is very dependent on the import of raw materials, energy and food, and the task of its foreign policy is to supplement the efforts of the private sector to secure them. While this is in principle no different from any other country, we have seen that Japan's political economy is substantially different in its structure and *modus operandi*. These differences as a whole give Japan considerable economic advantages in comparison with other Western countries which the latter perceive as unfair and which therefore lead to frictions. Japan benefited in the past from a very protectionist regime to develop its economy while keeping foreigners out. Its economic political system even kept out Japanese smaller companies or newcomers. The *keiretsu* system and the close cooperation between business, bureaucrats and politicians, to mention just a few features, has allowed Japanese industry to maximize its gains while being protected from outside competition. While this is now all changing and we experience an unprecedented shift towards convergence with other major Western countries, not least helped by a deep structural economic crisis, the changes are not fast enough (at least for many outsiders) and do not take away all advantages on which Japanese industry can now build worldwide. The task of Japan's foreign policy therefore is not only to facilitate the external interactions of business, but to cope with the frictions with its partners resulting from these advantages. It is ironic and it aggravates these tensions that due to historical circumstances the major ally of Japan with which is has built up a most comprehensive relationship in the postwar period happens to be a country which is not only so different in physical and economic size, but which has also a political economic system and political culture at the other end of the spectrum.

A fair solution of the problem of differences is very difficult because of the dangers and uncertainties inherent in any punitive measures (protectionism, managed trade), the narrowing gap between the political economic system of Japan and that of its major Western partners, the retributive power of Japan, and the importance of Japan's economy for the world economy. The problem with 'selective protectionism' as an answer is that proponents may not be those who want to use different ways to strengthen their country but who want only to protect particular interests and hide bureaucratic, social or industrial inertia. Refuting the differences by pointing at the ongoing changes, Japan is basically asking its trading partners to accept that it enjoyed for a considerable time an unfair advantage and to console themselves with 'but now it has changed' or 'we are going to change to become more like you'. We cannot take away from Japan the 'time lag advantage' it gained by adapting the country to the political economic system of other Western industrialized countries with a delay (in time and degree) which may be increasingly narrowing but will always be there. Above all, Japan has reached such an importance in the world economy and attained such power that it can wield power in many areas and defend itself against punitive measures. The only equitable solution out of this dilemma may be compensation for damages suffered during the periods of exclusion and transition to a more 'normal' regime.[1]

Japan's power is based on its economic performance. The recession, the political upheaval since 1993, the banking crisis or even the Kobe earthquake which affected the shipment of about 10 per cent of Japan's external trade has not significantly dented its economic power although it has put economic restructuring on the agenda very forcefully. We have seen how

Japan uses this economic power to pursue its economic interests, be it trade, investment or development aid. The changes in the international environment have provided pressure and incentives to expand the use of this economic power to wider goals. The US as a global hegemon is no longer willing or able, at least not on its own, to provide the public goods which secured an international environment conducive to Japan's national interest. We have seen that many factors are preventing Japan from being pushed into translating its economic power into commensurate military power although it has achieved the posture of a major military power, at least in the regional context, by virtue of the quality of the SDF and its arms production ability. Instead of becoming a military superpower, it is relying on US military force (some unkindly refer already to a Japan-paid mercenary force) and using its ODA to foster a stable and economically Japan-oriented regional environment, but also increasingly reaching out to other regions to be seen as contributing to a peaceful international environment.[2]

Pressures and opportunities resulting from the changing international environment have increasingly led Japan to add to the pursuit of economic goals, objectives of a more political nature. These political goals range from influencing the various international regimes affecting everything from trade to international relations to more specific and narrow aims. We have illustrated the former with Japan's attitude towards GATT and the new WTO, and analysed Japan's actions in the UN system, including PKO and the UNSC. Nothing can be undertaken in international organizations if Japan does not financially support a given action, helps to garner a majority for a vote, or at least is seen in agreement with it. This new power has also provided opportunities to protect more narrow or parochial political goals, be it the protection of an economically insignificant industrial sector like whaling or boosting the prestige of Japan through the forceful promotion of Japanese staff in international organizations.

The total impact of Japan's comprehensive power – economic, political and cultural – is considerable, although its scope and effectiveness depends on factors such as geographic contiguity, historical circumstances and the economic strength of other countries and players. Japan's influence on Asian countries is naturally particularly strong and is supplemented by cultural power on a scale unknown to Japan's Western partners. Based on its comprehensive economic power, Japan has become at least regionally a political superpower. Asian countries, including China, are now looking to Japan as a model, be it industrial policy, the organization of financial institutions or approaches to environmental issues. They are attracted by Japan's success and its financial enticements to emulate the model. When considering the impact of Japan's power one has also to take into account the relative decline of Japan's major competitors. Some of them have been less able to cope with the worldwide recession, and many are decreasing ODA or funding for cultural diplomacy while Japan is increasing it and supplementing it with private sector support.

Japan's cultural influence may not look impressive, particularly outside of Asia, but it is shaping trends and it has to be seen in the context of its economic benefits and influence on working practices and management. Japan's cultural and economic influence may ultimately contribute to the creation of a new universal societal model which at the very least would make Japan's international economic activities more acceptable and consensual. This would be no mean achievement, particularly if it is politically so much less onerous than using military power. It could help other Western countries with their access to Asia.

Based on Japan's economic success there are now increasing Japanese voices promoting Japanese ways, be it the manner of giving aid, running a factory or organizing society. Hamaguchi Eshun even speaks of the advantages of Japan's societal model, which he calls a network-type societal system, and predicts that the Japanese type of control through inducement and persuasion in our highly information oriented societies will dominate. Of course, the information may not be related at all to Japan, but it is the procedures which may appear so attractive and necessary in an increasingly competitive international environment that the forces to adopt them may become irresistible. This may have a significant impact on how we non-Japanese organize our societies and have to abandon cherished behaviours and institutions. Change is, of course, normal and vital, but the point is that we increasingly find the origin of pressure for change in Asia because it is not only Japan but all the other Asian countries, emulating and encouraged by Japan to do so, which feed the whirlwind of competitive power.

But does this all amount to some kind of leadership? Is Japan taking over from the US, at least in East Asia?

The classical notion of one hegemon dominating the global landscape seems to be outdated because no single power, not even the US, can any longer muster the power and followership which the US was able to do during the first two postwar decades in a bipolar world system. Japan looms large in Asia, but Japan has still more trade and investments in the US and Europe than in Asia, and Asia even without Japan is trading more with the US and Europe than within Asia, let alone with Japan. We have seen the barriers to Japanese leadership, whether we refer to domestic or international leadership, which range from political arrangements to Japan's inability to address adequately its past in Asia. The open character of Asia's regionalization, the strong dependence on extra-regional trade, and the rise of new intra-regional power centres, notably China, will soon relativize Japan's economic domination.

But, on the other hand, Japan is exerting leadership in an incremental, low-profile way. Influencing international regimes settles the structure through which conflicts of interests are settled and the more Japan shapes these regimes according to its needs and preferences, the better Japan can weather storms which result from clashes of interests with other countries. The confrontation with the US on cars and car part imports shows on the one hand how much Japan has already achieved by influencing the dispute settlement procedures and excluding from WTO rules those features of its political economic system which contribute to trade conflicts. On the other hand, it also shows the limits of this kind of leadership if the other side does not accept these regimes and can put pressure on Japan because of other common interests and a strong tendency towards unilateralism.

In view of the fact that Japan is mostly using its economic power and has predominantly economic interests the concept of 'civilian power' (*minsei taikoku*) or 'global civilian power' has been proposed to characterize Japan's status. Richard Rosecrance speaks of the 'trading state' to define this new paradigm of the civilian state.[3] Comparing Japan and Germany, Hanns Maull speaks of the two countries as prototypes of 'civilian powers' and defines 'civilian power' as

> (1) acceptance of the necessity of cooperation with others in the pursuit of international objectives; (2) the concentration on non-military, primarily economic, means of international interaction; and (3) a willingness to develop supranational structures to address critical issues of international management.[4]

Very similar but more specific on the actual modalities is what Michael Lind has called the 'catalytic state' as opposed to the 'integral state'.[5] Faced with a situation where a superpower like the United States can no longer play a predominant role as it could before, and a new major power like Japan can no longer hope to achieve nor would wish to achieve such a predominant role, what is being achieved is the status of a state which 'seeks its goals less by relying on its own resources than by acting as a dominant element in coalitions of other states, transnational institutions, and private sector groups, while detaining its distinct identity and its own goals'.[6]

Lacking the qualities and will for leadership, on an individual as well as organizational level, but being well endowed with economic power and a cultural propensity to work in groups, Japan's leaders feel more at ease forming coalitions of other states, transnational institutions and private sector groups rather than replacing the weakening American hegemon. This is also politically the least onerous way (the means ranging from quid pro quo proposals to blackmail) to establish linkages between issues in order to achieve economic as well as political objectives.

This concept of the 'catalytic state' bears an interesting resemblance to Hamaguchi Eshun's paradigm of the 'methodological relatum-ism' which is more based on society as a relational than an individual-centred concept.[7] Such a concept would also explain why states in general are said to be losing power, including the Japanese state, but somehow they still matter more than anything else for outcomes. As can be shown in economic interaction at a global level, state agencies and state-controlled agencies (for example, central banks) have established a network among themselves of dialogue and cooperation. Japanese agencies have shown that they are particularly apt at working at this level, either globally (for example, cooperation among central banks) or regionally (for example, MITI and the Ministry of Finance establishing networks with their Asian counterparts). This relational leadership of the 'catalytic state' is even functional during serious economic difficulties and at a time of political upheaval and transition when politicians delegate considerable political tasks to the bureaucracy.

Such leadership by stealth is, however, not without certain risks. It suffers from a considerable degree of democratic deficit which cannot be good for the long-term health of Japan's democracy. It means that outside actors, whether Japanese or non-Japanese, can only with great difficulty influence decisions or even predict outcomes. Incremental leadership functions well only in the case of relatively uncontentious political issues. Any potentially contentious issues, or issues which offer themselves for ambitious politicians to make their mark (for example, the normalization of relations with North Korea) can create stalemate in the leadership and worsen relations with the outside world. Incremental leadership is also hardly able to reduce the frustration of other countries who expect Japan, either with or without justification, to shoulder more responsibility (for example PKO) or to come clean on difficult issues like the legacy of the past or the government's position on the EAEC.

Avoiding clear decisions and positions ('thinking fuzzily') can lead to the unchecked influence of particular interests which gradually shape the agenda and the processes of policy-making, thus increasingly narrowing the scope for rational alternatives, political innovation and crisis management. The handling of the legacy of the past is such an example. By placating relatively minor interest groups for many years and by poor leadership Japan has become structurally as well as in terms of public opinion unable to solve the greatest obstacle for Japan's leadership role in Asia while contributing at the same time to the rise of nationalism in Japan. Reactive diplomacy also supports this rise of nationalism. Although we have seen how Japan has begun to shape the rules of international trade and is opposing managed trade demands, it still relies very much on outside pressure for change.

Lack of domestic and international leadership and innovation allows the uncontrolled and unchannelled growth of expectations (in Japan as well as abroad), opportunities, capabilities and needs which accompany the increase of hard and soft power. It may for example lead to giving undue weight to prestige in Japan's foreign policy and thus strengthen nationalism. Asking for a permanent seat on the UNSC may be a justifiable request (and this author personally supports it), but is it wise to spend so much political capital on a request fraught with many political complexities? Failure to achieve a permanent seat may only fan nationalism by withholding what many Japanese perceive to be a status befitting their country. Precious political capital has also been spent on a prestige-related issue like the government's demand for changing Victory over Japan Day to Victory in the Pacific Day. Prestige is, of course, a very simple notion and can be sold easily and with great political benefit to the domestic constituency.

Japan's regional and global environment is changing fast and Japan's actions and non-actions dynamically interact with this environment. The greatest challenge for Japan's foreign policy is to come from the emergence of several East Asian countries which are successfully following the Japanese model, and, beginning with China, will make it more difficult for Japan to translate economic power into political influence and to rely on leadership by stealth. Japan's deep structural economic crisis and the growing frictions with the US over bilateral and regional issues (for example, US–Chinese relations) can only compound this challenge. The irony therefore is that at the time when we see Japan move from economic superpowerhood to political superpowerhood, from followership to leadership by stealth and networking, the limitations and potential pitfalls of this foreign policy approach have never been more obvious.

Notes

INTRODUCTION

1. Kuriyama, Takakazu, *'Gekido no 90 nendai to Nihon gaiko no shin tenkai'* (The turbulent 1990s and new developments in Japan's foreign policy), *Gaiko Foramu*, no. 20 (May 1990), p. 16. Translation in Tanaka, Akihiko, 'Rhetorics and Limitations of Japan's New Internationalism', in: *Japanese Studies Bulletin (Australia)*, vol. 14, no. 1 (1994), p. 15.
2. See, for example, Jack Snyder, *Myths of Empire. Domestic Politics and International Ambition* (Ithaca: Cornell University Press, 1991), p. 319.
3. Huntington, Samuel, 'Why international primacy matters', *International Security*, vol. 17, no. 4 (Spring 1993), p. 72.
4. Nye, Joseph, 'Soft power', *Foreign Policy*, no. 80 (Fall 1990), p. 157.
5. Miyagawa, Makio, 'The employment of economic strength for foreign policy goals', *Japan Review of International Affairs*, vol. 6, no. 3 (Fall 1992), p. 275.
6. Okabe, Tatsumi, 'A proposal for lasting security in East Asia', *Japan Review of International Affairs*, vol. 6, no. 3 (Fall 1992), p. 236.
7. Discussion between Kuroda Makoto and Okamoto Yukio, 'Cold hearted America. What is wrong with a "faceless Japan"? Who can say that foreign countries will be pleased upon seeing its real face?', *Bungei Shunju*, July (1991). Translated in *Summary of Selected Japanese Magazines*, December (1991).
8. Waltz, Kenneth, 'The emerging structure of international politics', *International Security*, vol. 18, no. 2 (Fall 1993), p. 66.
9. Hanami, Andrew K., 'Japan and the military balance of power in Northeast Asia', *The Journal of East Asian Affairs*, vol. viii, no. 2 (Summer/Fall 1994), p. 393.
10. Chin, Kin Wah, 'Changing global trends and their effects on the Asia-Pacific', *Contemporary Southeast Asia*, vol. 13, no. 1 (June 1991), p. 7.
11. Baldwin, David A., 'Power analysis and world politics: New trends versus old tendencies', *World Politics*, vol. 31, no. 2 (January 1979), 161–94.
12. Inoguchi, Takashi, *Japan's Foreign Policy in an Era of Global Change* (London: Pinter, 1993), p. ix.
13. Kataoka, Tetsuya, *The Price of a Constitution. The Origin of Japan's Postwar Politics* (New York: Crane Russak, 1991), p. 3.
14. van Wolferen, Karel, *The Enigma of Japanese Power* (London: Macmillan, 1989), Chapter 2.
15. van Wolferen, Karel, *The Enigma of Japanese Power*, p. 5.
16. Johnson, Chalmers, 'South Korean democratization: The role of economic development', *The Pacific Review*, vol. 2, no. 1 (1989), pp. 1–10.
17. van Wolferen, Karel, *The Enigma of Japanese Power*, p. 21.
18. Eisenstadt, S.N. and Ben-Ari, Eyal, *Japanese Models of Conflict Resolution* (London: Routledge, 1990), pp. 12–13.

19. Baldwin, David A., *Power Analysis and World Politics*, pp. 180–1.
20. *The Japan Times* (13 September 1986).
21. *Asahi Shimbun* (16 March 1987).
22. The conference took place on 24 March 1987, and I owe this observation to Shiina Motoo whom I interviewed shortly thereafter.
23. *Asahi Shimbun* (15 May 1992).
24. Kaji, Motoo, 'Japan's long-range economic plans: From quantity to quality', *Japan Review of International Affairs*, vol. 6, no. 3 (Fall 1992), 213–23. There are plenty of other examples: The Komei-Party wants Japan to become a '*kankyo taikoku*' (meaning a country which cares about the environment). A discussion with Ogata Sadako and Homma Nagayo on refugees is entitled '*Keizai taikoku' kara 'Jindo taikoku' e* (From big economic power to big humanitarian power), *Gaiko Foramu* (April 1991), 72–9.
25. Nye, Joseph, 'Soft power', *Foreign Policy*, no. 80 (Fall 1990), p. 166.
26. Nye, Joseph, 'Soft power', p. 155.
27. Nye, Joseph, 'Soft power', pp. 153–71. See also: Joseph Nye, *Bound to Lead: The Changing Nature of American Power* (New York: Basic Books, 1989).
28. Guzzini, Stefano, 'Structural power: The limits of neorealist power analysis', *International Organization*, vol. 47, no. 3 (Summer 1993), p. 468.
29. Kroll, John A., 'The complexity of interdependence', *International Studies Quarterly*, vol. 37, no. 3 (September 1993), 321–48.
30. Otte/Grimes, quoted in: Maull, Hanns (ed.), *Japan und Europa. Getrennte Welten?* (Frankfurt: Campus Verlag, 1993), p. 117.
31. Gilpin, Robert, *The Political Economy of International Relations* (Princeton: Princeton University Press, 1987), p. 23 and p. 31.
32. Keohane, Robert O. and Nye, Joseph S., *Power and Interdependence* (Boston: Little, Brown, 1977).
33. Gilpin, Robert, *The Political Economy of International Relations*, p. 72.
34. Gilpin, Robert, *The Political Economy of International Relations*, p. 376.
35. Fukai, Shigeko, 'Japan, ASEAN and the Asian NIEs', in: Mason, David T. and Turay, Abdul M. (eds), *Japan, NAFTA and Europe, Trilateral Cooperation or Confrontation?* (London: Macmillan, 1994), p. 172.
36. Fukai, Shigeko, 'Japan, ASEAN and the Asian NIEs', p. 173.
37. Fukai, Shigeko, 'Japan, ASEAN and the Asian NIEs', p. 174.
38. Yamamura, Kozo, 'The deliberate emergence of a free trader: The Japanese political economy in transition', in: Garby, Craig C. and Brown Bullock, Mary (eds), *Japan. A New Kind of Superpower?* (Washington, DC: The Woodrow Wilson Center Press/The Johns Hopkins University Press, 1994), p. 36.
39. Major works on Japan's political economy are: Johnson, Chalmers, *MITI and the Japanese Miracle: The Growth of Industrial Policy, 1925–1975* (Stanford: Stanford University Press, 1982); Yamamura, Kozo and Yasuba, Yasukichi (eds), *The Political Economy of Japan, vol. 1, The Domestic Transformation* (Stanford: Stanford University Press, 1987); Sheridan, Kyoko, *Governing the Japanese Economy* (paperback edition) (Oxford: Polity Press, 1994); Calder, Kent, *Strategic Capitalism: Private Business and Public Purpose in Japanese Industrial Finance* (Princeton: Princeton University Press, 1993); Calder, Kent, *Crisis and Compensation: Public Policy and Political Stability in Japan, 1949–1986* (Princeton: Princeton University Press, 1989); Williams, David, *Japan: Beyond the End of History* (London: Routledge, 1994).

1   THE POLITICAL AND ECONOMIC FRAMEWORK OF JAPAN'S FOREIGN POLICY

1. The historical continuity has been best described for the case of MITI by Chalmers Johnson in *MITI and the Japanese Miracle. The Growth of Industrial Policy, 1925–1975* (Stanford: Stanford University Press, 1982).
2. For an analysis of Japan's structural corruption see: Johnson, Chalmers, *Japan. Who Governs? The Rise of the Developmental State* (New York: W.W. Norton, 1995), 183–234.
3. Numata, Sadaaki, '*Britain and Japan in the world*', Speech delivered to the Cambridge Anglo-Japanese Society, 12 May 1995.
4. For an overview of the political changes see: Bridges, Brian, 'Japan: Hesitant superpower', *Conflict Studies 264* (London: Research Institute for the Study of Conflict and Terrorism, September 1993), p. 29.
5. Ozawa, Ichiro, *Blueprint for Building a New Japan* (Tokyo: Kodansha, 1993).
6. van Wolferen, Karel, *The Enigma of Japanese Power*, p. 11.
7. Okabe, Tatsumi, 'A proposal for lasting security in East Asia', *Japan Review of International Affairs*, vol. 6, no. 3 (Fall 1992), p. 236.
8. How much contact Diet members had with Americans was measured by asking how often they met normally with the Americans in the following six categories: politicians, diplomats, media representatives, businessmen, interest groups or lobbyists, and personal friends. 'High levels' was defined as meeting normally with Americans in four or more categories at least once a year.
9. *The Japan Times* (2 May 1992).
10. For a discussion of the bureaucracy see: Johnson, Chalmers, *Japan. Who Governs? The Rise of the Developmental State*, pp. 115–56.
11. Calder, Kent E. 'Japanese foreign economic policy formation: Explaining the reactive state', *World Politics*, no. 40 (July 1988), p. 533.
12. Kitschelt, Herbert, 'Industrial governance structures, innovation strategies, and the case of Japan: sectoral or cross-national comparative analysis?', *International Organization* (Autumn 1991), 453–93.
13. News from the Economic and Social Research Council, *Social Sciences*, Issue 13 (February 1992), p. 5.
14. These problems are implicitly acknowledged in a report of the MFA which makes recommendations to improve communications and relations with other ministries and agencies. '*Gaiko kyoka kondankai hokoku*' (Report by the Advisory Board on the strengthening of diplomacy) (Tokyo: Ministry of Foreign Affairs, 2 December 1991), p. 3.
15. Figures supplied by the Japanese Embassy, London.
16. *Far Eastern Economic Review* (18 July 1991).
17. *Asahi Shimbun* (1 July 1987).
18. The following relies on Tanaka, Akihiko, in: Funabashi, Yoichi (ed.), *Japan's security policy in the 1990s*, in: *Japan's International Agenda* (New York: New York University, 1994), p. 51.
19. '*Gaiko kyoka kondankai hokoku*' (Report by the Advisory Board on the strengthening of diplomacy), p. 9. Figures for 1995 from Japanese Embassy, London.
20. Example of the Consulate-General in Hong Kong in 1992: Of a total of 32

diplomats, ten were from other ministries: three from the Ministry of Finance, two from the Ministry of Justice, one from MITI, two from the Police Agency, one from the local bureaucracy of Gifu prefecture, one judge from the Supreme Court. Figures supplied by the Consulate-General.

21. Interview with an MFA official in 1987 (Tokyo).
22. UNCTC Report, *Financial Times* (29 July 1991).
23. Eli, Max, *Japan Inc. Global Strategies of Japanese Trading Corporations* (London: McGraw-Hill Book Company, 1990), p. 130.
24. Upham, Frank K., 'The man who would import: A cautionary tale about bucking the system in Japan', *The Journal of Japanese Studies*, vol. 17, no. 2 (Summer 1991), 323–44.
25. A major case was revealed in 1992 in the Nagoya area, *Financial Times* (12 July 1992). Another case of bribery on a national scale in the construction industry was reported in March 1993, *International Herald Tribune* (30 March 1993). In April 1995 the Fair Trade Commission imposed the unprecedented penalty of a total of ¥1.86bn (£13.9 million) on 373 construction companies, *Financial Times* (18 April 1995).
26. *Financial Times* (10 February 1994).
27. '*Flickwerk von Brokern und Bürokraten*' (Patch work of brokers and bureaucrats), *Die Zeit* (19 March 1993), 41–2.
28. *International Herald Tribune* (24 May 1994).
29. Inoguchi, Takashi, 'Japan's response to the Gulf crisis: An analytical overview', *The Journal of Japanese Studies*, vol. 17, no. 2 (Summer 1990), 257–74.
30. This conceptual framework has been developed by the author in: Chapman, J.W.M., Drifte, R. and Gow, I.T.M., *Japan's Quest for Comprehensive Security* (London: Frances Pinter, 1983), p. 89.
31. Royama Michio argues that this trust of the Japanese people in the world's peace-loving people even at that time was not very convincing because of events after 1945. Royama, Michio, ' *"Reisengo" jidai ni okeru Nihon no heiwashugi*' (Japan's pacifism during the 'Cold War'), in: Usui, Hisakazu and Uchida, Takeo, *Tagen teki kyosei to kokusai network* (Pluralism, coexistence, international network) (Tokyo: Yushindo, 1991), p. 119.
32. Royama, Michio, ' *"Reisengo" jidai ni okeru Nihon no heiwashugi*' (Japan's pacifism during the 'Cold War').
33. Soichiro Tawara quotes Miyazawa Kiichi in this way in: '*Soren wa kowai desuka*' (Are you afraid of the Soviet Union?), *Bungei Shunju* (March 1980).
34. Quoted in: Wakaizumi, Kei, 'Japan's dilemma: To act or not to act', *Foreign Policy*, vol. 16 (Fall 1974), p. 31.
35. Quoted in: Romana, Elpidio R. Sta., 'Security, politicians and the public in Japan', in: Kendall, Harry H. and Joewono, Clara (eds), *Japan, ASEAN, and the United States* (Berkeley: Institute of East Asian Studies, Univ. of Calif. at Berkeley, 1991), p. 72.
36. Haga, Yasushi, '*Yoshida fukaku, Ishibashi no kosoryoku*' (The personality of Yoshida, the conceptional ability of Ishibashi), *This Is* (September 1992).
37. *International Herald Tribune* (22 August 1989), quoting *Nihon Keizai Shimbun*.
38. *Euro-Asia Centre News*, no. 22 (1992), p. 4.
39. *The Japan Times* (26 May 1993).

40. *News & Views from Japan* (1 May 1995).
41. US Congress, Office of Technology Assessment, *Multinationals and the US technology base, OTA-ITE-612* (Washington, DC: US Government Printing Office, September 1994), p. 2.
42. Bergsten, Fred and Noland, Marcus, *Reconcilable Differences? United States–Japan Economic Conflict* (Washington, DC: Institute for International Economics, 1993), pp. 90–2.
43. *Financial Times* (24 February 1995).
44. Young, Ross A., *Silicon Sumo: US–Japan Competition and Industrial Policy in the Semiconductor Equipment Industry* (Austin: The IC2 Institute of the University of Texas, 1994).
45. *Financial Times* (10 March 1995).
46. *Financial Times* (9 January 1992).
47. *International Herald Tribune* (2 January 1992).
48. For a general overview see: Balassa, B. and Noland, Marcus, *Japan in the World Economy* (Washington, DC: Institute for International Economics, 1988).
49. The data in this paragraph is from *Japan 1995. An International Comparison* (Tokyo: Keizai Koho Center, 1994).
50. Kubota, Isao, 'Tokyo financial center in decline?', *Look Japan* (December 1994), p. 13.
51. *Financial Times* (2–3 October 1993).
52. *Financial Times* (1 March 1995).
53. US Congress, Office of Technology Assessment, *Multinationals and the US Technology Base, OTA-ITE-612*, p. 3.
54. US Congress, Office of Technology Assessment, *Multinationals and the US Technology Base, OTA-ITE-612*, p. 136.
55. See for example: Emmott, Bill, *The Sun also Sets. Why Japan will not be Number One* (London: Simon & Schuster, 1989).
56. *Financial Times* (21 January 1992).
57. *Financial Times* (7 June 1995).
58. *Financial Times* (30 March 1995 and 18 May 1995).
59. Kubota, Isao, 'Tokyo financial center in decline?', *Look Japan* (December 1994), p. 12; *Financial Times* (19 October 1994).
60. *Financial Times* (28 February 1995).
61. *Financial Times* (19 October 1994).
62. *Financial Times* (1 March 1995).
63. *International Herald Tribune* (2 June 1992).
64. *International Herald Tribune* (18 April 1995).
65. West, Joel, 'Building Japan's information superhighway', in: *Japan Policy Research Institute Working Papers*, no. 7 (February 1995).
66. *Financial Times* (4 April 1995).
67. Emmott, Bill, 'The economic sources of Japan's foreign policy', *Survival*, vol. 34, no. 2 (Summer 1992), pp. 51–2.
68. Yoon, Young-Kwan, 'The political economy of transition. Japanese foreign direct investments in the 1980s', *World Politics*, vol. 43, no. 1 (1991), p. 12.
69. Matsumoto, Koji, *The Rise of the Japanese Corporate System. The Inside View of a MITI Official* (London: Kegan Paul International, 1991), p. 276.

174   *Notes*

70. *Financial Times* (4 March 1992), quoting Hu Yao-su, in: *California Management Review* (Winter 1992).
71. US Congress, Office of Technology Assessment, *Multinationals and the US Technology Base, OTA-ITE-612*, p. iii.
72. Bergsten, Fred and Noland, Marcus, *Reconcilable Differences? United States–Japan Economic Conflict*, pp. 7–12.
73. *Global competition: The new reality*. Report of the President's Commission on industrial competitiveness, vol. II (Washington, DC: US Government Printing Office, 1985), p. 6, quoted in Jeffrey A. Hart, 'The effects of state-societal arrangements on international competitiveness: Steel, motor vehicles and semiconductors in the United States, Japan and Western Europe', *British Journal of Political Sciences*, vol. 22, Part 3 (July 1992), p. 252.
74. van Marion, Marcel F., *Liberal Trade and Japan. The Incompatibility Issue* (Heidelberg: Physica-Verlag, 1993), p. 57.
75. *The Economist* (6 March 1993).
76. *Asahi Evening News* (30 August 1993).
77. For a critical summary of the advantages of the *keiretsu* system for Japanese companies see: Young, Ross A., *Silicon Sumo: US–Japan Competition and Industrial Policy in the Semiconductor Equipment Industry*, p. 27.
78. For a detailed overview see Young, Ross A., *Silicon Sumo: US–Japan Competition and Industrial Policy in the Semiconductor Equipment Industry*, chapter 5.
79. For an interesting discussion of Japanese writing on cultural aspects of Japan's economic performance see: Pyle, Kenneth B., *The Japanese Question. Power and Purpose in a New Era* (Washington, 1992), 51–8.
80. For a list of such NTBs see: von Stechow, Andreas, '*Binnen- und außenwirtschaftliche Entwicklung Japans im Jahre 1993*' (Domestic and foreign economic development of Japan in 1993), pp. 223–4, in: Pohl, Manfred (ed.), *Japan 1993/94. Politik und Wirtschaft* (Japan 1993/94. Politics and economics) (Hamburg: Institut für Asienkunde, 1994), 163–80.
81. *Far Eastern Economic Review* (22 December 1994), p. 53; *Financial Times* (15 December 1994).
82. Hollerman, Leon, 'The headquarters nation', *The National Interest* (Fall 1991), 16–25.
83. Bergsten, Fred and Noland, Marcus, *Reconcilable Differences? United States–Japan Economic Conflict*, p. 7.
84. For the neomercantilism interpretation see: Nester, William R., *The Foundation of Japanese Power. Continuities, Changes, Challenges* (London: Macmillan, 1990).
85. Johnson, Chalmers, 'Comparative capitalism: The Japanese difference', *California Management Review*, vol. 35, no. 4 (Summer 1993), 56–63.
86. *International Herald Tribune* (23 December 1992). See also: the report by the Tokyo Chamber of Commerce and Industry in 1993 which defends the *keiretsu* system while admitting some exclusive characteristics. *Japan Times* (9 April 1993).
87. Ushio, Jiro and Noguchi, Yukio, 'Reforming Japan's "war-footing" economic system', *Japan Echo*, vol. XXI, no. 2 (Summer 1994), 13–18.
88. *Financial Times* (22 May 1995).

89. 'Japan 2000', quoted in: *Far Eastern Economic Review* (27 June 1991), p. 15.
90. Johnson, Chalmers, 'Comparative capitalism: The Japanese difference', pp. 54–5.
91. Johnson, Chalmers, 'Comparative capitalism: The Japanese difference', pp. 52–3.
92. Fallows, James M., 'The myth of convergence. Acknowledging differences between Japan and the US', *Speaking of Japan* (December 1989), 1–5. See also conclusions of: Holstein, William J., *The Japanese Power: What it Means for America* (New York: Charles Scribner's Sons, 1990).
93. Friedman, George and Lebard, Meredith, *The Coming War with Japan* (New York: St Martin's Press, 1991).
94. Denman, Roy, 'Now read the rules to Japan', *International Herald Tribune* (17 June 1993).
95. Fodella, Gianni, 'Can Europe compete with Japan?', *Japan Forum*, vol. 4, no. 1 (1992), p. 12.
96. 'Keidanren's slogan for the year: Kyosei – economic symbiosis', *News & Views from Japan* (30 November 1992), pp. 3–4.
97. Interview with Hiraiwa Gaishi in: *Japan Echo*, vol. xx, no. 2 (Summer 1993), 55–9.
98. Morita, Akio, 'A critical moment for Japanese management', *Japan Echo*, xix, no. 2 (Summer 1992), 8–14, translated from *Bungei Shunju* (February 1992).
99. Quoted in: Johnson, Chalmers, 'Comparative Capitalism: The Japanese Difference', p. 58.
100. Ibid.
101. Nye, Joseph, 'Coping with Japan', *Foreign Policy*, no. 89 (Winter 1992–93), p. 102.
102. *International Herald Tribune* (2–3 June 1990).
103. *International Herald Tribune* (11 May 1990).
104. Bergsten, Fred and Noland, Marcus, *Reconcilable Differences? United States–Japan Economic Conflict*, p. 99.

2 THE INTERNATIONAL ENVIRONMENT AND JAPAN'S HARD POWER

1. The most representative work for this approach is: Friedman, George, and Meredith Lebard, *The Coming War with Japan* (New York: St Martin's Press, 1991).
2. For a very critical appraisal of this Soviet myopia see: Aliev, R. Sh., 'Polemic notes of a Japanese affairs specialist', *Far Eastern Affairs*, no. 3 (1989), 122–33.
3. Betts, Richard K., 'Wealth, power, and instability. East Asia and the United States after the cold war', *International Security*, vol. 18, no. 3 (Winter 1993–94), p. 43.
4. Akaha, Tsuneo, 'Japan's security agenda in the post-cold war era', *The Pacific Review*, vol. 8, no. 1 (1995), p. 50.
5. See Tanaka, Akihiko, 'Two faces of East Asian security and Japan's policy' in: *Proceedings of 'Korean Peninsula Trends and US–Japan–South Korea*

Relations' (Washington, DC: The Center for Strategic and International Studies, April 1994), pp. 92–3.

6. For an evaluation of this review in Japan see: Akaha, Tsuneo, 'Japan's security agenda in the post-cold war era', pp. 48–9.

7. *International Herald Tribune* (22 June 1990).

8. '*Sogo anzen hosho seisaku taiko*' (Outline for a comprehensive security policy), *Yomiuri Shimbun* (3 May 1995). *Asahi Shimbun* (3 May 1995), 13–15.

9. *The Modality of the Security and Defense Capability of Japan. The Outlook for the 21st Century* (Advisory Group on Defense Issues, 12 August 1994). Copy of the Japanese and English version of the report received from Professor Watanabe Akio, a member of the group.

10. *East Asia Strategy Report* (Washington, DC: US Department of Defense, Office of International Security Affairs, 1 March 1995).

11. *Far Eastern Economic Review* (13 April 1995), p. 25.

12. See for an excellent presentation of China's foreign and security policy and outlook: Shambaugh, David, 'Growing strong: China's challenge to Asian security', *Survival*, vol. 36, no. 2 (Summer 1994), 43–59.

13. Cossa, Ralph, *The Japan–US Alliance and Security Regimes in East Asia. A Workshop Report* (Tokyo and Alexandria VA: The Institute for International Policy Studies and the Center for Naval Analyses, January 1995).

14. On human rights see: Satoh, Yukio, *Motomerareru Nihon no hassotenkan* (A change in Japan's thinking is needed), *Gaiko Forum* (January 1993), 26–35.

15. Satoh, Yukio, *Motomerareru Nihon no hassotenkan* (A change in Japan's thinking is needed), p. 9.

16. *Mainichi Shimbun* (19 June 1981); Wolf, Jim, 'COCOM adopts new guidelines for China', *Jane's Defence Weekly* (10 May 1986), 842–3.

17. Kanayama, Hisahiro, *The Marketization of China and Japan's Response: Prospects for the Future. Policy Paper 115E* (Tokyo: Institute for International Policy Studies, November 1993), p. 28.

18. Takagi, Seiichiro, 'Human rights in Japanese foreign policy: Japan's policy towards China after Tiananmen', in: Tang, James T.H. (ed.), *Human Rights and International Relations in the Asia Pacific* (London/New York: Pinter, 1995), 97–111. For an official explanation of Japan's motives see: Tanino, Sakutaro, 'The recent situation in China and Sino-Japanese relations', *Japan Review of International Affairs*, vol. 4, no. 1 (Spring/Summer 1990), 20–41.

19. *The Independent* (22 January 1993); *International Herald Tribune* (6 April 1993); *Far Eastern Economic Review* (18 February 1993).

20. *Korea Times* (18 April 1994).

21. See the concern about the Chinese armament programme in: Funabashi, Yoichi, *Fuan yobu Chu-Ro 'Heiki kyosei'* (Anxiety causing Chinese–Russian 'Armament symbiosis'), *Asahi Shimbun* (1 July 1992).

22. *International Herald Tribune* (12 July 1994). For a good overview of various critical writings in Japan on China's security challenge see: Brown, Eugene, 'Japan's security policy in the post-Cold War world: Threat perceptions and strategic options', *The Journal of East Asian Affairs*, vol. viii, no. 2 (Summer/Fall 1994), 337–40.

23. *Far Eastern Economic Review* (14 April 1995), p. 25.

24. *Japan Times* (8 September 1992).

25. *Financial Times* (27 May 1993 and 1 June 1993).

26. *Financial Times* (11 January 1994).
27. *International Herald Tribune* (19 June 1992).
28. *International Herald Tribune* (4 April 1995); *Far Eastern Economic Review* (13 April 1995), p. 32.
29. *Japan Times* (28 March 1991).
30. *Financial Times* (7 October 1993; 5–6 March 1994 and 23 December 1994).
31. *International Herald Tribune* and *Financial Times* (23 May 1995).
32. *Korea Times* (10 December 1993).
33. *Asahi Shimbun* (20 February 1995).
34. Mason, T. David, 'Japan's future relations with China', in: *Japan, NAFTA and Europe, Trilateral Cooperation or Confrontation?* (London: Macmillan, 1994), p. 207.
35. Brown, Eugene, 'Japan's security policy in the post-Cold War world: Threat perceptions and strategic options', p. 334.
36. Zagorsky, Alexei, 'The post-cold war security agenda of Russia: implications for Northeast Asia', *The Pacific Review*, vol. 8, no. 1 (1995), 94–5.
37. *Korea Times* (20 February 1994).
38. 'NATO/Japan Security Conference', Report in *NATO Internet Public Data Service* (17 February 1995).
39. For the role of Russian nationalism see: Drifte, Reinhard and Zinberg, Yakov, 'Chaos in Russia and the territorial dispute with Japan', *The Pacific Review*, vol. 6, no. 3 (1993), 277–84.
40. Mekhov, Major-General Georgiy, 'Military aspects of the "Territorial Problem"', *Red Star* (22 July 1992). Summarized and commented by Prof. G. Jukes in an unpublished paper (7 August 1992).
41. Zagorsky, Alexei, 'The post-cold war security agenda of Russia: implications for Northeast Asia', *The Pacific Review*, vol. 8, no. 1 (1995), p. 83.
42. *International Herald Tribune* (31 July 1991).
43. *Looking Ahead. A Foreign Policy for a Changing World* (Tokyo: Ministry of Foreign Affairs, July 1993), p. 38.
44. For some examples of Soviet disregard see: Rozman, Gilbert, *Japan's Response to the Gorbachev Era, 1985–1991. A Rising Superpower Views a Declining One* (Princeton: Princeton University Press, 1992), p. 254. For a frank Soviet admission of its disregard of Japan see: Aliev, R. Sh., 'Polemic notes of a "Japanese affairs specialist"', *Far Eastern Affairs*, 122–33.
45. Kimura, Hiroshi, 'Yeltsin's visit and the outlook for Japanese–Russian relations', *Journal of Northeast Asian Studies*, vol. xiii, no. 2 (Summer 1994), p. 50.
46. *Pacific Research* (May 1990), p. 20, and (August 1990), p. 13.
47. *Japan Times* (18 June 1992).
48. *Korea Times* (25 February 1993).
49. For an up-to-date account see: Kim, Hong Nack, 'Japan's North Korea policy in the post-Cold War era', *Korea and World Affairs*, vol. 18, no. 4 (Winter 1994), 669–94.
50. *Korea Times* (25 September 1994).
51. *International Herald Tribune* (14–15 May 1994).
52. *Korea Herald* (8 November 1994).
53. *Wall Street Journal* (17 January 1995), as reported in 'Daily Report', *Nautilus Institute* (17 January 1995).

54. *International Herald Tribune* (29 January 1992).
55. *International Herald Tribune* (9 December 1993), quoting *Yomiuri Shimbun*.
56. Some of these points are proposed by Satoh, Yukio in: *Looking Ahead. A Foreign Policy for a Changing World* (Tokyo: Ministry of Foreign Affairs, July 1993), p. 38.
57. *Far Eastern Economic Review* (27 September 1988), p. 27.
58. For the most recent policy statement see: *East Asia Strategy Report* (US Department of Defense, March 1995).
59. *The Daily Yomiuri* (20 March 1990). A similar statement was made in October 1991 relating to Germany when General Robert Oakes, the commander of US Air Forces in Europe, with headquarters in Ramstein, said: 'I have had Germans tell me Germans are better people with Americans around'. *International Herald Tribune* (22 October 1991).
60. *International Herald Tribune* (25 May 1992).
61. *East Asia Strategy Report* (US Department of Defense, March 1995).
62. *Japan Times* (3 January 1983).
63. *Jane's Defence Weekly* (15 January 1994), p. 4; *Washington Times* (10 June 1994); *Asahi Shimbun* (21 February 1995); *Stars and Stripes* (11 March 1994) and *New York Times* (1 June 1994).
64. *Washington Times* (13 January 1995). .
65. Drifte, Reinhard, *Arms Production in Japan. The Military Applications of Civilian Technology* (Boulder Colorado: Westview Press, 1986), 79–87.
66. *Critical Technologies Plan* (Washington, DC: US Department of Defense, March 1990).
67. *Energizing Technologies: A Survey of Technical and Economic Opportunities* (Washington, DC: US Department of Commerce, Technology Administration, Spring 1990).
68. *International Herald Tribune* (18 April 1995).
69. According to a Business–Harris poll in 1989, 68 per cent of Americans viewed the 'economic threat from Japan' as a more serious threat to the US than the Soviet military threat, *International Herald Tribune* (13 October 1989). For more recent examples see: Akaha, Tsuneo, 'Japan's security agenda in the post-cold war era', p. 54.
70. Akaha, Tsuneo, 'Japan's security agenda in the post-cold war era', p. 90.
71. *Looking ahead. A Foreign Policy for a Changing World* (Tokyo: Ministry of Foreign Affairs, July 1993), p. 47.
72. Text of the agreements in: Drifte, Reinhard, *Arms Production in Japan. The Military Applications of Civilian Technology*, Appendix A and B.
73. *Far East Economic Review* (14 October 1993).
74. 'Japan's defense under a new world order', *Liberal Star*, vol. 21, no. 242 (May–June 1992), p. 5.
75. Cossa, Ralph, *The Japan–US Alliance and Security Regimes in East Asia. A Workshop Report*, p. 14.
76. All figures from *The Military Balance 1994–1995* (London: The International Institute for Strategic Studies, 1994).
77. Friedman, David B. and Samuels, Richard J., *How to Succeed Without Really Flying: The Japanese Aircraft Industry and Japan's Technology Ideology* (Cambridge: Center for International Studies, Massachusetts Institute of Technology, 1992), p. 4. On these points see also: Chinworth, Michael W.,

Strategic Technology Management in Japan: Commercial–Military Comparisons (Cambridge: Center for International Studies, Massachusetts Institute of Technology, 1989).

78. Tanaka, Akihiko, in: Funabashi, Yoichi (ed.), *Japan's Security Policy in the 1990s,* in: *Japan's International Agenda* (New York, 1994), p. 45.

79. Chinworth, Michael W., *Industry and Government in Japanese Defense Procurement: The Case of the Patriot Missile System* (Cambridge: Center for International Studies, Massachusetts Institute of Technology, 1989), pp. 3–4.

80. Keohane, Robert O. and Nye, Joseph S., *Power and Interdependence,* p. 228.

81. Owada, Hisashi, 'Japan's post Gulf international initiatives' (Ministry of Foreign Affairs, August 1991), p. 12.

82. Speech by Ambassador Kobayashi, 'Mission of Japan to the European Communities', Brussels, 11 May 1993, in: *News & Views from Japan* (31 May 1993), p. 3.

83. For a comprehensive account see: Drifte, Reinhard, *Japan's Rise to International Responsibilities. The Case of Arms Control* (London: Athlone Press, 1990).

84. *International Herald Tribune* (22 December 1994); Takamatsu, Akira, 'A call for nuclear disarmament', *Look Japan* (April 1995), p. 3.

85. Drifte, Reinhard, *China and the NPT,* in Goldblat, Joseph (ed.), *Non-Proliferation: The Why and the Wherefore* (London and Philadelphia: Taylor & Francis, 1985), pp. 45–55.

86. *The Nikkei Weekly* (5 September 1994 and 5 December 1994).

87. Kerr, Pauline, 'The security dialogue in the Asia Pacific', *The Pacific Review,* vol. 7, no. 4 (1994), 397–410.

88. Satoh, Yukio, *Gaiko Foramu* (January 1994), 14–15.

89. Ibid.

90. *Asahi Shimbun* (23 June 1992).

91. *Far Eastern Economic Review* (14 January 1993), p. 12.

92. Interview with Satoh Yukio, *International Herald Tribune* (30 March 1993).

93. *Japan Times* (23 October 1992).

94. Satoh, Yukio, *Looking Ahead. A Foreign Policy for a Changing World,* p. 43.

95. Statement by Parliamentary Vice Minister for Foreign Affairs, Hirata Yoneo, at the 2nd UN Hiroshima Conference on Disarmament Issues (24 May 1994).

96. *Asahi Shimbun* (13 March 1995).

97. Drifte, Reinhard, *Japan's Rise to International Responsibilities: The Case of Arms Control,* chapter 4.

98. 'Europe and Japan: The next steps', Communication of the Commission to the Council (1995).

99. 'NATO/Japan Security Conference', Report in *NATO Internet Public Data Service* (17 February 1995).

100. *International Herald Tribune* (20 June 1990).

101. Morimoto, Satoshi, '*Oshu anzen hosho no hirogari to Nihon*' (The broadening of Europe's security and Japan), *Asahi Shimbun* (8 June 1992).

102. *International Herald Tribune* (25 April 1995).

103. Katzenstein, Peter J. and Okawara, Nobuo, *Japan's National Security. Structures, Norms and Policy Responses in a Changing World* (Ithaca: East Asia Program, Cornell University, 1993), p. 2.

104. Hanami, Andrew K., 'Japan and the military balance of power in Northeast

Asia', *The Journal of East Asian Affairs*, vol. viii, no. 2 (Summer/Fall 1994), 363–95.

3 THE USE OF SOFT POWER IN JAPAN'S FOREIGN RELATIONS

1. Kono, Yohei, '*Nihon gaiko no shinro*' (A path for the future of Japan's foreign policy), *Gaiko Foramu* (January 1995), p. 13.
2. Okita, Saburo, 'Japan: Better to spend these billions on aid than on arms', *International Herald Tribune* (17 April 1991).
3. *Financial Times* (21 August 1991).
4. Quoted in: Pyle, Kenneth B., 'Can Japan lead the international system?', in: *Japan, NAFTA and Europe, Trilateral Cooperation or Confrontation?* (London: Macmillan, 1994), p. 236.
5. *International Herald Tribune* (12 April 1994).
6. *Financial Times* (17 July 1991).
7. *International Herald Tribune* (9–10 May 1992); *Asahi Shimbun* (8 May 1992).
8. For a translation of the Report see: *The Japan Times* (10 June and 11 June 1992).
9. *The Japan Times* (15 May 1992).
10. *Financial Times* (12 May 1993).
11. *Financial Times* (30–31 January 1993).
12. *Financial Times* (3 May 1995).
13. *Financial Times* (10 July 1992).
14. For a very up-to-date background on the issue see: Francks, Penny, 'The origins of agricultural protection in Japan', *Nissan Occasional Papers Series no. 22* (Oxford: Nissan Institute of Japanese Studies, 1995).
15. For background on these issues see: Moore, Richard H., *Japanese Agriculture. Patterns of Rural Development* (Boulder: Westview Press, 1988).
16. *The Nikkei Weekly* (24 October 1994).
17. *Mainichi Daily News* (9 December 1990); *Financial Times* (6 and 19 December 1990); *The Daily Yomiuri* (12 December 1988).
18. For an official and thus more charitable view of Japan's contribution by one of the Japanese participants see: Asakai, Kazuo, '*Uruguai raundo to wa na datta no ka?*' (What was the Uruguay Round?), *Gaiko Foramu* (April 1995), 44–7.
19. Helleiner, Eric, 'States and the future of global finance', *Review of International Studies*, 18 (1992), 31–49.
20. This is also confirmed by others, for example, *Far Eastern Economic Review* (29 September 1988), p. 25.
21. *International Herald Tribune* (20 September 1991).
22. Interview with a European banker of a major British bank (18 May 1995).
23. Reszat, Beate, '*Währungsentwicklung und Währungspolitik in Japan*' (Currency developments and currency policies in Japan), in Pohl, Manfred (ed), *Japan 1993/94. Politik und Wirtschaft* (Hamburg: Institut für Asienkunde, 1994), 237–57.
24. *International Herald Tribune* (17 May 1995).
25. *International Herald Tribune* (23 March 1992).

26. Young, Ross A., *Silicon Sumo: US-Japan Competition and Industrial Policy in the Semiconductor Equipment Industry*, p. 26.
27. Graham, Edward M. and Krugman, Paul R., *Foreign Direct Investment in the United States* (Washington, DC: Institute for International Economics, 1991), p. 24. The following account relies heavily on this book.
28. *International Herald Tribune* (17 May 1995).
29. *Financial Times* (17 May 1994).
30. *Financial Times* (27 April 1995).
31. Figures from Bank of England, interview (19 May 1995).
32. Naruse, Tomonori, *Britain and the New Europe: Working with Japan. Japanese finance: The European dimension*, speech given in November 1991.
33. *Far Eastern Economic Review* (15 June 1995).
34. *Financial Times* (6 May 1994).
35. *Financial Times* (14–15 May 1994).
36. News Release, Export–Import Bank of Japan (Tokyo, 11 November 1993).
37. News Release, Export–Import Bank of Japan (Tokyo, 9 April 1993).
38. Office of Science and Technology, *Collaboration into the 21st Century. The UK/Japan Relationship* (London: Office of Science and Technology, 1994), p. 12.
39. Radice, Giles, 'Labor Party wants Japan's business', *Japan Times* (19 December 1990).
40. Keizai Koho Center, *Japan 1995. An International Comparison*.
41. US Congress, Office of Technology Assessment, *Multinationals and the US Technology Base, OTA-ITE-612*, p. 102.
42. Figures for Fiscal Year 1994/95 from *International Herald Tribune* (17 May 1995).
43. *Financial Times* (21 Decembr 1992).
44. *Financial Times* (28 May 1993).
45. Jomo, K.S., *Japan and Malaysian Development. In the Shadow of the Rising Sun* (London: Routledge, 1994), pp. 34–5.
46. Jomo, K.S., *Japan and Malaysian Development. In the Shadow of the Rising Sun*, pp. 127–53.
47. Nomura Research Institute, *A Return to a Trade Surplus? The Impact of Japanese Investment on the UK* (London: Nomura Research Institute, 1989), p. 3.
48. van Marion, Marcel, *Liberal Trade and Japan. The Incompatibility Issue*, chapter viii in particular deals with colour television.
49. US Congress, Office of Technology Assessment, *Multinationals and the US Technology Base, OTA-ITE-612*, p. 2.
50. US Congress, Office of Technology Assessment, *Multinationals and the US Technology Base, OTA-ITE-612*, p. 88.
51. US Congress, Office of Technology Assessment, *Multinationals and the US Technology Base, OTA-ITE-612*, p. 152.
52. Holstein, William J., *The Japanese Power: What it Means for America* (New York: Charles Scribner's Sons, 1990), p. 211.
53. Hollerman, Leon, 'The headquarters nation', *The National Interest* (Fall 1991), 16–25.
54. Munday, Max, *Japanese Manufacturing Investment in Wales* (Cardiff: University of Wales Press, 1990), p. 115.

55. *Financial Times* (28 February 1995).
56. Moran, Theodore H., 'Foreign acquisition of critical US industries: Where should the US draw the line?', *The Washington Quarterly*, vol. 16, no. 2 (Spring 1993), 61–71.
57. Moran, Theodore H., 'Foreign acquisition of critical US industries: Where should the US draw the line?', p. 64.
58. Young, Ross A., *Silicon Sumo: US–Japan Competition and Industrial Policy in the Semiconductor Equipment Industry*, p. 15.
59. Young, Ross A., *Silicon Sumo: US–Japan Competition and Industrial Policy in the Semiconductor Equipment Industry*, p. 19.
60. Ibid.
61. Graham, Edward M. and Krugman, Paul R., *Foreign Direct Investment in the United States*, chapter 5.
62. For a presentation of various opinions on the dependence of the American military on Japanese high technology see: Murayama, Yuzo, *High-tech Weapons, Dual-use Technology and Strategic Alliance* (Cambridge: Center for International Studies, Massachusetts Institute of Technology, 1992).
63. The focus is more on civilian industry, as for example in: Seitz, K., *Die japanisch–amerikanische Herausforderung* (The Japanese–American challenge) (Bonn: Bonn Aktuell, 1990).
64. Yoda, Naoya, 'Technological innovation and globalization: Technonationalism and Japanese management', *TBR Intelligence*, vol. 3, no. 1 (1990), p. 25.
65. Graham, Edward M. and Krugman, Paul R., *Foreign Direct Investment in the United States*, p. 34.
66. Gerlach, Michael L., 'Twilight of the *Keiretsu*? A critical assessment', *The Journal of Japanese Studies*, vol. 18, no. 1 (Winter 1992), 79–118. See also: Milsome, Sue, *The Impact of Japanese Firms on Working and Employment Practices* (London: Employment Department, March 1993).
67. *Financial Times* (1 September 1992).
68. *Financial Times* (6 and 7–8 September 1991).
69. For an interesting evaluation of Japanese labour transfer processes in different countries see: Elger, Tony and Smith, Chris (eds), *Global Japanization? The Transnational Transformation of the Labour Process* (London: Routledge, 1994).
70. Garrahan, Philip and Stewart, Paul, *The Nissan Enigma. Flexibility at Work in a Local Economy* (London: Mansell, 1992), p. 116.
71. Garrahan, Philip and Stewart, Paul, *The Nissan Enigma. Flexibility at Work in a Local Economy*, p. 139.
72. Milsome, Sue, *The Impact of Japanese Firms on Working and Employment Practices*, pp. 116–7.
73. *International Herald Tribune* (23 December 1992).
74. In 1991 there was a dispute between Japan and the US over the inclusion of debt write-offs for a military loan in the overall ODA figure. Thanks to its insistence the US became again number one aid donor in 1990 because $1.3 billion of a written-off loan to Egypt for arms was included in the American aid figure. Since then Japan has been again number one aid donor without interruption. *Financial Times* (1 October 1991).
75. *Financial Times* (31 May 1995).
76. Hirabayashi, Hiroshi, '*Atarashii jidai no waga kuni no seifu kaihatsu enjo*

o motomete' (Call for governmental development aid in a new era), *Gaiko Foramu* (February 1995), p. 7.

77. See for example the series entitled *'Enjo taikoku Nihon'* (Japan as a development aid big power), *Asahi Shimbun* (starting 15 May 1992).

78. Nuscheler, Franz, *'Japan als "aid leader": Neue Entwicklungen in der japanischen Entwicklungspolitik'* (Japan as 'aid leader': New developments in Japanese development policies), in: Pohl, Manfred (ed.), *Japan 1993/94. Politik und Wirtschaft*, p. 165.

79. *News & Views from Japan* (29 June 1987).

80. Ministry of Foreign Affairs, *Looking ahead. A Foreign Policy for a Changing World* (Tokyo: Ministry of Foreign Affairs, July 1993), p. 5.

81. *The Japan Times* (7 November 1994).

82. Results of public opinion survey on diplomacy (Tokyo: Prime Minister's Office, 1994).

83. *Japan's Aid and the Developing Countries. Papers of the 1994 London Conference* (London: Overseas Development Institute, 1994), p. 12.

84. *Far Eastern Economic Review* (26 January 1995), p. 25.

85. *Financial Times* (18 April 1995). Figures based on Ministry of Finance, Tokyo.

86. *The Future of China in the Context of Asian Security, Policy Recommendations by the Japan Forum on International Relations* (Tokyo: Japan Forum on International Relations, January 1995), pp. 23–5.

87. *Financial Times* (3 May 1995).

88. *Le Monde* (2 April 1994).

89. *Nihon Keizai Shimbun* (13 November 1992).

90. *International Herald Tribune* (9 March 1992); *The Nikkei Weekly* (21 March 1992).

91. Speech by Fujii Hiroaki, ambassador to the UK, at a seminar organized by the British–Japanese Parliamentary Group (23 November 1994).

92. *Nikkei Weekly* (28 March 1992).

93. *Financial Times* (13 July 1992).

94. For a full text of the ODA Charter see: *News & Views from Japan* (29 June 1992).

95. *The Japan Times* (28 June 1992).

96. *The Daily Yomiuri* (5 January 1995); *Financial Times* (9 September 1994); *Financial Times* (28 March 1995).

97. *Financial Times* (17 January 1995).

98. For an official presentation see: Hanabusa, Masamichi, 'A Japanese perspective on aid and development', in Islam, Shafiqul, *Yen for Development. Japanese Foreign Aid and the Politics of Burden-Sharing* (New York: Council on Foreign Relations, 1991), pp. 88–104.

99. Islam, Shafiqul, *Yen for Development. Japanese Foreign Aid and the Politics of Burden-Sharing*, pp. 46–7.

100. Nuscheler, Franz, *'Japan als "aid leader": Neue Entwicklungen in der japanischen Entwicklungspolitik'* (Japan as 'aid leader': New developments in Japanese aid policies), pp. 172–3.

101. See, for example: *Keidanren Review on Japanese Economy* (April 1995), 13–18.

102. Kevenhörster, Paul, *'Japan als internationaler Akteur: das Instrument der multilateralen Entwicklungshilfe'* (Japan as international actor: the instrument

of multilateral development aid), in: Hummel, Hartwig and Drifte, Reinhard (eds), *Pax Nipponica? Die Japanisierung der Welt 50 Jahre nach dem Untergang des Japanischen Reichs* (Pax Nipponica? The Japanization of the world 50 years after the downfall of the Japanese imperium) (Bad Boll: Evangelische Akademie Bad Boll, 1995), p. 76.

103. Clifford, Bill, 'Japan presses World Bank on lending', *The Nikkei Weekly* (21 March 1992).

104. 'Implications of the World Bank's focus on structural adjustment', carried on the *Internet IPE List* (6 March 1995). The following quote and summary is from this document.

105. *Far Eastern Economic Review* (12 March 1992), p. 42.

106. *Korea Times* (11 December 1991).

107. *The East Asian Miracle. Economic Growth and Public Policy. A World Bank Policy Research Report* (Oxford: Oxford University Press, 1993). For a summary and discussion of the Report see: *Financial Times* (26 April 1993) and *Far Eastern Economic Review* (22 July 1993), pp. 79–80.

108. Terry, Edith, 'How Asia got rich: World Bank vs. Japanese industrial policy', *Japan Policy Research Institute Working Paper no. 10* (June 1995).

109. Nishimura, Kunio, 'The government's role in development', *Look Japan* (April 1995), 11–13.

110. For further details see: Terry, Edith, 'How Asia got rich: World Bank vs. Japanese industrial policy'.

111. Kevenhörster, Paul, '*Japan als internationaler Akteur: das Instrument der multilateralen Entwicklungshilfe*' (Japan as international actor: the instrument of multilateral development aid), p. 76.

112. Hirabayashi, Hiroshi, *Atarashii jidai no waga kuni no seifu kaihatsu enjo o motomete* (Call for governmental development aid in a new era), *Gaiko Foramu* (February 1995), p. 16.

113. Rix, Alan, *Japan's Foreign Aid Challenge. Policy Reform and Aid Leadership* (London: Routledge, 1993).

114. Weidner, Helmut, '*Japans globale Umweltpolitik: Merkmale und Perspektiven*' (Japan's global environmental policy: Characteristics and perspectives), in: Hummel, Hartwig and Drifte, Reinhard (eds), *Pax Nipponica? Die Japanisierung der Welt 50 Jahre nach dem Untergang des Japanischen Reichs* (Pax Nipponica? The Japanization of the world 50 years after the downfall of the Japanese imperium), 46–61.

115. *Basic facts on Japan's ODA* (Tokyo: Ministry of Foreign Affairs, July 1993).

116. Jomo, K.S., *Japan and Malaysian Development. In the Shadow of the Rising Sun*, p. 183.

117. Weidner, Helmut, '*Japans globale Umweltpolitik: Merkmale und Perspektiven*' (Japan's global environmental policy: Characteristics and perspectives), pp. 59–60.

118. *Far Eastern Economic Review* (26 January 1995), p. 26.

119. 'China, Japan agree to sign bilateral environment protection treaty', *BNA International Environment Daily* (20 December 1993). It was admitted by China for the first time in bilateral talks in April 1992. *Japan Times* (19 April 1992).

120. Maddock, Rowland T., 'Japan and global environmental leadership', *Journal of Northeast Asian Studies*, vol. xiii, no. 4 (Winter 1994), 21–36. Maull,

Hanns, 'Japan's global environmental policies', *The Pacific Review*, vol. 4, no. 3 (1991), 254–62.

121. See: Yasutomo, Dennis, *Japan and the Asian Development Bank* (New York: Praeger Special Studies, 1983).
122. *International Herald Tribune* (5 May 1993); *Korea Times* (9 May 1993).
123. *The Japan Times* (7 May 1992).
124. *Far Eastern Economic Review* (20 May 1993).
125. *Financial Times* (12 April 1995).
126. See, for example: *Financial Times* (7 February 1995); Terry, Edith, 'How Asia got rich: World Bank vs. Japanese industrial policy', *Japan Policy Research Institute Working Paper no. 10* (June 1995).
127. Hirabayashi, Hiroshi, '*Atarashii jidai no waga kuni no seifu kaihatsu enjo o motomete*' (Call for governmental development aid in a new era), p. 14. See also interview with the Indonesian ambassador to Japan, Peodji Koentarso, in the same issue of *Gaiko Foramu* on this subject.
128. *Japan's Aid and the Developing Countries. Papers of the 1994 London Conference* (London: Overseas Development Institute, 1994), p. 21.
129. Johnson, Chalmers, *MITI and the Japanese Miracle: The Growth of Industrial Policy, 1925–1975*.
130. *Japan's Aid and the Developing Countries. Papers of the 1994 London Conference* (London: Overseas Development Institute, 1994), p. 1.
131. Lincoln, Edward J., *Japan's New Global Role* (Washington, DC: The Brookings Institution, 1993), pp. 216–19.
132. Examples taken from Lee, Poh-Ping, in: Garby, Craig C. and Brown Bullock, Mary (eds), 'Japan and the Asia-Pacific region: A Southeast Asian perspective', in: *Japan. A new kind of superpower?* (Washington, DC: The Woodrow Wilson Center Press/The Johns Hopkins University Press, 1994), p. 134.
133. For the background and development of this policy see: Jomo, K.S., *Japan and Malaysian Development. In the Shadow of the Rising Sun*, pp. 3–10.
134. *Far Eastern Economic Review* (8 September 1994).
135. See: Chapman, J.W.M., Drifte, R., Gow, I.T.M., *Japan's Quest for Comprehensive Security* (London: Frances Pinter, 1983).
136. Yanagihara/Emig, in: Islam, Shafiqul, *Yen for Development. Japanese Foreign Aid and the Politics of Burden-Sharing*, p. 61.
137. For a purely economic appraisal of Japanese aid to the Philippines see: Pante, Filologo and Ryes, Romeo A., 'Japanese and US aid to the Philippines: A recipient-country perspective', in Islam, Shafiqul, *Yen for Development. Japanese Foreign Aid and the Politics of Burden-Sharing*, pp. 121–36.
138. *Daily Yomiuri Shimbun* (28 March 1991).
139. For a full text of the ODA Charter see: *News & Views from Japan* (29 June 1992).
140. Interview with a Japanese diplomat who had been involved in ODA (8 April 1991).
141. See, for example, a Ministry of Foreign Affairs-commissioned study on *Military Expenditure of Developing Countries and Aid Policy*, prepared for the Ministry of Foreign Affairs, by the International Development Center of Japan (March 1992).
142. Hirabayashi, Hiroshi, '*Atarashii jidai no waga kuni no seifu kaihatsu enjo*

o motomete' (Call for governmental development aid in a new era), p. 9.
Full text of the Guidelines of the Government Development Aid in: *Gaiko Foramu* (March 1993), p. 8.

143. Ministry of Foreign Affairs, *ODA Hakusho* (ODA White Paper) (1994), pp. 59–62.

144. Yasutomo, Dennis, *The Manner of Giving Strategic Aid and Japanese Foreign Policy* (Lexington: Lexington Books, 1986), p. 100.

145. Hanabusa, in: Islam, Shafiqul, *Yen for Development. Japanese Foreign Aid and the Politics of Burden-Sharing*, p. 98; Takagi, Seiichiro, 'Human rights in Japanese foreign policy: Japan's policy towards China after Tiananmen', in: Tang, James T. H. (ed.), *Human Rights and International Relations in the Asia Pacific* (London/New York: Pinter, 1995), 97–111.

146. On Iran see: *Korea Herald* (17 February 1995).

147. *The Japan Times* (8 October 1994); *Financial Times* (19 October 1994).

148. *The Nikkei Weekly* (7 November 1994); *Financial Times* (16 January 1995).

149. *Far Eastern Economic Review* (14 May 1992), pp. 17–18.

150. Hirabayashi, Hiroshi, *'Atarashii jidai no waga kuni no seifu kaihatsu enjo o motomete'* (Call for governmental development aid in a new era), pp. 9–10.

151. Deputy Prime Minister and Minister for Foreign Affairs, Kono Yohei, *A Path for the Future of Japan's Foreign Policy* (February 1995); see also the overview of the Japanese discussion about the issue in: Tanaka, Akihiko, 'Two faces of East Asian security and Japan's policy', in: *Proceedings of 'Korean Peninsula Trends and US–Japan–South Korea Relations'* (Washington, DC: The Center for Strategic and International Studies, April 1994), pp. 95–7.

152. *Far Eastern Economic Review* 11 July 1991, pp. 39–41; see also: Arase, David, 'Japanese policy toward democracy and human rights in Asia', *Asian Survey*, vol. xxxiii, no. 10 (October 1993), p. 946.

153. *Financial Times* (10 March 1995).

154. Ministry of Foreign Affairs, *Looking Ahead. A Foreign Policy for a Changing World* (Tokyo: Ministry of Foreign Affairs, July 1993), p. 7.

155. Ministry of Foreign Affairs press release (24 March 1995).

156. *International Herald Tribune* (16 December 1992).

157. US House of Representatives, Committee on Foreign Affairs, Subcommittee on Human Rights and International Organizations (Washington, DC: June 1982), p. 16. There were similar reports when the IWC considered a ban on whaling in the Antarctic Ocean in 1994. *Japan Times* (18 February 1994).

158. US House of Representatives, Committee on Foreign Affairs, Subcommittee on Human Rights and International Organizations (Washington, DC: September 1982), p. 44. For a list of alleged Japanese 'economic blackmail' see pp. 48–9.

159. *International Herald Tribune* (20 January 1993); *Financial Times* (21 January 1993); *International Herald Tribune* (22 January 1993); *Korea Times* (7 May 1993); *Die Zeit* (16 April 1993).

160. *International Herald Tribune* (8 July 1992); *The Independent* (8 July 1992).

161. Gelman, Harry, 'Japan and China as seen from Moscow today', *Journal of Northeast Asian Studies*, vol. xiii, no. 4 (Winter 1994), 49–60.

162. Hirono, Ryokichi, 'Japan's leadership role in the multilateral development institutions', in: Islam, Shafiqul, *Yen for Development. Japanese Foreign Aid and the Politics of Burden-Sharing*, pp. 171–81.

163. *Look Japan* (November 1993).
164. Figure from '*Hatarakigai aru ga tsukunai nakama*' (We are keen to work but have few companions), *AERA* (21 April 1992), pp. 33–4.
165. *Far Eastern Economic Review* (23 July 1987), p. 87.
166. *The Japan Times* (21 September 1992).
167. Saito, Yasuhiko, *Kokuren no 1503 tsuho tetsuzuki ni tsuite* (On the procedure of 1503 in the UN), *Horitsu Jippo* (November 1981).
168. Hicks, George, 'They won't allow Japan to push the "Comfort Women" aside', *International Herald Tribune* (10 February 1993); *Korea Times* (10 December 1992).
169. Takagi, Seiichiro, 'Human rights in Japanese foreign policy: Japan's policy towards China after Tiananmen', in: Tang, James T.H. (ed.), *Human Rights and International Relations in the Asia Pacific*, 97–111.
170. *The Japan Times* (23 April 1992).
171. *Korea Times* (7 May 1993); *Die Zeit* (16 April 1993).
172. *The Japan Times* (10 November 1973). Figures for present endowment fund and budget 1994–95 from UNU, June 1995.
173. Nagai, Michio, 'Why Tokyo? A Japanese scholar reminisces', *The UNU Newsletter*, vol. 5, no. 2 (1981).
174. Immerman, Robert M., 'Japan in the United Nations', in: Garby, Craig C. and Brown Bullock, Mary (eds), *Japan. A New Kind of Superpower?* (Washington, DC: The Woodrow Wilson Center Press/The Johns Hopkins University Press, 1994), p. 189.
175. For the latter view see: Tanaka, Hitoshi, *Tabu o koete kanjo ni nagasarenai gaiko rongi o* (Let's overcome the taboo and have an unemotional foreign policy debate), *Gaiko Foramu* (December 1993), pp. 66–7.
176. Results of public opinion survey on diplomacy (Tokyo: Prime Minister's Office, 1994).
177. Discussion in the Fifth Committee of the General Assembly in 1976, quoted in: Wakaizumi, Tsutsui, 'Japan and the Security Council', in: *The Japanese Annual of International Law*, no. 26 (1983), p. 21. See also: Ito, Kenichi, 'How ought Japan and Europe cope with uni-polarization of US? Meaning of tri-polar leadership set up among Japan, US and Europe in age of information revolution', in: *Chuo Koron* (July 1991), translated in *Summaries of Selected Japanese Magazines* (March 1992). Ito argues in the article that Japan has no obligation to participate in UN armed forces as long as it is not accepted as a permanent member of the Security Council.
178. *Far Eastern Economic Review* (25 August 1994), p. 23.
179. *Financial Times* (7 July 1993); *International Herald Tribune* (10–11 July 1993).
180. *The Japan Times* (1 March 1992); *Financial Times* (1–2 February 1992).
181. Kono, Yohei, '*Nihon gaiko no shinro*' (A path for the future of Japan's foreign policy), *Gaiko Foramu* (January 1995), pp. 12–19.
182. *Süddeutsche Zeitung* (28 July 1992); *International Herald Tribune* (25 September 1992).
183. Council of Ministers, *General Affairs* (29 May 1995).
184. *The Japan Times* (10 June 1994).
185. Tanaka, Akihiko, in Funabashi, Yoichi (ed.), 'Japan's security policy in the 1990s', in *Japan's International Agenda* (New York: New York University Press, 1994), p. 48.

186. *The Japan Times* (3 October 1984).
187. *International Herald Tribune* (29–30 August 1987); *FBIS-EAS-87–168* (31 August 1987).
188. *Asahi Evening News* (20 October 1989).
189. *Diplomatic Bluebook 1992* (Tokyo: Ministry of Foreign Affairs, 1993), p. 53.
190. This point is extensively discussed in: Tase, Yasuhiro, '*Kokuren ensetsu ni "gimon" ari*' (There are 'doubts' in the UN speech), *Foresight* (October 1994), 28–33.
191. Hummel, Hartwig, '*Japanische Blauhelme: Von der Golfkriegsdebatte zum "PKO-Gesetz"*' (Japanese Blue Helmets: From the Gulf debate to the 'PKO Law'), *INEF Report Heft 3* (Duisburg: Duisburg University, 1994), p. 5.
192. Results of public opinion survey on diplomacy (Tokyo: Prime Minister's Office, 1994).
193. Saito, Shiro, *Japan at the Summit. Japan's Role in the Western Alliance and Asian Pacific Cooperation* (London: Routledge, 1990), p. 97.
194. Arase, David, 'Japanese policy toward democracy and human rights in Asia', *Asian Survey*, vol. xxxiii, no. 10 (October 1993), p. 939.
195. See also: Takagi, Seiichiro, 'Human rights in Japanese foreign policy: Japan's policy towards China after Tiananmen', in: Tang, James T. H. (ed.), *Human Rights and International Relations in the Asia Pacific*, 97–111.
196. Brown, Eugene, 'The debate over Japan's strategic future. Bilateralism versus regionalism', *Asian Survey*, vol. xxxiii, no. 6 (June 1993), 543–59.
197. *Financial Times* (19 May 1989).
198. *Financial Times* (13 February 1992).
199. *Far Eastern Economic Review* (15 June 1995).
200. See: Kwan, C.H., *Economic Interdependence in the Asia Pacific Region* (London: Routledge, 1994).
201. Funabashi, Yoichi, 'Discovery of Asia', *Asahi Evening News* (7 February 1992); Frankel, Jeffrey A., 'Is a yen bloc forming in Pacific Asia?', *The AMEX Bank Review* (November 1991), 2–3.
202. Figures are from '*Hikaku kensho "EU vs. NAFTA vs EAEC"*' (Comparative investigation of 'EU vs. NAFTA vs. EAEC'), *Foresight* (April 1995), p. 75. 'East Asia' includes Japan, China, ASEAN and the Asian NIEs.
203. *Keidanren Review* (May 1995).
204. Quoted in: Chin, Kin Wah, 'Changing global trends and their effects on the Asia-Pacific', p. 9.
205. For the background of the EAEC see: Jomo, K.S., *Japan and Malaysian Development. In the Shadow of the Rising Sun*, pp. 10–13 and pp. 326–34.
206. *International Herald Tribune* (15–16 April 1995).
207. Interview with a former high official of the Ministry of Finance, Tokyo (June 1992).

4 JAPAN AS A CULTURAL SUPERPOWER?

1. *International Herald Tribune* (29–30 August 1992).
2. *International Herald Tribune* (26 November 1993); *Financial Times* (25 May 1995).

3. *International Herald Tribune* (7–8 December 1991).

4. For a general discussion of cultural relations and cultural diplomacy see: Mitchell, J.M., *International Cultural Relations* (London: Allen & Unwin/ British Council, 1986).

5. Whitehead, Sir John, 'Education and culture in the context of Japan–UK relations'. A paper for the UK–Japan 2000 Group (January 1994), p. 2.

6. The Japan Foundation, *Overview of Programs for Fiscal 1991. Annual Report for Fiscal 1990* (Tokyo: Japan Foundation, 1991).

7. *Die Zeit* (14 April 1995).

8. *The Guardian* (31 May 1990).

9. *Reaching Out. Japan's Global Initiatives* (Tokyo: Ministry of Foreign Affairs, July 1990).

10. Kokusai Koryu (Japan Foundation), *Kikin News*, no. 172 (March 1995), p. 1.

11. Wallace, William, 'Global change: New world disorder?', *International Affairs*, vol. 69, no. 3 (July 1993), p. 525.

12. *The Independent* (22 August 1991).

13. For an overview of Japanese sponsorship in Britain see: Joseph, Joe, *The Japanese. Strange but not Strangers* (London: Viking Press, 1993), pp. 261–8.

14. *Financial Times* (5 August 1991).

15. Hennessy, Elizabeth, 'Japanese sponsorship in Britain', *Insight Japan*, vol. 2, no. 3 (December 1993), 21–3.

16. Massarella, Derek, 'Japan Information superpower?' in: *The Japan Society, Proceedings 117* (Spring 1991), p. 7.

17. Ibid.

18. Ivy, Marilyn, 'Critical texts, mass artifacts: The consumption of knowledge in postmodern Japan', in: Miyoshi, Masao and Harootunian, H.D. (eds), *Postmodernism and Japan* (Durham/London: Duke University Press, 1989), p. 23.

19. Research Project Team for Japanese Systems, *Japanese Systems. An Alternative Civilization?* (Yokohama: Masuda Foundation SEKOTAC Ltd., 1992), p. 107.

20. This is, for example, illustrated by Endymion Wilkinson's book which in its Japanese and English language version in Japan is simply called 'Misunderstanding. Europe vs. Japan' whereas the British publisher seemed not to have been sure that such a simple title was intelligible to people outside of Japan and therefore called it 'Japan versus Europe. A history of misunderstanding'. Wilkinson, Endymion, *Gokai. Yoroppa vs. Nihon* (Misunderstanding. Europe vs. Japan) (Tokyo: Chuo Koronsha, 1980); *Misunderstanding. Europe vs. Japan* (Tokyo: Chuo Koronsha, 1981); *Japan versus Europe. A history of misunderstanding* (London: Penguin Books, 1983).

21. Sugimoto, Yoshio, '*Kaigai no Nihonzo ni futatsu no choryu*' (Two developments in the overseas image of Japan), *Asahi Shimbun* (2 November 1994).

22. Sugiyama, Yasushi, 'Internal and external aspects of internationalization', in: Glenn D. Hook and Michael A. Weiner (eds), *The Internationalization of Japan* (Routledge: London 1992), p. 89.

23. *News & Views from Japan* (October 31 1994), pp. 5–6.

24. The Japan Foundation, *Overview of Programs for Fiscal 1991. Annual Report for Fiscal 1990*, p. 63.

25. Katherine E. Jankowski (ed.), *Inside Japanese support* (Rockville: The Taft Group, 1992), p. xxxiv.

26. This and the following information is based on: Holstein, William J., *The Japanese Power: What it Means for America*, pp. 222–40.

27. *International Herald Tribune* (3 November 1993).

28. The most known source on this subject is: Choate, Pat, *Agents of influence* (New York: Alfred A Knopf, 1990). For special case studies on the Toshiba scandal, the semiconductor industry and the construction industry see: Arakawa, Jun, *Japanese Corporations' Lobbying in the US. Under Intense Frictions*, M. Phil thesis (Yamato: International University of Japan, 1989).

29. Tanaka, Akihiko, 'Rhetorics and limitations of Japan's new internationalism', in *Japanese Studies Bulletin (Australia)*, vol. 14, no. 1 (1994), p. 14.

30. For a good overview of it see: *Chicago Tribune* (11 December 1994); see also: Tanaka, Akihiko, 'Two faces of East Asian security and Japan's policy', in: *Proceedings of 'Korean Peninsula Trends and US–Japan–South Korea Relations'* (Washington, DC: The Center for Strategic and International Studies, April 1994), pp. 92–7.

31. Sasae, Kenichiro, *Rethinking Japan–US Relations, Adelphi Paper 292* (London: International Institute for Strategic Studies, December 1994), p. 50.

32. Soeya, Yoshihide, 'The "Re-Asianization" of Japan', *Look Japan* (March 1995), p. 17; *Asahi Shimbun* (27 April 1992).

33. Takagi, Seiichiro, 'Human Rights in Japanese Foreign Policy: Japan's Policy towards China after Tiananmen', in: Tang, James T.H. (ed.), *Human Rights and International Relations in the Asia Pacific* (London/New York: Pinter, 1995), pp. 97–111.

34. Kogawara, Tetsu and Lummis, Douglas, 'The psychology of "travel" ', in *AMPO*, vol. 17, no. 2 (1985), p. 52.

35. Ikeda, Tadashi, 'Asian diplomacy without Asianism', *Gaiko Foramu* (February 1994).

36. Hohmann, Uwe, '*Japans Einfluss in Ost- und Südostasien am Beispiel populärkultureller Elemente*' (Japan's influence in East and Southeast Asia shown by the example of popular cultural elements), in Hummel, Hartwig and Drifte, Reinhard (eds), *Pax Nipponica? Die Japanisierung der Welt 50 Jahre nach dem Untergang des Japanischen Reichs* (Pax Nipponica? The Japanization of the world 50 years after the downfall of the Japanese imperium), pp. 62–72.

37. Tanaka, Akihiko, 'Two faces of East Asian security and Japan's policy', in: *Proceedings of 'Korean Peninsula Trends and US–Japan–South Korea Relations'*, p. 97.

38. For an excellent article on the way the past has been pushed aside in connection with Emperor Hirohito and his war responsibility see: Bix, Herbert P., 'The Showa Emperor's "Monologue" and the problem of war guilt', in: *The Journal of Japanese Studies*, vol. 18, no. 2 (Summer 1992), 295–363.

39. For a thorough discussion of these issues see: Buruma, Ian, *The Wages of Guilt. Memories of War in Germany and Japan* (London: Jonathan Cape, 1994).

40. *International Herald Tribune* (8 March 1995).

41. *International Herald Tribune* (11–12 July 1992); 'Conference on Disarmament (Geneva)', *Procès Verbale*, 614 (27 February 1992).

42. *Far Eastern Economic Review* (8 September 1994).

43. *Nikkei Weekly* (25 April 1992).

44. Takagi, Seiichiro, 'Human Rights in Japanese Foreign Policy: Japan's Policy towards China after Tiananmen', p. 102.
45. See, for example, a Japanese account of 'low-brow' culture in Thailand: Kawamura, Tetsuo, *'Sashimi ya Kenzo ga hayatte. Tai ban Yappi mo dehajimeta'* (Sashimi and Kenzo is fashionable. The magazine 'Yappi' has started a Thai edition), *AERA* (9 June 1992), pp. 30–1. For Malaysia see: Jomo, K.S., *Japan and Malaysian Development. In the Shadow of the Rising Sun*, pp. 345–63.
46. *The Japan Times* (22 October 1992).
47. Joseph Tobin (ed.), *Re-made in Japan* (New Haven: Yale University Press, 1992), p. 6.
48. Honda, Shiro, *'Higashi Ajia ni hirogaru Nihon no popiura bunka'* (The spreading of Japan's popular culture in East Asia), *Gaiko Foramu* (September 1994), pp. 63–70. Translation in *Japan Echo*, vol. 21, no. 4 (Winter 1994).
49. *Financial Times* (27 January 1994).
50. For details on the music and publishing scene see: Hohmann, Uwe, *'Japans Einfluss in Ost- und Südostasien am Beispiel populärkultureller Elemente'* (Japan's influence in East and Southeast Asia shown by the example of popular cultural elements), in: Hummel, Hartwig and Drifte, Reinhard (eds), *Pax Nipponica? Die Japanisierung der Welt 50 Jahre nach dem Untergang des Japanischen Reichs* (Pax Nipponica? The Japanization of the world 50 years after the downfall of the Japanese imperium), p. 68.
51. Hohmann, Uwe, *'Japans Einfluss in Ost- und Südostasien am Beispiel populärkultureller Elemente'* (Japan's influence in East and Southeast Asia shown by the example of popular cultural elements), p. 70.
52. The Japan Foundation, *Overview of Programs for Fiscal 1991. Annual Report for Fiscal 1990*, p. 141. For a case study on Japanese official cultural diplomacy in Malaysia see: Jomo, K.S., *Japan and Malaysian Development. In the Shadow of the Rising Sun*, pp. 343–4.
53. The Japan Foundation, *Overview of Programs for Fiscal 1991. Annual Report for Fiscal 1990*, p. 59.
54. There has been, for example, the report about substantial funding from Japanese monks to several Sri Lankan temples which follow the Mahayana school and the conversion of one Sri Lankan monk who serves as a channel of Japanese money to the Shingon sect, *Far Eastern Economic Report* (14 June 1990), p. 18.
55. *Japan Times* (24 May 1992).
56. *International Herald Tribune* (3 February 1994).
57. *Financial Times* (3 September 1991).

CONCLUSIONS

1. An example is the Automotive Committee of the European Business Chamber which asked in its Japan Report (August 1993) for the deregulation and abolishment of all taxes on net import car purchases to 'compensate for long-standing discrimination of the Japanese distribution system'. *Japan Report* (EBC Automotive Committee, Tokyo, August 1993), p. 31.
2. An example of the term mercenary used for the US forces in Japan see:

Clemens, Steven C., 'Japan adrift without moral mission', *The Daily Yomiuri* (25 April 1995).

3. Richard Rosecrance, *Rise of the Trading State* (New York: Basic Books, 1986).
4. Maull, Hanns W., 'Germany and Japan: The new civilian powers', *Foreign Affairs*, vol. 69 no. 5 (1990), 91–106.
5. Lind, Michael, 'The catalytic state', *The National Interest*, no. 27 (Spring 1992), 3–12.
6. Lind, Michael, 'The catalytic state', p. 3.
7. Research Project Team for Japanese Systems, *Japanese Systems. An Alternative Civilization?* (Yokohama: Masuda Foundation SEKOTAC Ltd., 1992), p. 10.

Index